Learning Python Application Development

Take Python beyond scripting to build robust, reusable, and efficient applications

Ninad Sathaye

[PACKT] open source✳
PUBLISHING   community experience distilled

BIRMINGHAM - MUMBAI

Learning Python Application Development

First published: August 2016

Production reference: 1290816

Published by Packt Publishing Ltd.
Livery Place
35 Livery Street
Birmingham B3 2PB, UK.

ISBN 978-1-78588-919-6

www.packtpub.com

Credits

Author
Ninad Sathaye

Reviewer
Will Ware

Commissioning Editor
Priya Singh

Acquisition Editor
Kevin Colaco

Content Development Editor
Deepti Thore

Technical Editors
Kunal Chaudhari

Sunith Shetty

Copy Editor
Zainab Bootwala

Project Coordinator
Shweta H Birwatkar

Proofreader
Safis Editing

Indexer
Tejal Daruwale Soni

Graphics
Abhinash Sahu

Production Coordinator
Melwyn Dsa

Cover Work
Melwyn Dsa

Disclaimers

The names, characters, businesses, places, events, and incidents mentioned in this book are either the products of the author's imagination or used in a fictitious manner. Any resemblance to actual persons, living or dead, or actual events is purely coincidental.

The views and opinions expressed in this book are solely of the author and do not reflect those of author's employer or its clients.

For this book, the cartoons representing imaginary game characters, such as the Dwarf, Knight, Orc, Fairy, Elf, and so on, are created and copyrighted by Packt Publishing.

About the Author

Ninad Sathaye has spent several years of his professional career designing and developing performance-critical engineering applications written in a variety of languages, including Python and C++. He has worked as a software architect in the semiconductor industry, and more recently in the domain of Internet of Things. He holds a master's degree in mechanical engineering.

I would like to thank my wife, Arati, for her creative input on the book's game theme. This book wouldn't have been possible without her continued support. I would also like to express my sincere gratitude to Will Ware for technically reviewing this book. His feedback was valuable and really helped me take this book to the next level! Thank you Deepti, Kunal, Zainab, and the whole Packt Publishing team for your hard work and support. I owe a special thanks to Abhinash Sahu from Packt Publishing for creating the awesome graphics art for all the fictional characters in this book. My sincere thanks to Steve Furkay, Neeshma, and Kevin for their valuable feedback during the initial phase of this book. Finally, I would like to thank my whole family for their encouragement and support!

About the Reviewer

Will Ware is a software engineer in the Boston area. He has worked with embedded systems, mobile phones, and web development. He received degrees in electrical engineering and mathematics from M.I.T. His interests include STEM education and 3D printing.

www.PacktPub.com

eBooks, discount offers, and more

Did you know that Packt offers eBook versions of every book published, with PDF and ePub files available? You can upgrade to the eBook version at www.PacktPub.com and as a print book customer, you are entitled to a discount on the eBook copy. Get in touch with us at customercare@packtpub.com for more details.

At www.PacktPub.com, you can also read a collection of free technical articles, sign up for a range of free newsletters and receive exclusive discounts and offers on Packt books and eBooks.

https://www2.packtpub.com/books/subscription/packtlib

Do you need instant solutions to your IT questions? PacktLib is Packt's online digital book library. Here, you can search, access, and read Packt's entire library of books.

Why subscribe?

- Fully searchable across every book published by Packt
- Copy and paste, print, and bookmark content
- On demand and accessible via a web browser

To my daughter, Anvita

Table of Contents

Preface

Python is one of the most widely used dynamic programming languages. It supports a rich set of libraries and frameworks that enable rapid development. Such fast-paced development often comes with its own baggage that can bring down the overall quality, performance, and extensibility of the application. This book will help you push your Python skill level by teaching you how to build and deploy interesting applications.

Starting with a simple program, the book takes you all the way through designing and developing robust and efficient applications. It touches upon several important topics in an accessible and fun way.

A fantasy theme is used as a vehicle to explain various concepts. During the course of this book, you will meet many fictional game characters. While you learn different topics, these imaginary characters will talk to you, ask questions, and request new features.

Each chapter targets a different aspect of application development. A few initial ones focus on software robustness, packaging, and releasing the application code. The next few chapters are about improving the application's lifetime by making the code extensible, reusable, and readable. You will learn about refactoring, unit testing, design patterns, documentation, and best practices.

Techniques for identifying bottlenecks and improving performance are covered in a series of three chapters devoted to performance. The last chapter introduces you to GUI development.

Important things to note

- The book uses a fun, text-based game theme as a vehicle to explain various application development aspects. However, the book itself is not about developing game applications!

- Every chapter will have its own set of Python source files. Although we will talk through most of the code, you should keep the relevant files at hand. See the *Downloading the example code* section for more details.

- The following is relevant if you are reading the electronic version of this book. Most of the code illustrated in this book is created as images. Try to use 100% zoom for a better reading experience as these code snapshots should appear crisp at zoom level.

- The solutions to the exercises (if any) are generally not provided.

- This book provides several external links (URLs) for further reading. Over time, some of these links might end up being broken. If that ever happens, try searching the web with the appropriate search terms.

- Some experienced readers may find the code explanation a bit verbose. In this case, you can review the code provided in the supporting material for the book.

Very important note for e-book readers

The code illustrations that you see in this book are actually image files or code snapshots.

The rendering quality of these images will vary depending on your PDF reader's page display resolution and the zoom level.

If you have trouble clearly reading this code, you may try the following in your PDF or e-book reader:

- Set the zoom level to 100%
- Use the page display resolution of 96 pixels/inch or similar

If the problem still persists, you can try with a different resolution.

How do you set this resolution? It will depend on your e-book reader. For example, if you are using Adobe Reader, go to **Edit** | **Preferences** and then select **Page Display** from the left panel. You will see **Resolution** as an option in the right panel. Select **96 pixels/inch** or similar and see if that helps render the images better.

What this book covers

Chapter 1, Developing Simple Applications, starts with installation prerequisites and the theme of the book. The first program is a fantasy text-based game presented as a script. An incremental version of this program with new features is then developed using functions. With more features added, the code becomes difficult to manage. To address this, the game application is redesigned using OOP concepts. This application now becomes the reference version for the next few chapters.

Chapter 2, Dealing with Exceptions, will teach you how to fix the obvious issues that the code written in the previous chapter has. You will learn how to add exception handling code to make the application robust. You will also learn about the `try...except...finally` clause, raising and re-raising exceptions, creating and using custom exception classes, and so on.

Chapter 3, Modularize, Package, Deploy!, will teach you how to modularize and package the code written in the earlier chapters. After preparing a package, it will show you how to deploy a source distribution, make incremental releases, set up a private Python package repository, and bring the code under version control.

Chapter 4, Documentation and Best Practices, dives into coding standards, which are a set of guidelines that you should follow while developing the code. Complying with these standards can make a significant impact on code readability and the life of the code. In this chapter, you will learn about another important aspect of software development, code documentation, and best practices. It starts with an introduction to the reStructuredText format and uses it to write docstrings. You will create HTML documentation for the code using the Sphinx document generator. The chapter also talks about some important coding standards for writing a Python code and using PyLint to check the code quality.

Chapter 5, Unit Testing and Refactoring, starts with an introduction to the unit testing framework in Python. You will write some unit tests for the game application developed so far. It covers many other topics, such as using Mock library in unit tests and measuring effectiveness of the unit tests with code coverage. The later part of the chapter talks about many code refactoring techniques. This is the last chapter that makes use of the code developed in the earlier chapters. The following chapters will have their own simplified examples tied to the same high-fantasy theme.

Chapter 6, Design Patterns, tells you how, during development, you often encounter a recurring problem. Many times, a general solution or recipe exists, which just works for this problem. This is often referred to as a design pattern. This chapter introduces you to some commonly used design patterns. It covers the strategy, simple and abstract factory, and adapter patterns. For each pattern, a simple game scenario will demonstrate a practical problem. You will learn how the design pattern can help solve this problem. Each of these patterns will be implemented using a Pythonic approach.

Chapter 7, Performance – Identifying Bottlenecks, is the first one in a series of three chapters on performance improvements. You will write a simple program called *Gold Hunt* that looks harmless until you tweak some parameters. The parameter tweaking reveals performance problems. In this chapter, you will identify the time-consuming blocks of the code. It covers the basic ways to clock the application runtime, profiling the code to identify performance bottlenecks, the basics of memory profiling, and using big-O notation to represent computational complexity.

Chapter 8, Improving Performance – Part One, teaches you how to fix some of the performance bottlenecks identified in the previous chapter. Additionally, you will also learn about several techniques, such as algorithm changes, list comprehension, generator expressions, the right choice of data structures, and so on, to improve the application performance.

Chapter 9, Improving Performance – Part Two, NumPy and Parallelization, is the final chapter on performance improvements, wherein you will drastically improve the performance of the *gold hunt* application. The chapter will introduce you to the `NumPy` package. It will also introduce you to parallel processing using Python.

Chapter 10, Simple GUI Applications, is the final chapter and introduces you to simple GUI application development. The chapters so far covered several key aspects of application development using command-line programs. In this chapter, however, you will learn about the `Tkinter` module, MVC architecture, and develop a GUI version of the first application developed in *Chapter 1, Developing Simple Applications*.

What you need for this book

The code illustrated in this book is compatible with Python version 3.5. The supporting code bundles also provide files compatible with version 2.7.9; however, throughout the book, Python version 3.5 is assumed. See the *Installation prerequisites* section of *Chapter 1, Developing Simple Applications*, for details on the basic packages that need to be installed. Additionally, there are some Python package dependencies that need to be installed. Most of these packages can be installed using pip (Python package manager). These dependencies are mentioned in the chapters that require them.

Who this book is for

Do you know the basics of Python and object-oriented programming?

Do you wish to go the extra mile and learn techniques to make your Python application robust, extensible, and efficient?

This is the book for you if you answered yes to these questions. It is also for those with a different programming background (for instance, C++ or Java) and wish to get to grips with Python application development.

This book is not for you if either of the following statements apply to you:

- You are completely new to Python or do not have any background in OOP. The first chapter covers some basics but further understanding will be required.
- You are looking for a reference on specific application domains, such as Web, GUI, database, or game applications. Except for GUI, this book does not cover such domain-specific topics. Nonetheless, the techniques you will learn in this book should provide a solid foundation to all such domains.

Conventions

In this book, you will find a number of text styles that distinguish between different kinds of information. Here are some examples of these styles and an explanation of their meaning.

Code words in text, database table names, folder names, filenames, file extensions, pathnames, dummy URLs, user input, and Twitter handles are shown as follows: "There are some changes to the `GoldHunt.find_coins` method."

A block of code is set as follows:

```
results = pool.starmap_async(self.find_coins,
                            zip(itertools.repeat(x_list),
                                itertools.repeat(y_list),
                                x_centers,
```

Any command-line input or output is written as follows:

```
export PATH=$PATH:/usr/bin/
```

New terms and **important words** are shown in bold. Words that you see on the screen, for example, in menus or dialog boxes, appear in the text like this: "As mentioned earlier, at the time of installation, you should select the **Add Python 3.5 to PATH option**."

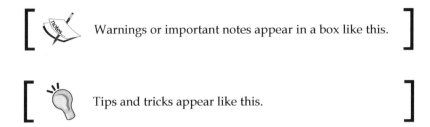

Warnings or important notes appear in a box like this.

Tips and tricks appear like this.

Reader feedback

Feedback from our readers is always welcome. Let us know what you think about this book—what you liked or disliked. Reader feedback is important for us as it helps us develop titles that you will really get the most out of.

To send us general feedback, simply e-mail feedback@packtpub.com, and mention the book's title in the subject of your message.

If there is a topic that you have expertise in and you are interested in either writing or contributing to a book, see our author guide at www.packtpub.com/authors.

Customer support

Now that you are the proud owner of a Packt book, we have a number of things to help you to get the most from your purchase.

Downloading the example code

You can download the example code files for this book from your account at http://www.packtpub.com. If you purchased this book elsewhere, you can visit http://www.packtpub.com/support and register to have the files e-mailed directly to you.

You can download the code files by following these steps:

1. Log in or register to our website using your e-mail address and password.
2. Hover the mouse pointer on the **SUPPORT** tab at the top.
3. Click on **Code Downloads & Errata**.
4. Enter the name of the book in the **Search** box.
5. Select the book for which you're looking to download the code files.
6. Choose from the drop-down menu where you purchased this book from.
7. Click on **Code Download**.

You can also download the code files by clicking on the **Code Files** button on the book's webpage at the Packt Publishing website. This page can be accessed by entering the book's name in the **Search** box. Please note that you need to be logged in to your Packt account.

Once the file is downloaded, please make sure that you unzip or extract the folder using the latest version of:

- WinRAR / 7-Zip for Windows
- Zipeg / iZip / UnRarX for Mac
- 7-Zip / PeaZip for Linux

The code bundle for the book is also hosted on GitHub at `https://github.com/PacktPublishing/Learning-Python-Application-Development`. We also have other code bundles from our rich catalog of books and videos available at `https://github.com/PacktPublishing/`. Check them out!

Downloading the color images of this book

We also provide you with a PDF file that has color images of the screenshots/diagrams used in this book. The color images will help you better understand the changes in the output. You can download this file from `http://www.packtpub.com/sites/default/files/downloads/LearningPythonApplicationDevelopment_ColorImages.pdf`.

Errata

Although we have taken every care to ensure the accuracy of our content, mistakes do happen. If you find a mistake in one of our books—maybe a mistake in the text or the code—we would be grateful if you could report this to us. By doing so, you can save other readers from frustration and help us improve subsequent versions of this book. If you find any errata, please report them by visiting `http://www.packtpub.com/submit-errata`, selecting your book, clicking on the **Errata Submission Form** link, and entering the details of your errata. Once your errata are verified, your submission will be accepted and the errata will be uploaded to our website or added to any list of existing errata under the Errata section of that title.

To view the previously submitted errata, go to `https://www.packtpub.com/books/content/support` and enter the name of the book in the search field. The required information will appear under the **Errata** section.

Piracy

Piracy of copyrighted material on the Internet is an ongoing problem across all media. At Packt, we take the protection of our copyright and licenses very seriously. If you come across any illegal copies of our works in any form on the Internet, please provide us with the location address or website name immediately so that we can pursue a remedy.

Please contact us at `copyright@packtpub.com` with a link to the suspected pirated material.

We appreciate your help in protecting our authors and our ability to bring you valuable content.

Questions

If you have a problem with any aspect of this book, you can contact us at `questions@packtpub.com`, and we will do our best to address the problem.

1
Developing Simple Applications

Python is one of the most widely used dynamic programming languages. It supports a rich set of packages, GUI libraries, and web frameworks that enable you to build efficient cross-platform applications. It is an ideal language for rapid application development. Such fast-paced development often comes with its own baggage that could bring down the overall quality, performance, and extensibility of the code. This book will show you ways to handle such situations and help you develop better Python applications. The key concepts will be explained with the help of command-line applications, which will be progressively improved in subsequent chapters.

This chapter will be an introductory one. It will serve as a refresher to Python programming. That being said, it is expected you have some knowledge of Python language, as well as **object-oriented programming** (OOP) concepts.

Here is how this chapter is organized:

- We will start with installation prerequisites and set up a proper environment for Python development.

- To set the tone right for the rest of the book, the next section will be a brief introduction to the *high fantasy theme* of the book.

- What follows next is our first program. It is a simple text-based fantasy game, presented as a Python script.

- We will add some complexity to this game and develop an incremental version of the game using simple functions.

- Moving ahead, we will add more features to the game and redesign the code by applying OOP concepts.

- The last topic will briefly cover **Abstract Base Classes** (ABCs) in Python.

The code explanation will be a bit verbose. More experienced readers can breeze past the examples and go to the next chapter, but be sure to understand the theme of the book and review the code in the `ch01_ex03.py` file. In the next few chapters, you will learn techniques to progressively improve this code.

Important housekeeping notes

Before diving into the rest of the chapter, let's get some housekeeping out of the way. If you haven't already, you should read the *Preface*, which documents most of the following things:

- Every chapter will have its own set of Python source files. Although we will talk through most of the code, you should keep the relevant files at hand.

- The source code can be downloaded from the Packt Publishing website. Follow the instructions mentioned in the *Preface*.

- The code illustrated in this book is compatible with Python version 3.5.1. The supporting code bundles also provide files compatible with version 2.7.9.

- As noted before, it is assumed that you are familiar with basics of the Python language and know OOP concepts.

- The book uses a fun, text-based game theme as a vehicle to explain various application development aspects. However, the book itself is not about developing game applications!

- The solutions to the exercises (if any) are generally not provided.

- The book provides several external links (URLs) for further reading. Over time, some of these links might end up being broken. If that ever happens, try searching the web with appropriate search terms.

Installation prerequisites

Let's make sure that we have installed the prerequisites. Here is a table that summarizes the basic tools we need for this chapter and beyond; more verbose installation instructions follow in the next section:

Tool	Notes
Python 3.5	The code illustrated in this book is compatible with version 3.5. See the next table for available Python distributions. Supporting code bundles also provide 2.7.9 compatible files.
pip (package manager for Python)	The pip is already available in the official distribution for versions 3.5 and 2.7.9.
IPython	Optional installation. IPython is an enhanced Python interpreter.
Integrated development environment (IDE)	Use the Python editor or any IDE of your choice. Some good IDEs are listed in a table later in this chapter.

In subsequent chapters, we will need to install some additional dependencies. The Python package manager (pip) will makes this a trivial task.

 Have you already set up the required Python environment or know how to do it? Just skip the setup instructions that follow and move on to the *The theme of the book* section, where the real action begins!

Installing Python

There are two options to install Python. You can either use the official Python version or one of the freely available bundled distributions.

Option 1 – official distribution

For Linux or Mac users, Python is probably already installed on your system. If not, you can install it using the package manager of your operating system. Windows OS users can install Python 3.5 by downloading the Python installer from the official Python website:

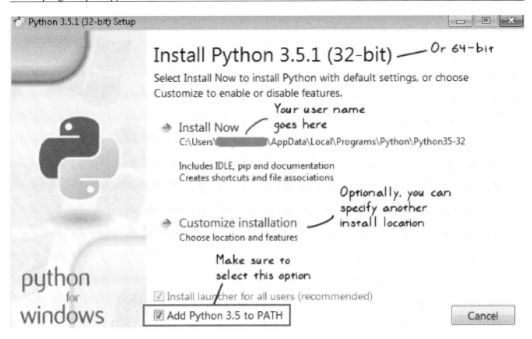

During the installation process, just make sure to select the option that adds Python 3.5 to the system environment variable, PATH, as shown in the preceding screenshot. You can also visit the official Python website, https://www.python.org/downloads, to get the platform-specific distribution.

Option 2 – bundled distribution

Alternatively, there are several freely available Python distributions that bundle together useful Python packages, including pip and IPython. The following table summarizes some of the most popular Python distributions, including the official one:

Distribution	Supported platforms	Notes
Official Python distribution `https://www.python.org`	Windows, Linux, Mac	• Freely available • Versions 2.7.9 and 3.5 include pip by default
Anaconda `http://continuum.io`	Windows, Linux, Mac	• Freely available • Includes pip, IPython and Spyder IDE • Bundles packages primarily for science, math, engineering, and data analysis
Enthought Canopy Express `https://www.enthought.com/canopy-express/`	Windows, Linux, Mac	• Freely available • Includes pip and IPython • Integrates a Python code editor and application development platform
Python(x, y) `https://python-xy.github.io/`	Windows	• Freely available • Includes pip, IPython, and Spyder IDE

Python install location

Let's briefly talk about the path where Python is installed, and how to make sure `python` is available as a command in your terminal window. Of course, things will widely vary, depending on where you install it and which Python distribution you choose.

 The official Python documentation page has comprehensive information on setting up the Python environment on different platforms. Here is a link, in case you need further help beyond what we have covered: `https://docs.python.org/3/using/index.html`.

Unix-like operating systems

On a Unix-like operating system such as Linux, the default location is typically `/usr/bin/python` or `/usr/local/bin/python`.

If you used your operating system's package manager to install Python, the command `python` or `python3` should be available in the terminal window. If it isn't, you need to update the `PATH` system environment variable to include the directory path to the Python executable. For example, if you have a **Bash** shell, add the following to the `.bashrc` file in your user home directory:

```
export PATH=$PATH:/usr/bin/
```

Specify the actual path to your Python installation in place of `/usr/bin`.

Windows OS

On Windows OS, the default Python installation path is typically the following directory: `C:\Users\name\AppData\Local\Programs\Python\Python35-32\python.exe`. Replace `name` with your Windows username. Depending on your installer and system, the Python directory can also be `Python35-64`. As mentioned earlier, at the time of installation, you should select the option **Add Python 3.5 to PATH** to make sure `python` or `python.exe` are automatically recognized as commands. Alternatively, you can rerun the installer with just this option checked.

Verifying Python installation

Open a terminal window (or command prompt on Windows OS) and type the following command to verify the Python version. This command will work if Python is installed and is available as a command in the terminal window. Otherwise, specify the full path to the Python executable. For instance, on Linux you can specify it as `/usr/bin/python`, if Python is installed in `/usr/bin`:

```
$ python -V
```

> Note that the $ sign in the previous command line belongs to the terminal window and is not part of the command itself! Put another way, the actual command is just `python -V`. The $ or % sign in the terminal window is a prompt for a normal user on Linux. For a root (admin) user, the sign is #. Likewise, on Windows OS, the corresponding symbol is >. You will type the actual command after this symbol.

The following is just a sample output, if we run the preceding command:

```
[user@hostname ~]$ python -V
Python 3.5.1 :: Anaconda 4.0.0 (64-bit)
```

Installing pip

The pip is a software package manager that makes it trivial to install Python packages from the official third party software repository, **PyPI**. The pip is already installed for Python-2 version 2.7.9 or higher and Python-3 version 3.4 or higher. If you are using a different Python version, check out `https://pip.pypa.io/en/stable/installing` for the installation instructions.

On Linux OS, the default location for the pip is same as that of the Python executable. For example, if you have `/usr/bin/python`, then pip should be available as `/usr/bin/pip`. On Windows OS, the default `pip.exe` is typically the following: `C:\Users\name\AppData\Local\Programs\Python\Python35-32\Scripts\pip.exe`. As mentioned earlier, replace `name` with your Windows username. Depending on your installer and the system, the Python directory can also be `Python35-64`.

Installing IPython

This is an optional installation. IPython is an enhanced version of the Python interpreter. If it is not already bundled in your Python distribution, you can install it with:

```
$ pip install ipython
```

After the installation, just type `ipython` in the terminal to start the IPython interactive shell. Here is a screenshot of the IPython shell using the Anaconda Python 3.5 distribution:

```
[user@hostname ~]$ ~/anaconda3.5/bin/ipython
Python 3.5.1 |Anaconda 4.0.0 (64-bit)| (default, Dec  7 2015, 11:16:01)
Type "copyright", "credits" or "license" for more information.

IPython 4.1.2 -- An enhanced Interactive Python.
?          -> Introduction and overview of IPython's features.
%quickref -> Quick reference.
help       -> Python's own help system.
object?    -> Details about 'object', use 'object??' for extra details.

In [1]: import os

In [2]: 
```

It is often very convenient to use the **Jupyter Notebook** to write and share interactive programs. It is a web application that enables an interactive environment for writing Python code alongside rich text, images, plots, and so on. For further details, check out the project homepage at `http://jupyter.org/`. The Jupyter Notebook can be installed with:

```
$ pip install "ipython[notebook]"
```

Choosing an IDE

Using an IDE for development is a matter of personal preference. Simply put, an IDE is a tool intended to accelerate application development. It enables developers to write efficient code quickly by integrating the most common tools they need. The Python installation comes with a program called **IDLE**. It is a basic IDE for Python, which should get you started. For advanced development, you can choose from a number of freely or commercially available tools. Any good Python IDE has the following minimum features:

- A source code editor with code completion and syntax highlighting features
- A code browser to browse through files, projects, functions, and classes
- A debugger to interactively identify problems
- A version control system integration such as **Git**

You can get started by trying out one of the freely available IDEs. Here is a partial list of popular IDEs. If you are just interested in a simple source code editor, you can check out `https://wiki.python.org/moin/PythonEditors`, for a list of available choices.

Python IDE	Notes

PyCharm Community Edition
 	
`https://www.jetbrains.com/`
`pycharm`
	Has a free community edition. Excellent tool to begin Python development!

Wing IDE 101
 	
`http://wingware.com/downloads/`
`wingide-101`
	Free for non-commercial purposes only. Commercial version available with additional features. Another excellent Python IDE.

Spyder `https://pythonhosted.org/` `spyder`	Freely available, open source. Also provided in bundled Python distributions such as Python(x,y) and Anaconda.
Eclipse PyDev `www.pydev.org`	Freely available, open source.
Sublime Text 2 or Sublime Text 3 (beta) `http://www.sublimetext.com/2`	Free for evaluation purposes only. Highly configurable IDE.

The theme of the book

Have you read high fantasy novels, such as *The Lord of the Rings* or *The Hobbit* by J. R. R. Tolkien? Or watched the films based on these novels? Well, here is a high fantasy, "Tolkienesque" themed book on Python application development.

 To find out more about J.R.R. Tolkien's work, see `https://`
`en.wikipedia.org/wiki/J._R._R._Tolkien`. The term *high fantasy* is often used to represent a fantasy theme set in an alternate fictional world. Check out `https.//en.wikipedia.org/wiki/`
`High_fantasy` for more information.

This book takes you to an imaginary world where you will develop a text game based on the aforementioned theme. Yes, you can continue being a developer even in this imaginary world! During the course of the book, you will be accompanied by many fictional characters. While you learn different aspects of Python development, these characters will talk to you, ask questions, request new features, and even fight with the enemy.

It should be noted that this book is not about developing game applications. It uses a simple text-based game just as a medium to learn various development aspects.

Off topic, if you are interested in playing a high fantasy theme game, there are quite a few to choose from. Among the open source ones, *Battle for Wesnoth* is one of the most highly rated, free, turn-based strategy games with a high fantasy theme. Check out `https://www. wesnoth.org`, for more details.

Meet the characters

Let's meet the imaginary characters who will accompany you in various chapters:

	Sir Foo A human knight who is portrayed as a grand knight guarding the southern plains. He is our main character and will be talking to us throughout the book.
	Orc Rider An Orc is a human-like imaginary creature. Here, it is portrayed as an enemy soldier. The Orc is seen riding a wild boar-like creature. You will see this creature in this chapter.
	Elf Rider An Elf is a supernatural mythical being. The Elf is mounted on an elvish horse. He is portrayed as a friendly. You will meet Mr. Elf in *Chapter 6, Design Patterns.*
	Fairy An intelligent fairy with an inherent capability for magic. She will use her magic just once while finding her enchanted locket in *Chapter 7, Performance Identifying Bottlenecks*, (See $O(log\ n)$). You will first meet her in *Chapter 6, Design Patterns.*
	Dwarf A Dwarf is a small human-like mythical being. He is portrayed as "The Great Dwarf" of the Foo mountains. He asks lots of questions. You will see him in the second half of the book, starting with *Chapter 6, Design Patterns.*

With this fun theme as a vehicle, let's start our journey with a simple command-line application. It will be a text-based game. The complexities added in subsequent chapters will challenge you with interesting problems. The book will show you how to gracefully handle such situations.

Simple script – Attack of the Orcs v0.0.1

We have the required tools and the environment set up. It is now time to write our first Python program. It will be a simple game of chance, developed as a command-line application. As we advance further, we will add more complexity to the game and learn new techniques to develop efficient applications. So, get ready for action!

The game – Attack of the Orcs v0.0.1

The war between humans and their arch enemies, the Orcs, was in the offing. A huge army of Orcs was heading toward the human establishments. They were virtually destroying everything in their way. The great kings of the human race joined hands to defeat their worst enemy for the great battle of their time. Men were summoned to join the rest of the army. Sir Foo, one of the brave knights guarding the southern plains, began a long journey toward the east, through an unknown dense forest. For two days and two nights, he moved cautiously through the thick woods. On his way, he spotted a small isolated settlement. Tired and hoping to replenish his food stock, he decided to take a detour. As he approached the village, he saw five huts. There was no one to be seen around. Hesitantly, he decided to enter a hut...

Problem statement

You are designing a simple game in which the player is required to choose a hut for Sir Foo. The huts are randomly occupied either by a friend or an enemy. It is also possible that some huts remain unoccupied. If the chosen one turns out to be an enemy hut, the player loses. In the other two scenarios, the player wins.

Pseudo code – version 0.0.1

Now that the goal is clear, open your favorite editor and note down the main steps. This is sometimes referred to as a pseudo code.

While the user wishes to keep playing the game:

- Print the game mission
- Create a `huts` list
- Randomly place `'enemy'` or `'friend'` or `'unoccupied'` in 5 huts
- Prompt the player to select a hut number
- `if enemy`: print `"you lose"`
- `else`: print `"you win"`

As you will notice, the key piece of the code is to randomly occupy the five huts with either enemy or friend and keep the remaining ones unoccupied. How do we do this? Let's quickly work this out using the Python interpreter. If you have installed IPython, start the IPython interpreter. Otherwise, just use the default Python interpreter by typing the command `python` in a terminal window. First, we need a Python list to hold all the occupant types. Next, we will use the built-in `random` module and call `random.choice` to pick one element randomly from this list. This code is shown in the following screen capture:

```
In [2]: import random

In [3]: occupants = ['enemy', 'friend', 'unoccupied']

In [4]: random.choice(occupants)
Out[4]: 'unoccupied'

In [5]: random.choice(occupants)
Out[5]: 'friend'

In [6]:
```

Now, we just need to write the surrounding code. Let's review it next.

Reviewing the code

Download the source code, `ch01_ex01.py`, from the supplementary code bundle provided for this chapter. The file extension, `.py`, indicates that it is a Python file. Open it in a Python editor or an IDE of your choice. It is recommended that you keep this file handy while reading the following discussion. It is often easier to glance at the full code to understand it better. Observe the following code snippet. It is just a small portion of the code inside the `if __name__ == '__main__'` condition block in the aforementioned file.

 If you have Python 2.7.9 installed, there is a separate Python 2.7.9 compatible source provided in the supporting code bundle.

```
import random
import textwrap

if __name__ == '__main__':
    keep_playing = 'y'
    occupants = ['enemy', 'friend', 'unoccupied']
    width = 72
    dotted_line = '-' * width
    print(dotted_line)
    print("\033[1m" + "Attack of The Orcs v0.0.1:" + "\033[0m")
```

Let's review the code snippet in the preceding screenshot:

- The first two lines import two built-in modules to gain access to the functionality provided within these modules. The textwrap module essentially provides features to nicely format the messages printed on the command line.

- The if condition block, if __name__ == '__main__', is invoked only when the file is run as a standalone script. In other words, the code inside this condition block won't be executed if you import this file in some other file.

- Now, let's look at the code in this condition block. First, we will initialize a few variables. As demonstrated earlier, the list occupants stores the potential occupant types for the hut.

- The last few lines are just to format the text printed in the terminal window. The dotted_line is a string that will show a 72-character long line with hyphen symbols.

- The ASCII escape sequence is used to print the text in bold. The sequence "\033[1m" is to make bold text, and "\033[0m" is to go back to normal printing style.

The next few lines essentially print further information about the game in the console:

```
msg = (
    "The war between humans and their arch enemies, Orcs, was in the "
    "offing. Sir Foo, one of the brave knights guarding the southern "
    "plains began a long journey towards the east through an unknown "
    "dense forest. On his way, he spotted a small isolated settlement."
    " Tired and hoping to replenish his food stock, he decided to take"
    " a detour. As he approached the village, he saw five huts. There "
    "was no one to be seen around. Hesitantly, he  decided to enter..")

print(textwrap.fill(msg, width=width))
print("\033[1m" + "Mission:" + "\033[0m")
print("\tChoose a hut where Sir Foo can rest...")
print("\033[1m" + "TIP:" + "\033[0m")
print("Be careful as there are enemies lurking around!")
print(dotted_line)
```

Let's have a look at the code from the preceding screenshot:

- The variable `msg` is a very long string. This is where the `textwrap` module is used.

- The `textwrap.fill` function wraps the message in such a way that each line is 72 characters long, as specified by the `width` in our code.

Now, let's review the following `while` loop.

For Python 2.7.9, the only change required in the first example is to replace all the calls to the built-in function `input` with `raw_input`:

```
# For Python 2.7
user_choice = raw_input(msg)
```

```python
while keep_playing == 'y':
    huts = []
    # Randomly append 'enemy' or 'friend' or None to the huts list
    while len(huts) < 5:
        computer_choice = random.choice(occupants)
        huts.append(computer_choice)

    # Prompt user to select a hut
    msg = "\033[1m" + "Choose a hut number to enter (1-5): " + "\033[0m"
    user_choice = input("\n" + msg)
    idx = int(user_choice)

    # Print the occupant info
    print("Revealing the occupants...")
    msg = ""
    for i in range(len(huts)):
        occupant_info = "<%d:%s>"%(i+1, huts[i])
        if i + 1 == idx:
            occupant_info = "\033[1m" + occupant_info + "\033[0m"
        msg += occupant_info + " "
    print("\t" + msg)
    print(dotted_line)
    print("\033[1m" + "Entering hut %d... " % idx + "\033[0m", end=' ')

    # Determine and announce the winner
    if huts[idx-1] == 'enemy':
        print("\033[1m" + "YOU LOSE :( Better luck next time!" +
            "\033[0m")
    else:
        print("\033[1m" + "Congratulations! YOU WIN!!!" + "\033[0m")
    print(dotted_line)
    keep_playing = input("Play again? Yes(y)/No(n):")
```

- This top-level loop gives the player an option to play the game again.
- Using `random.choice`, we randomly pick an occupant from the list of `occupants` and add it to the `huts` list. This was illustrated earlier.
- The built-in `input` function accepts a hut number of the user's choice as an integer. The `idx` variable stores a number.

Next, it reveals the occupants by printing related information. Finally, it determines the winner by checking the list item corresponding to the hut number. Note that the `huts` list index starts at 0. Therefore, to retrieve the list element for a given hut number, `idx`, we need to check the list index at `idx-1`.

Running Attack of the Orcs v0.0.1

Assuming you already have Python in your system environment variable, PATH (available as either python or python3), run the program from the command line as:

```
$ python ch01_ex01.py
```

That's all! Just play the game and try to save Sir Foo by choosing the right hut! The following snapshot of a Linux terminal window shows our game in action:

```
[user@hostname src_ch1]$ python ch01_ex01.py
-------------------------------------------------------------------
Attack of The Orcs v0.0.1:
The war between humans and their arch enemies, Orcs, was in the offing.
Sir Foo, one of the brave knights guarding the southern plains began a
long journey towards the east through an unknown dense forest. On his
way, he spotted a small isolated settlement. Tired and hoping to
replenish his food stock, he decided to take a detour. As he approached
the village, he saw five huts. There was no one to be seen around.
Hesitantly, he  decided to enter..
Mission:
        Choose a hut where Sir Foo can rest...
TIP:
Be careful as there are enemies lurking around!
-------------------------------------------------------------------

Choose a hut number to enter (1-5): 1
Revealing the occupants...
        <1:unoccupied> <2:friend> <3:unoccupied> <4:enemy> <5:unoccupied>
-------------------------------------------------------------------
Entering hut 1...  Congratulations! YOU WIN!!!
-------------------------------------------------------------------
Play again? Yes(y)/No(n):y
```

Using functions – Attack of the Orcs v0.0.5

In the last section, you wrote a quick set of instructions to create a nice little command-line game. You asked your friends to try it out and they kind of liked it (perhaps they were just trying to be nice!). You received the first feature request for the game.

> *"I think this game has good potential to grow. How about including combat in the next version of the game? When Sir Foo encounters an enemy, he should not just give up that easily. Fight with the enemy! Let the combat decide the winner. "-your friend*

You liked the idea and decided to add this capability to the code in the next version. Additionally, you also want to make it more interactive.

The script you wrote for the first program was small. However, as we go on adding new features, it will soon become a maintenance headache. As a step further, we will wrap the existing code into small functions so that the code is easier to manage. In functional programming, the focus is typically on function arrangement and their composition. For example, you can build complicated logic using a simple set of reusable functions.

Revisiting the previous version

Before adding any new features, let's revisit the script that you wrote in the previous version (version 0.0.1). We will identify the blocks of code that can be wrapped into functions. Such code chunks are marked in the two code snippets that follow:

```python
if __name__ == '__main__':
    keep_playing = 'y'
    occupants = ['enemy', 'friend', 'unoccupied']
    width = 72
    dotted_line = '-' * width
    print(dotted_line)
    print("\033[1m" + "Attack of The Orcs v0.0.1:" + "\033[0m")
    msg = (
        "The war between humans and their arch enemies, Orcs, was in the "
        "offing. Sir Foo, one of the brave knights guarding the southern "
        "plains began a long journey towards the east through an unknown "
        "dense forest. On his way, he spotted a small isolated settlement."
        " Tired and hoping to replenish his food stock, he decided to take"
        " a detour. As he approached the village, he saw five huts. There "
        "was no one to be seen around. Hesitantly, he  decided to enter..")
    print(textwrap.fill(msg, width=width))
    print("\033[1m" + "Mission:" + "\033[0m")
    print("\tChoose a hut where Sir Foo can rest...")
    print("\033[1m" + "TIP:" + "\033[0m")
    print("Be careful as there are enemies lurking around!")
    print(dotted_line)
```

1

2

We will wrap most of the highlighted code into individual functions, as follows:

```
1:    show_theme_message
2:    show_game_mission
3:    occupy_huts
4:    process_user_choice
5:    reveal_occupants
6:    enter_hut
```

```
while keep_playing == 'y':
    huts = []
    while len(huts) < 5:
        computer_choice = random.choice(occupants)
        huts.append(computer_choice)
```

3

```
    msg = "\033[1m" + "Choose a hut number to enter (1-5): " + "\033[0m"
    user_choice = input("\n" + msg)
    idx = int(user_choice)
    print("Revealing the occupants...")
    msg = ""
```

4

```
    for i in range(len(huts)):
        occupant_info = "<%d:%s>"%(i+1, huts[i])
        if i + 1 == idx:
            occupant_info = "\033[1m" + occupant_info + "\033[0m"
        msg += occupant_info + " "

    print("\t" + msg)
    print(dotted_line)
```

5

```
    print("\033[1m" + "Entering hut %d... " % idx + "\033[0m", end=' ')

    if huts[idx-1] == 'enemy':
        print("\033[1m" + "YOU LOSE :( Better luck next time!" +
            "\033[0m")
    else:
        print("\033[1m" + "Congratulations! YOU WIN!!!" + "\033[0m")

    print(dotted_line)
    keep_playing = input("Play again? Yes(y)/No(n):")
```

6

In addition to these six blocks of code, we can also create a few top-level functions to handle all this logic. In Python, the function is created using the `def` keyword, followed by the function name and arguments in parentheses. For example, the `reveal_occupants` function requires the information about the `huts` list. We also need to optionally pass the `dotted_line` string if we do not want to recreate it in the function. So, we will pass the hut number `idx`, the `huts` list, and the `dotted_line` string as function arguments. This function can be written as follows:

```python
def reveal_occupants(idx, huts):
    """Print the occupants of the hut"""
    msg = ""
    print("Revealing the occupants...")
    for i in range(len(huts)):
        occupant_info = "<%d:%s>" % (i+1, huts[i])
        if i + 1 == idx:
            occupant_info = "\033[1m" + occupant_info + "\033[0m"
        msg += occupant_info + " "

    print("\t" + msg)
    print_dotted_line()
```

After this initial work, the original script can be rewritten as:

```python
def run_application():
    keep_playing = 'y'
    width = 72
    dotted_line = '-' * width

    show_theme_message(dotted_line, width)  ──────── 1
    show_game_mission(dotted_line)__ 2

    while keep_playing == 'y':
        huts = occupy_huts()  ──────── 3
        idx = process_user_choice()──────── 4
        reveal_occupants(idx, huts, dotted_line)──── 5
        enter_hut(idx, huts, dotted_line) ──────────────── 6
        keep_playing = input("Play again? Yes(y)/No(n):")

if __name__ == '__main__':
    run_application()
```

This is much easier to read now. What we just did is also referred to as **refactoring**; more on various refactoring techniques in a later chapter. It makes it easier to do changes to the individual methods. For example, if you want to customize the mission statement or scenario description, you do not need to open the main function, `run_application`. Similarly, `occupy_huts` can be expanded further without any clutter in the main code.

> The initial refactored version of the code is not perfect. There is plenty of room for improvement. Can you reduce the burden of passing the `dotted_line` parameter or think of some other way to handle the printing of bold text?

Pseudo code with attack feature – Version 0.0.5

In the previous section, we wrapped the game logic into individual functions. This not only improved the code readability, but also made it easier to maintain. Let's move on and include the new `attack()` function in the game. The following steps show the logic of the game with the attack feature included.

While the user wishes to keep playing the game:

- Print game mission
- Create a `huts` list
- Randomly place `'enemy'`, `'friend'`, or `'unoccupied'` in 5 huts
- Prompt the player to select a hut number
- `if` the hut has an enemy, do the following:

    ◦ `while` the user wishes to continue the attack, use the `attack()` method on the enemy

       After each attack, update and show the health of Sir Foo, and of the enemy too; `if enemy health <= 0:` print `"You Win"`.

       But, `if Sir Foo health <= 0:` print `"You Lose"`.

- `else` (hut has a friend or is unoccupied) print `"you win"`

Initially, Sir Foo and the Orc will have full health. To quantify health, let's assign hit points to each of these characters (or the game units). So, when we say the character has full health, it means it has the maximum possible hit points. Depending on the character, the default number of hit points will vary. The following image shows Sir Foo and the Orc with the default number of hit points, indicated by the **Health** label:

The bar above the **Health** label in the image represents a health meter. Essentially, it keeps track of the *hit points*. In the discussion that follows, we will use the terms hit points and health meter interchangeably. During the combat, either the player or the enemy will get injured. For now, neglect the third possibility where both escape unhurt. An injury will reduce the number of available hit points for the injured unit. In the game, we will assume that in a single attack turn only one of the characters is hit. The following image will help you imagine one such attack turn:

Here, Sir Foo's health meter is shown as the maximum and the Orc has sustained injuries!

Hmm, the Orc thinks he can defeat Sir Foo! This is interesting. Let's develop the game first and then see who has a better chance of winning!

With this understanding of the problem, let's review the code that implements this feature.

Reviewing the code

Download the source file, ch01_ex02.py, from the chapter's code bundle and skim through the code. The key logic will be in the attack() function. We will also need a data structure to keep the health record of Sir Foo and the enemy. Let's start by introducing the following utility functions that take care of some print business:

```python
def print_bold(msg, end='\n'):
    """Print a string in 'bold' font"""
    print("\033[1m" + msg + "\033[0m", end=end)


def print_dotted_line(width=72):
    """Print a dotted (rather 'dashed') line"""
    print('-'*width)
```

Now, look at the main function, `run_application`, and the supporting function, `reset_health_meter`. In addition to introducing the dictionary `health_meter`, we have also encapsulated the game logic in `play_game`:

```python
def run_application():
    """Top level control function for running the application."""
    keep_playing = 'y'
    health_meter = {}
    reset_health_meter(health_meter)
    show_game_mission()

    while keep_playing == 'y':
        reset_health_meter(health_meter)
        play_game(health_meter)
        keep_playing = input("\nPlay again? Yes(y)/No(n): ")
```

Create empty dictionary to keep track of health

Write initial health record for Sir Foo and the potential enemy

At the start of a new game, the values of the `health_meter` dictionary are set back to the initial ones by calling `reset_health_meter`:

```python
def reset_health_meter(health_meter):
    """Reset the values of health_meter dict to the original ones"""
    health_meter['player'] = 40
    health_meter['enemy'] = 30
```

Next, let's review the `play_game` function. If the hut has the enemy, the player will be asked if the attack should be continued (the start of the `while` loop). Based on the user input, the code calls the `attack` function or exits the current game:

```python
def play_game(health_meter):
    huts = occupy_huts()
    idx = process_user_choice()          ── as before...
    reveal_occupants(idx, huts)

    if huts[idx - 1] != 'enemy':
        print_bold("Congratulations! YOU WIN!!!")
    else:
        print_bold('ENEMY SIGHTED! ', end='')
        show_health(health_meter, bold=True)
        continue_attack = True

        while continue_attack:
            continue_attack = input(".......continue attack? (y/n): ")
            if continue_attack == 'n':
                print_bold("RUNNING AWAY with following health status...")
                show_health(health_meter, bold=True)
                print_bold("GAME OVER!")
                break
                                    function to fight the combat and
                attack(health_meter) ──── update the health meter
check if
we have a
winner!    ─── if health_meter['enemy'] <= 0:
                print_bold("GOOD JOB! Enemy defeated! YOU WIN!!!")
                break

            if health_meter['player'] <= 0:
                print_bold("YOU LOSE  :(  Better luck next time")
                break
```

The enemy is attacked repetitively using the interactive `while` loop, which accepts user input. Execution of the `attack` function may result in injury to Sir Foo, or the enemy, or both. It is also possible that no one gets hurt. For simplicity, we will only consider two possibilities: a single attack that will injure either the enemy or Sir Foo. In the previous section, we used the built-in random number generator to randomly determine the occupants of the huts. We can use the same technique to determine who gets hurt:

```
injured_unit = random.choice(['player', 'enemy'])
```

But hold on a minute. Sir Foo has something to say:

We should take into account the chance of an injury to the player and to the enemy. In the `attack` function shown next, we will assume that for about *60%* of the time, the enemy will get hit and for the remaining *40%*, it is Sir Foo who is on the receiving end.

The simplest way is to create a list with 10 elements. This list should have six entries of `'enemy'` and four entries of `'player'`. Then, let `random.choice` select an element from this list. You can always introduce a difficulty level in the game and change this distribution:

```
def attack(health_meter):
    hit_list = 4 * ['player'] + 6 * ['enemy']
    injured_unit = random.choice(hit_list)
    hit_points = health_meter[injured_unit]
    injury = random.randint(10, 15)
    health_meter[injured_unit] = max(hit_points - injury, 0)
    print("ATTACK! ", end='')
    show_health(health_meter)
```

Get the current hit points for the randomly picked injured unit

update the health_meter for injured_unit

Once the `injured_unit` is selected randomly, the `injury` is determined by picking a random number between `10` and `15`, inclusive. Here, we use the `random.randint` function. The final important step is to update the `health_meter` dictionary for the injured unit by reducing its number of hit points.

Running Attack of the Orcs v0.0.5

We have discussed the most important functions in this game. Review the other supporting functions from the downloaded file. The following screenshot shows the game in action:

```
[user@hostname src_ch1]$ python ch01_ex02.py
Mission:
        Choose a hut where Sir Foo can rest...
TIP:
Be careful as there are enemies lurking around!
---------------------------------------------------------------------

Choose a hut number to enter (1-5): 1
Revealing the occupants...
        <1:enemy> <2:unoccupied> <3:enemy> <4:friend> <5:friend>
---------------------------------------------------------------------
ENEMY SIGHTED! Health: Sir Foo: 40, Enemy: 30
.......continue attack? (y/n): y
ATTACK! Health: Sir Foo: 40, Enemy: 17
.......continue attack? (y/n): y
ATTACK! Health: Sir Foo: 40, Enemy: 4
.......continue attack? (y/n): y
ATTACK! Health: Sir Foo: 40, Enemy: 0
GOOD JOB! Enemy defeated! YOU WIN!!!

Play again? Yes(y)/No(n): █
```

Using OOP – Attack of the Orcs v1.0.0

The attack feature that you added in the previous game has made it a lot more interesting. You can see some friends coming back again and again to play the game. The new feature requests have started pouring in.

Here is a partial list of the requested features:

1. New mission to acquire all the huts and defeat all the enemies. This also means the hut occupants should be revealed right at the beginning of the game.
2. Ability to get healed in a friendly or unoccupied hut.
3. Ability to abandon combat (or run away from the enemy). This is a strategic move to run away, get healed in a friendly hut, and resume combat.
4. Introduce one or more horse riders to assist Sir Foo. They can take turns to acquire huts. Ideally, a user-configurable option.
5. Ability to configure the maximum hit points for each enemy unit and each of the horse riders.
6. Configurable total number of huts; for example, increase it to 10.
7. Each hut can have either some gold or a weapon inside that Sir Foo and his friends can pick up.
8. Have an elf rider join Sir Foo. His abilities give him a very high chance of winning with fewer attacks.

This is quite a long list. You are preparing a plan. Here is a partial list of things you will need to add to the existing code to implement some of these features:

- Keeping track of the hit points of multiple enemy units occupying various huts
- Maintaining the health record of Sir Foo and all accompanying horse riders
- Monitoring how many huts are acquired by Sir Foo's army
- Another dictionary or list to keep track of the gold in each hut, and another one for weapons; additionally, what if someone wants to put armor in the hut?
- Not to forget, yet another list of dictionary for each unit that accepts any of these goodies
- Ah! So they want an elf rider with its own traits and abilities...nice...thanks for the additional trouble!

That is already a long list. While you could still continue to use the functional programming approach, in such scenarios it will get tougher as the game evolves and new features get added.

Thankfully, object-oriented programming comes to the rescue. How about making Sir Foo an instance of a `Knight class`? With this, it should be easy to manage parameters relevant to Sir Foo. For example, an attribute, `hitpoints`, can be used to keep track of Sir Foo's health instead of using the `health_meter` dictionary in the earlier example. Similarly, the other attributes in the class can keep track of the amount of gold or weapons collected while acquiring the huts (another requested feature).

There is a lot more beyond this bookkeeping. The various methods of the class would enable a specific implementation of behaviors, such as attack, run, heal, and so on. The horse riders accompanying Sir Foo can also be instances of the class `Knight`. Alternatively, you can create a new class called `HorseRider` for all these units that accept commands from Sir Foo.

Prioritize the feature requests

For this new version, let's hand pick a few requested features from the earlier list. In fact, Sir Foo should be the one who makes this call:

As you wish, Sir Foo...we will only add the new `heal` feature in this version.

Problem statement

It is now time to clearly define the targets for this release. You are not just adding new features to your application, but also making some fundamental changes to the code to accommodate future requests.

In this version, the mission is to acquire all of the five huts. Here, you will implement a new `heal` feature to regain all the hit points for Sir Foo. You will also implement some strategic controls, such as running away from combat, getting healed in a friendly hut, and then returning rejuvenated to defeat the enemy.

Redesigning the code

We already discussed how creating a `Knight` class will help simplify the handling of data and all other things related to Sir Foo, be it the hit points or the way he attacks enemies.

What other classes can be carved out? How about having the enemy as an object? The enemy could occupy multiple huts. Remember that we need to defeat all the enemies. Imagine the following scenario: Sir Foo injures an enemy in hut number 2, thereby reducing its hit points. Then, he moves on to another hut occupied by another enemy. Now, we need to maintain two separate hit point counters for each of these enemy units.

In a future version, you can expect users to ask for different enemy types with the ability to attack or heal, just like how we have it for Sir Foo. So, at this point, it makes sense to have a separate class, instances of which represent the enemy units. We will name this class `OrcRider`. It will have similar attributes to the `Knight` class. However, for simplicity, we will not give the enemy capabilities such as healing, changing huts, and so on.

> *Sir Foo says he is delighted to read that the enemy has been denied some important capabilities. (But you can't see his happy face behind the helm.)*

There is something else we should consider. So far, `huts` was just a simple Python `list` object holding information about the occupant types as strings.

Looking at the requested features list, we also need bookkeeping for the amount of gold and armor in the hut and to update its occupant, depending on the result of the fight. In a future version, you may also want to show some statistics, such as a historic record of the occupants, changes in the amount of gold, and so on. For all this and more, we will create a class, `Hut`.

Painting the big picture

Take a pen and paper and write down the important attributes we need for each class discussed so far. At this point, do not worry about classifying whether it is an instance variable or a class method that encapsulates instructions to perform specific tasks. Just write down what you think belongs to each class.

The following schematic shows a list of potential attributes for the Knight, Hut, and OrcRider classes. The attribute names in strikethrough text indicate the potential attributes that won't be implemented in this illustration. But, it is always good to think ahead and keep it at the back of your mind during the design phase of the application:

Orc Rider   Hut   Knight

Orc Rider	Hut	Knight
name	number	name
health_meter	occupant	health_meter
show_health	occupant_type	show_health
info	acquire	info
~~attack~~	~~weapons~~	attack
~~heal~~	~~gold~~	heal
~~acquire_hut~~	~~food~~	acquire_hut
~~run_away~~	~~history~~	run_away
~~weapons~~		~~weapons~~
~~gold~~		~~gold~~

This is not a complete specification, but we have a good starting point now. When Sir Foo enters an enemy hut, we have a choice to call the attack method of the Knight class. As before, the attack method will randomly pick who gets injured and deduct the hit points for that character. In the Knight class, it is convenient to have a new attribute, enemy, that will represent the active opponent. In this example, enemy will be an instance of the OrcRider class.

Let's develop this design further. Did you notice that the `Knight` and `OrcRider` classes have several things in common? We will use the **inheritance** principle to create a superclass for these classes, and call it `GameUnit`. We will move the common code to the superclass, and let the subclasses override the things they want to implement differently. In the next section, we will represent these classes with a **Unified Modeling Language** (**UML**)-like diagram.

Pseudo UML representation

The following diagram will help develop a basic understanding of how the various components talk to each other:

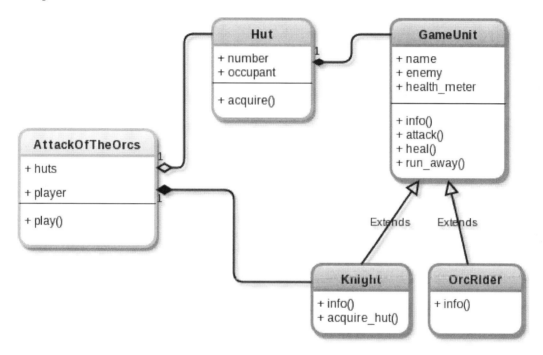

The preceding diagram is similar to a UML representation. It helps create a visual representation of a software design. In this book, we will loosely follow the UML representations. Let's call the diagrams used here pseudo UML diagrams (or UML-like diagrams).

Understanding the pseudo UML diagram

An explanation is in order for the UML-like convention used here. We will represent each class in the schematics as a rounded rectangle. It shows the class name followed by its attributes. The plus sign (**+**) before the attribute indicates that it is public. A protected or private method is generally represented with a negative sign (**-**). All the attributes shown in this diagram are public attributes. So, optionally, you could add a plus sign next to each attribute. In later chapters, we will follow this convention. For ease of illustration, only a few relevant public attributes will be listed. Observe that we are using different types of connectors in this diagram:

- The arrowhead with an empty triangle symbol represents inheritance; for example, the `Knight` class inherits from the `GameUnit` class

- The arrowhead with a filled diamond symbol represents **object composition**, for example, a `Hut` instance has an object of the `GameUnit` class (or its subclasses)

- The arrowhead with an empty diamond symbol represents **object aggregation**

Now, let's talk about the individual components of the diagram presented earlier.

The `Knight` and `OrcRider` classes inherit from `GameUnit`. The `Knight` class, in this case, will override default methods, such as `attack`, `heal`, and `run_away`. The `OrcRider` class will not have such overridden methods, as we will not give these capabilities to the enemy.

The `Hut` class will have an occupant. The occupant can either be an instance of the `Knight` or the `OrcRider`, or the `None` type if the hut is unoccupied. The filled diamond connector in the diagram indicates composition.

Object composition

It is an important OOP principle. It implies a has-a relationship. In this case, `Hut` contains, or is composed of, some other object that is to be used to perform specific tasks. Just say it out loud; a `Hut` has-a `Knight`, a `Hut` has-an `OrcRider`, and so on.

In addition to the four classes discussed, we will introduce another one to encapsulate the top-level code. Let's call it `AttackOfTheOrcs`. As there are five huts, a class method in `AttackOfTheOrcs` creates that number of `Hut` instances. This is object aggregation, shown by the empty diamond shaped arrow in the preceding diagram.

Have you noticed another has-a relationship in `AttackOfTheOrcs`? The `player` attribute in this class is an instance of the `Knight` class, but in the future, this could change. This relationship is indicated by the filled diamond-head connector joining the `Knight` and `AttackOfTheOrcs` boxes.

Reviewing the code

With this high-level understanding, let's begin developing the code. Download the Python source file, `ch01_ex03.py`. We will review only a few important methods in the code. Refer to this source file for the complete code.

 The code for this example, `ch01_ex03.py`, is all squished inside a single file. Is it good practice? Certainly not! As we go along, you will learn about best practices. Later in the book, we will discuss some important building blocks of application development, namely refactoring, coding standards, and design patterns. As an exercise, try to split the code into smaller modules and add code documentation.

The main execution code is shown here, along with some details of the `AttackOfTheOrcs` class. In the `__init__` method, we will initialize some instance variables and later update the values they hold. For example, `self.player` represents the instance of the `Knight` class when the game begins:

```python
class AttackOfTheOrcs:
    def __init__(self):
        self.huts = []
        self.player = None

    def get_occupants(self):...

    def show_game_mission(self):...

    def _process_user_choice(self):...

    def _occupy_huts(self):...

    def play(self):...


if __name__ == '__main__':
    game = AttackOfTheOrcs()
    game.play()
```

a list to hold the instances of class Hut to be created later.

The player to be instantiated later

various methods of the class (code is not shown)

create an instance of the class and call its play method

Just as a refresher, the __init__ method is somewhat similar to a constructor in languages such as C++; however, keep in mind some differences. For example, you cannot overload __init__ as you might do in these languages. Instead, you can easily accomplish this using optional arguments or the classmethod decorator. We will cover some aspects later in the book.

Let's quickly review the play and _occupy_huts methods:

Create an instance of the Knight class

```python
def play(self):
    self.player = Knight()
    self._occupy_huts()
    acquired_hut_counter = 0

    self.show_game_mission()
    self.player.show_health(bold=True)

    while acquired_hut_counter < 5:
        idx = self._process_user_choice()
        self.player.acquire_hut(self.huts[idx-1])

        if self.player.health_meter <= 0:
            print_bold("YOU LOSE  :(  Better luck next time")
            break

        if self.huts[idx-1].is_acquired:
            acquired_hut_counter += 1

    if acquired_hut_counter == 5:
        print_bold("Congratulations! YOU WIN!!!")
```

An underscore at the start indicates you intend to use this privately. But this is not enforced' in Python...

self. player takes it from here...

The self.player is an instance of the Knight class. We will call the acquire_hut method of this instance where most of the high-level action happens. After this, the program simply looks for the health parameters of the player and the enemy. It also queries the Hut instance to see if it is acquired.

Moving ahead, in the _occupy_hut method, the objects of Hut are created and appended to the self.huts list. This method is shown in the following figure:

```
def _occupy_huts(self):
    """Randomly occupy the huts with one of: friend, enemy or 'None'"""
    for i in range(5):
        choice_lst = ['enemy', 'friend', None]
        computer_choice = random.choice(choice_lst)
        if computer_choice == 'enemy':
            name = 'enemy-' + str(i+1)
            self.huts.append(Hut(i+1, OrcRider(name)))
        elif computer_choice == 'friend':
            name = 'knight-' + str(i+1)
            self.huts.append(Hut(i+1, Knight(name)))
        else:
            self.huts.append(Hut(i+1, computer_choice))
```

Create an instance of Hut. As the second argument for Hut, we create instance of a GameUnit

Public, protected, and private in Python

You will notice that some methods of the AttackOfTheOrcs class start with an underscore, for example, _process_user_choice(). That is a way to say that this method is not meant for public use. It is intended to be used from within the class. Languages such as C++ define class access specifiers, namely, private, protected, and public. These are used to put restrictions on the access of class attributes.

There is no such thing in Python. It allows outside access to the attributes with a single underscore as game._process_user_choice(). If the attribute name starts with double underscores, you can't call it directly. For example, you can't directly call game.__process_user_choice(). That being said, there is another way to access such attributes from outside. But let's not talk about it. Although Python allows you to access such attributes, it is is not good practice to do so!

Observe the `acquire_hut` method of the Knight class:

```python
def acquire_hut(self, hut):
    """Fight the combat (command line) to acquire the hut"""
    print_bold("Entering hut %d..."%hut.number, end=' ')
    is_enemy = (isinstance(hut.occupant, GameUnit)
                and hut.occupant.unit_type == 'enemy')
    continue_attack = 'y'
    if is_enemy:
        print_bold("Enemy sighted!")
        self.show_health(bold=True, end=' ')
        hut.occupant.show_health(bold=True, end=' ')
        while continue_attack:
            continue_attack = input(".......continue attack? (y/n): ")
            if continue_attack == 'n':
                self.run_away()
                break

            self.attack(hut.occupant)

            if hut.occupant.health_meter <= 0:
                print("")
                hut.acquire(self)
                break
            if self.health_meter <= 0:
                print("")
                break
    else:
        if hut.get_occupant_type() == 'unoccupied':
            print_bold("Hut is unoccupied")
        else:
            print_bold("Friend sighted!")
        hut.acquire(self)
        self.heal()
```

logic to see if the occupant is an enemy

self.attack() takes enemy as an argument. Pass the occupant object of the hut class. in our case it is an instance of OrcRider

update the 'occupant' attribute of the hut with an instance of this class

Let's talk through this method next:

- First, we need to check whether the hut's occupant is a friend or an enemy. This is determined by the variable `is_enemy`, as shown in the preceding figure.
- The hut's occupant can be of the following types: an instance of the `Knight` class, an instance of the `OrcRider` class, or set to `None`.
- The `GameUnit` class, and its subclasses `Knight` and `OrcRider`, define a `unit_type` attribute. This is just a string that is set as either `'friend'` or `'enemy'`.

- Thus, to determine whether there is an enemy hiding in the hut, we will first check whether the `hut.occupant` is an instance of the superclass `GameUnit`. If true, we will know it has a `unit_type` parameter. So, we will check whether `hut.occupant.unit_type` is equal to `'enemy'`. For the `OrcRider` class, `unit_type` is set to `'enemy'` by default.

- The rest of the logic is simple. If the occupant is an enemy, it asks the user what to do next: attack or run away.

- The `Knight.attack` method is similar to the one discussed earlier. One change here is that we can access the `health_meter` attribute of the injured unit and update it.

- If `hut.occupant` happens to be `'friend'` or `None`, it calls `hut.acquire()`.

What happens when the `Hut.acquire()` method is called? Here is the code snippet for the `Hut` class:

```python
class Hut:
    """Class to create hut object(s) in the game Attack of the Orcs"""
    def __init__(self, number, occupant):
        self.occupant = occupant
        self.number = number
        self.is_acquired = False

    def acquire(self, new_occupant):
        """Update the occupant of this hut"""
        self.occupant = new_occupant
        self.is_acquired = True
        print_bold("GOOD JOB! Hut %d acquired" % self.number)

    def get_occupant_type(self):
        """Return a string giving info on the hut occupant"""
        if self.is_acquired:
            occupant_type = 'ACQUIRED'
        elif self.occupant is None:
            occupant_type = 'unoccupied'
        else:
            occupant_type = self.occupant.unit_type

        return occupant_type
```

The `acquire` method simply updates the `occupant` attribute with the object passed as an argument to this method.

Running Attack of the Orcs v1.0.0

It's play time! We have reviewed the most important methods of the new classes. You can review the rest of the code from the ch01_ex03.py file, or better try to write these methods on your own. Run the application from the command line, like we did earlier. The following screenshot shows the game in action:

```
[user@hostname src_ch1]$ python ch01_ex03.py
Mission:
  1. Fight with the enemy.
  2. Bring all the huts in the village under your control
-----------------------------------------------------------------

Health: Sir Foo: 40
Current occupants: ['unoccupied', 'enemy', 'friend', 'friend', 'unoccupied']
Choose a hut number to enter (1-5): 2
Entering hut 2... Enemy sighted!
Health: Sir Foo: 40 Health: enemy-2: 30 .......continue attack? (y/n): y
ATTACK! Health: Sir Foo: 40  Health: enemy-2: 18  .......continue attack? (y/n): y
ATTACK! Health: Sir Foo: 40  Health: enemy-2: 5  .......continue attack? (y/n): y
ATTACK! Health: Sir Foo: 29  Health: enemy-2: 5  .......continue attack? (y/n): y
ATTACK! Health: Sir Foo: 14  Health: enemy-2: 5  .......continue attack? (y/n): n
RUNNING AWAY
Current occupants: ['unoccupied', 'enemy', 'friend', 'friend', 'unoccupied']
Choose a hut number to enter (1-5): 1
Entering hut 1... Hut is unoccupied
GOOD JOB! Hut 1 acquired
You are HEALED! Health: Sir Foo: 40
Current occupants: ['ACQUIRED', 'enemy', 'friend', 'friend', 'unoccupied']
Choose a hut number to enter (1-5): 2
Entering hut 2... Enemy sighted!
Health: Sir Foo: 40 Health: enemy-2: 5 .......continue attack? (y/n): y
ATTACK! Health: Sir Foo: 40  Health: enemy-2: 0
GOOD JOB! Hut 2 acquired
Current occupants: ['ACQUIRED', 'ACQUIRED', 'friend', 'friend', 'unoccupied']
Choose a hut number to enter (1-5): 3
```

healed! Go back to hut 2 and attack again!

injured earlier

yey!

Abstract base classes in Python

In the previous section, we redesigned the code using the OOP approach. We also demonstrated the use of inheritance by defining a superclass GameUnit, and inheriting from it to create the Knight and OrcRider subclasses. As the last topic in this chapter, let's talk about using abstract base classes in Python.

This section is intended to provide a basic understanding of ABCs in Python. The discussion here is far from being comprehensive but will be just enough to implement an ABC in our application code. For further reading, check out the Python documentation at https://docs.python.org/3/library/abc.html.

If you are familiar with OOP languages such as Java or C++, you probably already know the concept of an ABC.

A base class is a parent class from which other classes can be derived. Similarly, you can have an abstract base class and create other classes that inherit this class. So, where is the difference? One of the major differences is that an ABC can't be instantiated. But that is not the only difference. An ABC forces the derived classes to implement specific methods defined within that class. This much knowledge about an ABC should be good enough to work through the examples in this book. For more details, see the aforementioned Python documentation link. Let's review a simple example that shows how to implement an abstract base class in Python and how it differs from an ordinary base class. The abc module provides the necessary infrastructure. The following code snippet compares the implementation of an ABC to an ordinary base class:

```python
from abc import ABCMeta, abstractmethod          ①

class AbstractGameUnit(metaclass=ABCMeta):        class GameUnit:
    def __init__(self):                               def __init__(self):
        pass                   ②                           pass

    @abstractmethod  ╌╌╌
    def info(self):           ③                       def info(self):
        pass                                              print("INFO: GameUnit")

class Knight(AbstractGameUnit):                   class Knight(GameUnit):
    def __init__(self):                               def __init__(self):
        pass                                              pass
    def info(self):                                   def info(self):
        print("INFO: Knight")                             print("INFO: Knight")

if __name__ == "__main__":                        if __name__ == "__main__":
    # Inherits from ABC                               # inherits simple base class
    k1 = Knight()                                     k2 = Knight()
    k1.info()                                         k2.info()
```

The class on the left, AbstractGameUnit, is the abstract base class, whereas the GameUnit class on the right is an ordinary base class. The three differences in the ABC implementation are marked with numbers, as shown in the preceding screenshot.

- The argument metaclass=ABCMeta is used to define AbstractGameUnit as an ABC.

- The ABCMeta is a **metaclass** to define the abstract base class. It is a broad discussion topic, but the simplified meaning of a metaclass is as follows: to create an object, we use a class. Likewise, imagine a metaclass as one used to create a class.

- A Python **decorator** provides a simple way to dynamically alter the functionality of a method, a class, or a function. This is a special Python syntax that starts with an @ symbol followed by the decorator name. A decorator is placed directly above the method definition.

- The @abstractmethod is a decorator that makes the method defined on the next line an abstract method.

- The abstract method is the one that the ABC requires all the subclasses to implement. In this case, AbstractGameUnit requires its Knight subclass to implement the info() method. If the subclass does not implement this method, Python simply doesn't instantiate that subclass and will throw TypeError. You can try this by removing the Knight.info method and running the code.

- There is no such restriction if the Knight class inherits from an ordinary base class, such as GameUnit.

 The code illustrated here is for Python version 3.5. For version 2.7, the syntax is different. Refer to the ch01_ex03_AbstractBaseClass.py file in the Python2 directory of the supporting material for an equivalent example.

Exercise

In the ch01_ex03.py file, you will see some comments. These are intentionally kept to give you an opportunity to improve portions of the code. There is plenty of room for improvement in this code. See if you can rewrite portions of the code to make it more robust. If you prefer a well-defined problem, here is one:

The Knight and OrcRider classes inherit from the GameUnit superclass. This exercise is about converting GameUnit to AbstractGameUnit, an abstract base class. Here is a cheat sheet for you; the skeleton code shown in the following figure is with the Python 3.5 syntax.

Refer to the `ch01_ex03_AbstractBaseClass.py` file:

```python
class AbstractGameUnit(metaclass=ABCMeta):
    def __init__(self, name=''):...

    @abstractmethod
    def info(self):...

    def attack(self, enemy):...

    def heal(self, heal_by=2, full_healing=True):...

    def reset_health_meter(self):...

    def show_health(self, bold=False, end='\n'):...
```

 Note that for Python 2.7, there is a separate version of this code. Refer to the `src_ch1_Python2` directory in the supporting code bundle.

Summary

In this chapter, we touched upon some introductory concepts in Python to develop a simple command-line application. We first equipped ourselves by setting up a Python development environment.

The first program we wrote was a simple Python script. We soon realized that a simple script would be hard to maintain if more features are added. As a next step, we did a bit of refactoring and wrapped the code inside functions. This improved the code readability and also made it easier to manage. The proposed introduction of more features to the application made us rethink the design. We learned how to transform the code into an object-oriented design and implemented a few of these new features.

And how can we forget Sir Foo! He will accompany us throughout this book.

Is the code developed free from bugs? You might have already noticed some problems while playing the game! In the next chapter, we will see how to make the application more robust by handling exceptions.

Very important note for e-book readers

The code illustrations that you see in this book are actually image files or code snapshots.

The rendering quality of these images will vary depending on your PDF reader's page display resolution and the zoom level.

If you have trouble clearly reading this code, you may try the following in your PDF or e-book reader:

- Set the zoom level to 100%
- Use the page display resolution of 96 pixels/inch or similar

If the problem still persists, you can try with a different resolution.

How do you set this resolution? It will depend on your e-book reader. For example, if you are using Adobe Reader, go to **Edit | Preferences** and then select **Page Display** from the left panel. You will see **Resolution** as an option in the right panel. Select **96 pixels/inch** or similar and see if that helps render the images better.

2
Dealing with Exceptions

In the previous chapter, we started with a simple command-line script and gradually transformed it into an object-oriented code. Several new features were added in the process. So far, we have paid little attention to the application quality. We neglected to look for any obvious errors encountered during the program execution. Such errors detected during the application runtime are referred to as **exceptions**. In this chapter, you will learn techniques to make the application more robust by handling exceptions.

Specifically, we will cover the following topics:

- What are the exceptions in Python?
- Controlling the program flow with the `try...except` clause
- Dealing with common problems by handling exceptions
- Creating and using custom exception classes

Let's start by reviewing the feedback you received from the users.

Revisiting Attack of the Orcs v1.0.0

The heal feature added in v1.0.0 became a hit among the core users. The OOP approach put you in a better position to implement new features (or so you thought!). As the feature requests started pouring in, so did the reported bugs.

> *The game is OK, but there are several annoyances. For example, when prompted to choose a hut, sometimes I input a number greater than 5 or input a character by mistake. After this, it just prints some weird error message and the application terminates. Can you fix this?*

Debugging the problem

Let's try to reproduce the reported problem. Run the example from *Chapter 1, Developing Simple Applications*:

```
$ python ch01_ex03.py
```

When prompted for the hut number, enter any character, as shown in the following screenshot:

```
Health: Sir Foo: 40
Current occupants: ['unoccupied', 'friend', 'enemy', 'enemy', 'friend']
Choose a hut number to enter (1-5): y
Traceback (most recent call last):
  File "ch01_ex03.py", line 319, in <module>
    game.play()
  File "ch01_ex03.py", line 303, in play
    idx = self._process_user_choice()
  File "ch01_ex03.py", line 266, in _process_user_choice
    idx = int(user_choice)
ValueError: invalid literal for int() with base 10: 'y'
```

Entering any character instead of a number between 1-5 results in a ValueError

The application is terminated with an error **traceback** in the console. A traceback is a snapshot of the call stack at the point where the exception (the error) occurred. In this particular example, the _process_user_choice method is called by the play method, which is called directly from the module. The line numbers show where these calls occur. It is useful for debugging. The reported error in this case is ValueError. It occurred because we assumed the user choice as an integer. The other problem reported is when the hut number does not fall in the range 1 to 5. The traceback error received is IndexError. It occurs while accessing the entry in the huts list corresponding to the user input:

```
Choose a hut number to enter (1-5): 8 ———— out of range !
Traceback (most recent call last):
  File "ch01_ex03.py", line 319, in <module>
    game.play()                              error occurs in
  File "ch01_ex03.py", line 303, in play
    idx = self._process_user_choice() ——— this method
  File "ch01_ex03.py", line 267, in _process_user_choice
    if self.huts[idx-1].is_acquired:
IndexError: list index out of range
```

If you look at the two tracebacks closely, both these errors occur in the _process_user_choice method of the AttackOfTheOrcs class. Let's review the original method:

```python
def _process_user_choice(self):
    """Process the user input for choice of hut to enter"""
    verifying_choice = True                   'ValueError' if user inputs a
    idx = 0                                    character such as 'y'
    print("Current occupants: %s" % self.get_occupants())
    while verifying_choice:
        user_choice = input("Choose a hut number to enter (1-5): ")
        idx = int(user_choice)
        if self.huts[idx-1].is_acquired:
            print(
                "You have already acquired this hut. Try again."
                "<INFO: You can NOT get healed in already acquired hut.>")
        else:
            verifying_choice = False    'IndexError' if the 'idx-1' is a
                                        number that exceeds the length
    return idx                          of the 'huts' list
```

Good! We have pinpointed where the problem is. Now, the next task is to fix these bugs.

Fixing the bugs...

Sir Foo has some thoughts on fixing bugs...

Sure. One way to fix the reported problems is to add conditional blocks which ensure that the user input is a number between 1 and 5.

But like many other languages, Python provides an elegant way to handle such situations using the `try...except` clause. It is based on the **Easier to Ask for Forgiveness than Permission (EAFP)** principle.

The EAFP principle

When coding, you assume some things exist and try writing the code accordingly. But if this turns out to be a wrong assumption, you ask for forgiveness by catching that exception. This is a very common approach used in Python development. You can check out the Python 3 documentation (`https://docs.python.org/3/glossary.html`) that defines this idiom. In some cases, exception handling can affect the performance when compared to the use of the `if` condition blocks; however, you will most likely find more good things than bad ones when using the `try...except` clause.

Exceptions

Before jumping straight into the code and fixing these issues, let's first understand what an exception is and what we mean by handling an exception.

What is an exception?

An **exception** is an object in Python. It gives us information about an error detected during the program execution. The errors noticed while debugging the application were **unhandled exceptions** as we didn't see those coming. Later in the chapter, you will learn the techniques to handle these exceptions.

The `ValueError` and `IndexError` exceptions seen in the earlier tracebacks are examples of built-in exception types in Python. In the following section, you will learn about some other built-in exceptions supported in Python.

Most common exceptions

Let's quickly review some of the most frequently encountered exceptions. The easiest way is to try running some buggy code and let it report the problem as an error traceback! Start your Python interpreter and write the following code:

```
>>> import non_existant
Traceback (most recent call last):
  File "<stdin>", line 1, in <module>
ImportError: No module named 'non_existant'
>>>
>>> x
Traceback (most recent call last):
  File "<stdin>", line 1, in <module>
NameError: name 'x' is not defined
>>>
>>> assert(2 == 10)
Traceback (most recent call last):
  File "<stdin>", line 1, in <module>
AssertionError
```

Here are a few more exceptions:

```
>>> some_list = []
>>> some_list[1]
Traceback (most recent call last):
  File "<stdin>", line 1, in <module>
IndexError: list index out of range
>>>
>>> y = 10
>>> y.thing
Traceback (most recent call last):
  File "<stdin>", line 1, in <module>
AttributeError: 'int' object has no attribute 'thing'
>>>
>>> y/0
Traceback (most recent call last):
  File "<stdin>", line 1, in <module>
ZeroDivisionError: division by zero
```

As you can see, each line of the code throws an error traceback with an exception type (shown highlighted). These are a few of the built-in exceptions in Python. A comprehensive list of built-in exceptions can be found at https://docs.python.org/3/library/exceptions.html#bltin-exceptions.

Python provides BaseException as the base class for all built-in exceptions. However, most of the built-in exceptions do not directly inherit BaseException. Instead, they are derived from a class called Exception that in turn inherits from BaseException. The built-in exceptions that deal with program exit (for example, SystemExit) are derived directly from BaseException. You can also create your own exception class as a subclass of Exception. You will learn about that later in this chapter.

Exception handling

So far, we saw have seen the exceptions occur. Now it is time to learn how to use the try...except clause to handle these exceptions. The following pseudocode shows a very simple example of the try...except clause:

```
try:
    things_you_hope_will_execute_fine()
except:
    print("Uh oh..an exception occurred.")
    exception_handling_code()
    print("Gracefully handled!")

print("Done with the exception handling code...move on!")
```

Let's review the preceding code snippet:

- First, the program tries to execute the code inside the try clause.

- During this execution, if something goes wrong (if an exception occurs), it jumps out of this try clause. The remaining code in the try block is not executed.

- It then looks for an appropriate exception handler in the except clause and executes it.

The except clause used here is a universal one. It will catch all types of exceptions occurring within the try clause. Instead of having this "catch-all" handler, a better practice is to catch the errors that you anticipate and write an exception handling code specific to those errors. For example, the code in the try clause might throw an AssertionError. Instead of using the universal except clause, you can write a specific exception handler, as follows:

```
try:
    things_you_hope_will_execute_fine()
except AssertionError:
    print("Uh oh..an exception occurred.")
    exception_handling_code()
    print("Gracefully handled!")

    print("Done with the exception handling code...move on!")
```

Here, we have an except clause that exclusively deals with AssertionError. What it also means is that any error other than the AssertionError will slip through as an unhandled exception. For that, we need to define multiple except clauses with different exception handlers. However, at any point in time, only one exception handler will be called. This can be better explained with an example. Let's take a look at the following code snippet:

```
def solve_something():
    a = int(input("Enter a number 'a':"))
    # Raises AssertionError if a <= 0
    assert a > 0 ──────────────────────────────▶  Entering a <=0
                                                   results in an
                                                   assertion failure
    print("Number entered is OK.")
    # Raises NameError                                  │
    d = x + a                                           ▼
    e = 2*d                    if a > 0. it reaches  rest of the code
                               here and calls the   is skipped
def some_function():           other exception
    try:                       handler                   │
        solve_something()                                 ▼
    except NameError as e:                           calls this
        print("Uh oh..Name Error.", e.args)          exception handler
    except AssertionError:
        print("Uh oh..Assertion Error.")

if __name__ == '__main__':
    some_function()
```

The try block calls solve_something(). This function accepts a number as a user input and makes an assertion that the number is greater than zero. If the assertion fails, it jumps directly to the handler, except AssertionError.

In the other scenario, with a > 0, the rest of the code in solve_something() is executed. You will notice that the variable x is not defined, which results in NameError. This exception is handled by the other exception clause, except NameError. Likewise, you can define specific exception handlers for anticipated errors.

Raising and re-raising an exception

The raise keyword in Python is used to force an exception to occur. Put another way, it raises an exception. The syntax is simple; just open the Python interpreter and type:

```
>>> raise AssertionError("some error message")
```

This produces the following error traceback:

```
Traceback (most recent call last):
  File "<stdin>", line 1, in <module>
AssertionError :  some error message
```

In some situations, we need to re-raise an exception. To understand this concept better, here is a trivial scenario. Suppose, in the `try` clause, you have an expression that divides a number by zero. In ordinary arithmetic, this expression has no meaning. It's a bug! This causes the program to raise an exception called `ZeroDivisionError`. If there is no exception handling code, the program will just print the error message and terminate.

What if you wish to write this error to some log file and then terminate the program? Here, you can use an `except` clause to log the error first. Then, use the `raise` keyword without any arguments to re-raise the exception. The exception will be propagated upwards in the stack. In this example, it terminates the program. The exception can be re-raised with the `raise` keyword without any arguments.

Here is an example that shows how to re-raise an exception:

```
def solve_something():
    b = 0
    a = int(input("Enter a number 'a':"))
    assert a > 0
    print("Number entered is OK.")
    print("a = {}, b = {}, Now doing a/b".format(a, b))
    a += a/b  ←         Causes division by zero
    d = x + a           ZeroDivisionError Is raised.
    e = 2*d

def some_function():
    try:
        solve_something()            goes to the 'catch-all'
    except NameError as e:           exception clause
        print("Uh oh..Name Error.", e.args)
    except AssertionError:
        print("Uh oh..Assertion Error.")
    except Exception as e:
        print("Unhandled exception. Logging the error")
        # Some function that writes the error (not shown here)
        #log_the_error(e)
        raise
                            Log the error (do something useful).
if __name__ == '__main__':      Then 're-raise' the exception.
    some_function()
```

As can be seen, a division by zero exception is raised while solving the a/b expression. This is because the value of variable b is set to 0. For illustration purposes, we assumed that there is no specific exception handler for this error. So, we will use the general except clause where the exception is re-raised after logging the error. If you want to try this yourself, just write the code illustrated earlier in a new Python file, and run it from a terminal window. The following screenshot shows the output of the preceding code:

```
[user@hostname src_ch2]$ python test_zerodiv.py
Enter a number 'a':10
Number entered is OK.
a = 10, b = 0, Now doing a/b
Unhandled exception. Logging the error
Traceback (most recent call last):
  File "test_zerodiv.py", line 41, in <module>
    some_function()
  File "test_zerodiv.py", line 30, in some_function
    solve_something()
  File "test_zerodiv.py", line 24, in solve_something
    a += a/b
ZeroDivisionError: division by zero
```

The else block of try...except

There is an optional else block that can be specified in the try...except clause. The else block is executed only if no exception occurs in the try...except clause. The syntax is as follows:

```
try:
    things_you_hope_will_execute_fine()
except AssertionError:
    print("Uh oh..Assertion error occurred.")
else:
    print("Nice! Not exception raised so far.")
```

The else block is executed before the finally clause, which we will study next.

finally...clean it up!

There is something else to add to the try...except...else story: an optional finally clause. As the name suggests, the code within this clause is executed at the end of the associated try...except block. Whether or not an exception is raised, the finally clause, if specified, will certainly get executed at the end of the try...except clause. Imagine it as an all-weather guarantee given by Python! The following code snippet shows the finally block in action:

```
def some_function():
    try:
        a = int(input("Enter a number 'a':"))      = -1 (user input)
        assert a > 0
    except AssertionError:
        print("Uh oh..Assertion Error.")
    finally:
        print("Do some special cleanup")    in the end execute
                                             the 'finally' clause
if __name__ == '__main__':
    some_function()
```

Running this simple code will produce the following output:

```
$ python finally_example1.py
Enter a number: -1
Uh oh..Assertion Error.
Do some special cleanup
```

The last line in the output is the print statement from the finally clause.

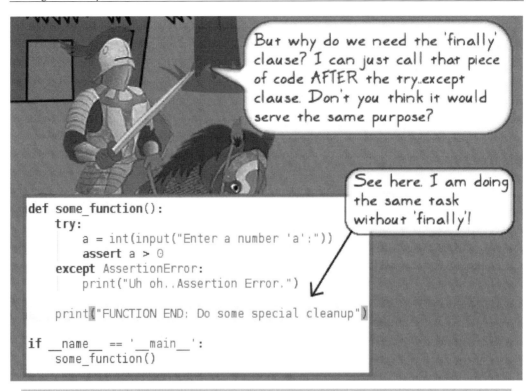

That's a good question! Let's add a twist to the tale. What if the new code in the except *clause forces a return from the function? In such a scenario, will your solution execute the last line of code shown in the earlier screenshot?*

The code snippets with and without the `finally` clause are shown in the following screenshot. The code in the `finally` clause is assured to be executed in the end, even when the `except` clause instructs the code to return from the function.

```
def some_function():
    try:
        a = int(input("Enter a number 'a':"))
        assert a > 0
    except AssertionError:
        print("Uh oh..Assertion Error.")
        print("Returning from the the function")
        return

    print("FUNCTION END: Do some special cleanup")

if __name__ == '__main__':
    some_function()
```

WITHOUT finally clause: Early return from the function. Code after try...except not run

```
Enter a number 'a':-1
Uh oh..Assertion Error.
Returning from the the function
```

```
def some_function():
    try:
        a = int(input("Enter a number 'a':"))
        assert a > 0
    except AssertionError:
        print("Uh oh..Assertion Error.")
        print("Returning from the the function")
        return
    finally:
        print("FINALLY: Do some special cleanup")

if __name__ == '__main__':
    some_function()
```

WITH finally clause: finally clause executed regardless of the return statement in the except clause

```
Enter a number 'a':-1
Uh oh..Assertion Error.
Returning from the the function
FINALLY: Do some special cleanup
```

The `finally` clause is typically used to perform clean-up tasks before leaving the function. An example use case is to close a database connection or a file. However, note that, for this purpose, you can also use the `with` statement in Python.

Back to the game – Attack of the Orcs v1.1.0

With this knowledge of the exception handling, let's work on the next incremental version of the application.

Preparatory work

Before writing any code, let's first understand how the rest of the section is organized. In a nutshell, we will start with v1.0.0 of the code from *Chapter 1, Developing Simple Applications,* progressively add the exception handling code, and call the new version v1.1.0.

 The Python files in the supporting code bundle already include the exception handling code to be discussed in this section as well as in a later section of this chapter, *Defining custom exceptions*

The following points elaborate further details:

- We will start by downloading the v1.0.0 of the game from *Chapter 1, Developing Simple Applications.* The file name is `ch01_ex03_AbstractBaseClass.py` (recall that this was provided as a solution to an exercise in *Chapter 1, Developing Simple Applications*). You can find this file in this chapter's code bundle.

- Compare the aforementioned file with `ch01_ex03.py`. The only difference here is the use of an abstract base class, `AbstractGameUnit`, instead of an ordinary base class, `GameUnit`. The rest of the code is identical.

- Let's copy `ch01_ex03_AbstractBaseClass.py` and save it as `attackoftheorcs_v1_1.py`. or give it any name you like. In the following discussion, we will refer to the file by this new name and incrementally add exception handling code to it.

- As noted before, the supporting code bundle has all the exception handling code that we will review. You will find a file by the same name (`attackoftheorcs_v1_1.py`) in the code bundle with all the changes included.

Adding the exception handling code

This will essentially be a bug-fix version with no new features added. The debugging done earlier has already helped us find where the problems are. Open the Python file (attackoftheorcs_v1_1.py) and update the _process_user_choice method of the AbstractGameUnit class. The updated version of this method with the new try... except clauses is shown in the following code snippet:

```python
def _process_user_choice(self):
    """Process the user input for choice of hut to enter"""
    verifying_choice = True
    idx = 0
    print("Current occupants: %s" % self.get_occupants())
    while verifying_choice:
        user_choice = input("Choose a hut number to enter (1-5): ")
        try:
            idx = int(user_choice)
        except ValueError as e:
            print("Invalid input, args: %s \n" % e.args)
            continue

        try:
            if self.huts[idx-1].is_acquired:
                print("You have already acquired this hut. Try again."
                    "<INFO: You can NOT get healed in already acquired hut.>")
            else:
                verifying_choice = False
        except IndexError:
            print("Invalid input : ", idx)
            print("Number should be in the range 1-5. Try again")
            continue

    return idx
```

Code that handles the ValueError exception when raised

Handle the `IndexError` exception

> In case you missed reading this earlier, you should copy the ch01_ex03_AbstractBaseClass.py file and name it attackoftheorcs_v1_1.py. Then work with this new file to add the preceding exception handling code. Alternatively, you can simply review the file with the same name provided in the code bundle for this chapter. It includes all the changes we will discuss next. The Python 2.7.9 compatible source file is also provided in the code bundle.

Let's review the preceding code:

- In the `try` clause, if the `user_choice` variable is not a number, the `ValueError` exception occurs, which is handled by `except ValueError as e`

- The `as` keyword is used to assign exception to an `e` object

- Alternatively, you can just use the syntax `except ValueError`

- The second `try...except` clause takes care of the situation where the input number goes out of range of the `huts` list

- When the `IndexError` exception occurs, the `continue` statement in the `except` clause makes the user re-enter the input

That's all we need. Now, let's run the application next.

Running Attack of the Orcs v1.1.0

It is time to run the application and see if these changes fix the reported problems. Run the program in a terminal window, as shown in the following code snippet:

```
$ python attackoftheorcs_v1_1.py
```

When prompted for an input, enter some unacceptable value for the hut number:

```
Health: Sir Foo: 40
Current occupants: ['friend', 'unoccupied', 'enemy', 'enemy', 'unoccupied']
Choose a hut number to enter (1-5): 8 ✕
Invalid input :  8
Number should be in the range 1-5. Try again ── Nice! it is going back
Choose a hut number to enter (1-5): hi ✕       to the while loop
Invalid input, args: invalid literal for int() with base 10: 'hi'

Choose a hut number to enter (1-5): 2 ✓
Entering hut 2... Hut is unoccupied
GOOD JOB! Hut 2 acquired
```

Looks good! At least the reported problems have been resolved. It is easy to find more such errors. For example, a user can still enter 0 or a negative number while choosing a hut, or, when the program asks for permission to attack the enemy, any input other than y or n is not handled gracefully. As an exercise, have a go at fixing these issues yourself!

Defining custom exceptions

You can define your own exception class by inheriting from the `Exception` base class or any other exception class. Why do we need such customization? Firstly, you can create an exception class with a descriptive name. This allows us to identify the purpose of the exception just by looking at the descriptive name. For example, instead of `ValueError`, a custom exception named `ValueGreaterThanFiveError` will immediately help identify the problem. There are other advantages as well. You can use such classes to add customized messages based on error subcategories, writing error logs, and so on. Let's learn how to define custom exceptions next.

Preparatory work

Here is a list of files we will use:

- `attackoftheorcs_v1_1.py`: This is the file from the previous section that we will use. As mentioned earlier, the supporting code bundle already has a file by the same name. It includes all the modifications we will discuss.

- `gameuniterror.py`: This is a new module to hold a custom exception class.

- `heal_exception_example.py`: This is where the top-level control code will be written. This is a simplified version of the game where we do not need to play the whole game in order to reproduce the problem.

You need to put all the aforementioned files in the same directory.

Custom exception – The problem

To demonstrate the use of custom exceptions, let's identify a trivial problem. Observe the `heal` method shown next (recall that it is defined in `AbstractGameUnit`, the superclass of `Knight`). You can find it in the `attackoftheorcs_v1_1.py` file.

```python
def heal(self, heal_by=2, full_healing=True):
    """Heal the unit replenishing all the hit points"""
    if self.health_meter == self.max_hp:
        return
    if full_healing:
        self.health_meter = self.max_hp
    else:
        self.health_meter += heal_by
    print_bold("You are HEALED!", end=' ')
    self.show_health(bold=True)
```

The method has two optional arguments. If `full_healing` is set to `True`, the game unit will regain all its lost hit points. The other option, `heal_by`, heals the game unit by a small amount. In this version, we are not using the `heal_by` option. But in a future version, you may want to introduce a turn-based feature in the game, where the injured units are healed by a small amount on every turn.

To demonstrate how to create and use custom exceptions, let's introduce an artificial bug in the `heal_by` feature! Save the following code as `heal_exception_example.py` and place this file in the same directory as `attackoftheorcs_v1_1.py`.

```python
from attackoftheorcs_v1_1 import Knight
if __name__ == '__main__':
    print("Creating a Knight..")
    knight = Knight("Sir Bar")
    # Assume the knight has sustained injuries in the combat.
    knight.health_meter = 10
    knight.show_health()
    # Heal the knight by 100 hit points. This is the 'artificial bug'!
    # The Knight can have a maximum of 40 hit points.
    knight.heal(heal_by=100, full_healing=False)
    knight.show_health()
```

This is a simplified version of the game where we do not need to play the whole game in order to create this artificial bug! It is a top-level control code that creates a `Knight` instance, forcefully reduces the hit points (check out `knight.health_meter`) as if the knight has fought a combat and sustained injuries. In the end, it calls the `heal` function with the `heal_by` argument.

Have you noticed a problem here? Recall that the `knight` instance can have a maximum of `40` hit points (check out the instance attribute `Knight.max_hp`). The preceding code is trying to `heal` the knight by `100` points using the `heal_by` argument. Clearly, it will exceed the limit. One way of preventing this is to add an assertion statement in the `heal` method, as shown in the following code snippet:

```python
assert (self.health_meter + heal_by  <= self.max_hp)
```

This will raise an `AssertionError`. This is an acceptable solution. Another way to accomplish this is to use a custom exception class. It is demonstrated next.

Writing a new exception class

It is trivial to create a new exception class derived from Exception. Open your Python interpreter and create the following class:

```
>>> class GameUnitError(Exception):
...      pass
...
>>>
```

That's all! We have a new exception class, GameUnitError, ready to be deployed. How to test this exception? Just raise it. Type the following line of code in your Python interpreter:

```
>>> raise GameUnitError("ERROR: some problem with game unit")
```

Raising the newly created exception will print the following traceback:

```
>>> raise GameUnitError("ERROR: some problem with game unit")
Traceback (most recent call last):
  File "<stdin>", line 1, in <module>
__main__.GameUnitError: ERROR: some problem with game unit
```

Copy the GameUnitError class into its own module, gameuniterror.py, and save it in the same directory as attackoftheorcs_v1_1.py.

Next, update the attackoftheorcs_v1_1.py file to include the following changes:

- First, add the following import statement at the beginning of the file:

  ```
  from gameuniterror import GameUnitError
  ```

- The second change is in the AbstractGameUnit.heal method. The updated code is shown in the following code snippet. Observe the highlighted code that raises the custom exception whenever the value of self.health_meter exceeds that of self.max_hp.

```
def heal(self, heal_by=2, full_healing=True):
    """Heal the unit replenishing all the hit points"""
    if self.health_meter == self.max_hp:
        return
    if full_healing:
        self.health_meter = self.max_hp
    else:
        self.health_meter += heal_by

    # raise a custom exception.
    if self.health_meter > self.max_hp:
        raise GameUnitError("health_meter > max_hp!")

    print_bold("You are HEALED!", end=' ')
    self.show_health(bold=True)
```

With these two changes, run `heal_exception_example.py` created earlier. You will
see the new exception being raised, as shown in the following screenshot:

```
[user@hostname ch]$ python heal_exception_example.py
Creating a Knight..
Health: Sir Bar: 10
Traceback (most recent call last):
  File "heal_exception_example.py", line 45, in <module>
    knight.heal(heal_by=100, full_healing=False)
  File "/home/ch/attackoftheorcs_v1_1.py", line 135, in heal
    raise GameUnitError("health_meter > max_hp!")
gameuniterror.GameUnitError: health_meter > max_hp!
```

Expanding the exception class

Can we do something more with the GameUnitError class? Certainly! Just like any other class, we can define attributes and use them. Let's expand this class further. In the modified version, it will accept an additional argument and some predefined error code. The updated GameUnitError class is shown in the following screenshot:

```python
class GameUnitError(Exception):
    """Custom exceptions class for the `AbstractGameUnit` and its subclasse
    def __init__(self, message='', code=000):
        super().__init__(message)
        self.error_message = '~'*50 + '\n'          # a new instance
        self.error_dict = {                         # attribute to hold
                                                    # error code info
            000: "ERROR-000: Unspecified Error!",
            101: "ERROR-101: Health Meter Problem!",
            102: "ERROR-102: Attack issue! Ignored",
        }
        try:                                        # prepare
            self.error_message += self.error_dict[code]   # the error
        except KeyError:                                  # message
            self.error_message += self.error_dict[000]
        self.error_message += '\n' + '~'*50
```

Let's take a look at the code in the preceding screenshot:

- First, it calls the __init__ method of the Exception superclass and then defines some additional instance variables.

- A new dictionary object, self.error_dict, holds the error integer code and the error information as key-value pairs.

- The self.error_message stores the information about the current error depending on the error code provided.

- The try...except clause ensures that error_dict actually has the key specified by the code argument. It doesn't in the except clause; we just retrieve the value with the default error code of 000.

Now, let's take look at the consumer of this class. Observe the modified `heal` method. The only change here is the additional argument to the `GameUnitError` instance. Here, we pass an error code as the second argument:

```python
def heal(self, heal_by=2, full_healing=True):          attackoftheorcs_v1_1.py
    """Heal the unit replenishing all the hit p
    if self.health_meter == self.max_hp:
        return

    if full_healing:
        self.health_meter = self.max_hp           Pass an `error code` as
    else:                                         an additional parameter
        self.health_meter += heal_by
    # -----------------------------------------------------------------
    # raise a custom exception. Refer to chapter on exception handling
    # -----------------------------------------------------------------
    if self.health_meter > self.max_hp:
        raise GameUnitError("health_meter > max_hp!", 101)

    print_bold("You are HEALED!", end=' ')
    self.show_health(bold=True)
```

So far, we have made changes to the `GameUnitError` class and the `AbstractGameUnit.heal` method. We are not done yet. The last piece of the puzzle is to modify the `main` program in the `heal_exception_example.py` file. The code is shown in the following screenshot:

```python
from attackoftheorcs_v1_1 import Knight          heal_exception_example.py
from gameuniterror import GameUnitError

if __name__ == '__main__':
    print("Creating a Knight..")             Will raise
    knight = Knight("Sir Bar")               GameUnitError
    knight.health_meter = 10                 exception
    knight.show_health()
    try:
        knight.heal(heal_by=100, full_healing=False)
    except GameUnitError as e:
        print(e)                             Retrieve the error info
        print(e.error_message)               with the new exception
                                             handler for GameUnitError
    knight.show_health()
```

Let's review the code:

- As the `heal_by` value is too large, the `heal` method in the `try` clause raises the `GameUnitError` exception.

- The new `except` clause handles the `GameUnitError` exception just like any other built-in exceptions.

- Within the `except` clause, we have two `print` statements. The first one prints `health_meter > max_hp!` (recall that, when this exception was raised in the `heal` method, this string was given as the first argument to the `GameUnitError` instance). The second `print` statement retrieves and prints the `error_message` attribute of the `GameUnitError` instance.

We have got all the changes in place. We can run this example from a terminal window as:

```
$ python heal_exception_example.py
```

The output of the program is shown in the following screenshot:

```
try:
    knight.heal(heal_by=100, full_healing=False)
except GameUnitError as e:
    print(e)
    print(e.error_message)
```
code snippet from,
`heal_exception_example.py`

```
[user@hostname src_ch2]$ python heal_exception_example.py
Creating a Knight..
Health: Sir Bar: 10
health_meter > max_hp!
~~~~~~~~~~~~~~~~~~~~~~~~~~~~~~~~~~~~~~~~~~
ERROR-101: Health Meter Problem!
~~~~~~~~~~~~~~~~~~~~~~~~~~~~~~~~~~~~~~~~~~
Health: Sir Bar: 110
```

unacceptable value, raises GameUnitError exception. In the except clause, we print the error message.

In this simple example, we have just printed the error information to the console. You can further write verbose error logs to a file and keep track of all the error messages generated while the application is running.

Inheriting from the exception class

Sir Foo has something to say about the error codes maintained in `GameUnitError.error_dict` *seen earlier...*

You are right. While raising an exception, you need to remember what each error number corresponds to. Let's discuss a few alternatives.

One option is to use unique strings as keys of `error_dict` in place of the error numbers, for example:

```
self.error_dict = {
    'health_meter_problem':"ERROR: Health meter problem!"}
```

This alleviates the problem of remembering the error codes. However, this approach is not suitable if you want to do something beyond just printing a message. For example, depending on the error type, you may want to do some additional processing.

A better approach is to use `GameUnitError` as a base exception class and derive new classes that target specific errors. The descriptive names of these exception classes should help convey the same information. The following code snippet shows an example of how to do it. You can replace the existing code in `gameuniterror.py` with the one shown in the following screenshot:

```python
class GameUnitError(Exception):
    """Custom exceptions class for the `AbstractGameUnit` and its subclasses"""
    def __init__(self, message=''):
        super().__init__(message)
        self.padding = '~'*50 + '\n'
        self.error_message = " Unspecified Error!"


class HealthMeterException(GameUnitError):
    """Custom exception to report Health Meter related problems"""
    def __init__(self, message=''):
        super().__init__(message)
        self.error_message = (self.padding +
                              "ERROR: Health Meter Problem" +
                              '\n' + self.padding )
```

gameuniterror.py

Now, in the `heal` method, instead of raising the `GameUnitError` exception, just raise the `HealthMeterException`. Be sure to `import` the `HealthMeterException` module as indicated in the following code snippet:

```
from gameuniterror import HealthMeterException        attackoftheorcs_v1_1.py

Method of class AbstractGameUnit                    Import statement at the
                                                    top of the file

    def heal(self, heal_by=2, full_healing=True):
        """Heal the unit replenishing all the hit points"""
        if self.health_meter == self.max_hp:
            return

        if full_healing:
            self.health_meter = self.max_hp
        else:
            self.health_meter += heal_by
        # - - - - - - - - - - - - - - - - - - - - - - - - - - - - - - - - - -
        # raise a custom exception. Refer to chapter on exception handling
        # - - - - - - - - - - - - - - - - - - - - - - - - - - - - - - - - - -
        if self.health_meter > self.max_hp:
            raise HealthMeterException("health_meter > max_hp!")

        print_bold("You are HEALED!", end=' ')
        self.show_health(bold=True)
```

Running the code with the aforementioned changes produces a similar output. It is just that we have revised `error_message` of the `HealthMeterException` class. The output is shown as follows:

```
$ python heal_exception_example.py
Creating a Knight..
Health: Sir Bar: 10
health_meter > max_hp!
~~~~~~~~~~~~~~~~~~~~~~~~~~~~~~~~~~~~~~~~~~~~~~~~~~~~~~~~~~
ERROR: Health Meter Problem
~~~~~~~~~~~~~~~~~~~~~~~~~~~~~~~~~~~~~~~~~~~~~~~~~~~~~~~~~~

Health: Sir Bar: 110
```

Likewise, you can create other subclasses to deal with specific issues.

Exercise

Identify any code that can benefit from exception handling. For example, create a new `HutError` exception, and use it to raise errors related to the `Hut` class. Here is a cheat sheet:

```python
class HutError(Exception):
    def __init__(self, code):
        self.error_message = ''
        self.error_dict = {
            000: "E000: Unspecified Error code",
            101: "E101: Out of range: Number > 5",
            102: "E102: Out of range, Negative number",
            103: "E103: not a number!"
        }
        try:
            self.error_message = self.error_dict[code]
        except KeyError:
            self.error_message = self.error_dict[000]
        print("\n Error message:", self.error_message)
```

Instead of using `error_dict`, you can also create subclasses, such as:

```python
class HutNumberGreaterThanFiveError(HutError): pass
class NegativeHutNumberError(HutError): pass
```

Summary

This chapter served as an introduction to the basics of exception handling in Python. We saw how the exceptions occur, learned about some common built-in exception classes, and wrote simple code to handle these exceptions using the `try...except` clause. By handling exceptions, we fixed some obvious bugs in the *Attack of the Orcs* game.

The chapter also demonstrated techniques, such as raising and re-raising exceptions, using the `finally` clause, and so on. The later part of the chapter focused on implementing custom exception classes. We defined a new exception class and used it for raising custom exceptions for our application.

With exception handling, the code is in a better shape. However, we still have the majority of the code squished inside a single file (`attackoftheorcs_v1_1.py`). In the next chapter, you will learn how to package the application code and release it to a broader audience.

3
Modularize, Package, Deploy!

In the past few chapters, you wrote a simple application, added new features to it, and made sure that some commonly encountered bugs were fixed. Now, it is time to make it available to a broader audience. In this chapter, you will learn the following topics:

- Modularizing and packaging the code written in earlier chapters
- Preparing and deploying a source distribution
- Setting up a private Python package repository
- Making incremental releases
- Bringing your code under version control

Thanks to word of mouth publicity, the high fantasy game application is gaining further attention. More and more people are requesting access to the code, either to use the functionality in their own application or to simply play the game. So far, you have sent the complete source code to the users requesting it. But, it is silly to continue doing that because you have made quite a few frequent upgrades.

There are several ways to handle this. The most basic option is to host the code on some server and ask the users to download it from that location. Another option is to use a version control system such as **Git** to manage the code and let others clone it. Yet another option, which we will see next, is to deploy this as a Python package.

Not so fast, Sir Foo! We have to do some preparatory work first. Hold on to your enthusiasm for now. By the way, your army is still far away. You will be reunited with your comrades in arms in Chapter 6, Design Patterns.

Selecting a versioning convention

How do we name new versions of the code? There are several versioning schemes in use. Let's quickly review a few popular ones.

Serial increments

In this scheme, you just increment the version number in a serial manner for each upgrade, for example, v1, v2, v3, and so on. However, this does not give any information on what a particular release is about. Just by looking at the version number, it is tough to tell whether a particular version introduces a revolutionary feature or just fixes a minor bug. It does not give any information on API compatibility. You can choose this simple versioning scheme if it is a small application with a small user base and a very limited scope.

API compatibility

An **Application Programming Interface (API)**, in simple terms, enables a piece of a program, say a library or an application, to talk to another one using a standard set of functions, methods, or objects.

Imagine a software library `car` that stores some data on a fancy car. You have an application that wishes to get some information on the car color. The library says, "just call my `color()` method to get what you need." Here, the `color()` method is an API method of the `car` library. With this information, you have started using `car.color()` within your application.

In the latest version of the `car` library, `color()` has been renamed to `get_color()`. If you switch to this new version, it will break your application code as you are still using `car.color()` to retrieve the color information from the library. In this case, the new API is said to be incompatible with the older releases of the library. Conversely, a **backward compatible** API is where applications using the older version of the library will continue to run smoothly even with the newer one. This is just one way to look at API compatibility.

Using a date format

In this convention, the release name is tagged by embedding information on when it was released. For example, it may follow the YYYY-MM convention to include the year and month of release. Such a convention helps determine how old a particular release is. However, as before, the release name itself does not give any information about API compatibility unless you follow some hybrid naming convention. This scheme is typically useful if you are following a regular release schedule or have some time sensitive features in the release.

Semantic versioning scheme

This is a recommended versioning convention. In the application we have developed so far, we loosely followed the semantic versioning scheme. In this scheme, the release is represented by three numbers (**MAJOR.MINOR.PATCH**). For example, when we say version 1.2.4, it implies that the major version number is 1, minor version is 2, and patch or maintenance version number is 4. The major version number is incremented when you introduce incompatible changes to the API that access functionality from your package. The minor version is incremented when some new minor functionality is added to the package while keeping the code backward compatible. For example, you add a new internal feature to the next version, but that does not break any code from the previous version. The API to access functionality from the package remains the same as before. The last number represents the patch. It is incremented when some bugs are fixed.

> Python *PEP 440* specification talks in depth about the semantic versioning scheme for Python distributions. This is what the Python community recommends. You can find this specification at https://www.python.org/dev/peps/pep-0440/. Choose the versioning convention that best suits your application.
>
> The versioning scheme illustrated in this book only loosely follows semantic versioning. For instance, in earlier illustrations, after fixing some important bugs, we updated the minor version number instead of the patch version number.

With this understanding of various versioning conventions, let's go back to the *Attack of the Orcs* code and split it into independent modules. This would be our first step toward creating a package.

Modularizing the code

We have been referring to modules in the earlier chapters. An explanation is in order. A single Python file with a `.py` extension is a **module**. You can use this module in some other source code using an `import` statement. The module name is the same as the file name, except the `.py` extension. For example, if the file name is `knight.py`, then `import knight` will import the module into your source file.

In this section, we will split the code in the `attackoftheorcs_v1_1.py` file into individual modules. You can find this file in the supporting code bundle for the previous chapter.

Attack of the Orcs v2.0.0

We will name this version 2.0.0. The major version is incremented to 2 as we are about to make some API level changes. The way we access functionality from the code will change after introduction of the new modules. Let's review the source file, `attackoftheorcs_v1_1.py`, from *Chapter 2, Dealing with Exceptions*. The first step is to create a module (a new file) for each of the classes. The module name should preferably be all lowercase.

```
def weighted_random_selection(obj1, obj2):...

def print_bold(msg, end='\n'):...                    > gameutils.py

class AbstractGameUnit(metaclass=ABCMeta):...  —  abstractgameunit.py

class Knight(AbstractGameUnit):...        —  knight.py

class OrcRider(AbstractGameUnit):...      —  orcrider.py

class Hut:...    —  hut.py

class AttackOfTheOrcs:...
                                         > attackoftheorcs.py
if __name__ == '__main__':
    game = AttackOfTheOrcs()
    game.play()
```

Let's take a look at the code in the preceding screenshot:

- Create a new module called `gameutils.py` and copy the utility functions `weighted_random_selection` and `print_bold` into this module.

- The `attackoftheorcs.py` file holds the `AttackOfTheOrcs` class. In the same file, copy the main execution code that runs the game. Optionally, create a new module for the main code.

- Refer to the code from the previous screenshot and put the other classes in their own modules.

We are not done yet. Splitting the code into a bunch of modules gives rise to unresolved references. We need to fix these new errors now. This was not a problem earlier as the entire code was in a single file. For example, while creating `Hut` instances in the `AttackOfTheOrcs` class, Python could find the `Hut` class definition right in the same file. Now, we need to import these classes from their respective modules.

 If you are using an IDE such as PyCharm, it is very easy to detect such unresolved references using the **code inspection** feature. The IDE will show a visual indication (for example, a red underline) for all problematic references. Additionally, the Inspect Code feature lets you find all the problem code in one go.

Add the following `import` statements at the beginning of the `attackoftheorcs.py` file:

```
import random
from hut import Hut                    ─────── attackoftheorcs.py
from knight import Knight
from orcrider import OrcRider
from gameutils import print_bold
```

Here, we import the `Hut` class from the new module called `hut`, and so on. The following code screenshot shows the `import` statements in the `knight.py` file:

```
from abstractgameunit import AbstractGameUnit        ─────── knight.py
from gameutils import print_bold
```

The following code screenshot shows the `import` statements in the `abstractgameunit.py` file:

```
import random
from abc import ABCMeta, abstractmethod
from gameutils import print_bold, weighted_random_selection
from gameuniterror import GameUnitError
```

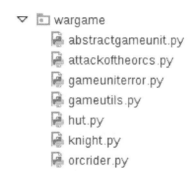

Likewise, you have to update all the remaining files and include the necessary `import` statements. Those changes are not discussed here. For further details, you can refer to the corresponding files in this chapter's supporting code bundle.

Put all the new modules in a directory, call it `wargame` or give it any name you like. Recall that in *Chapter 2*, *Dealing with Exceptions*, we had created a class called `GameUnitError` in a `gameuniterror.py` file. Make sure to copy this file into the new directory. The directory structure after copying `gameuniterror.py` is shown in the next screenshot:

▽ 🗀 wargame
    📄 abstractgameunit.py
    📄 attackoftheorcs.py
    📄 gameuniterror.py
    📄 gameutils.py
    📄 hut.py
    📄 knight.py
    📄 orcrider.py

As the last step, let's verify that the application runs smoothly by executing the following command:

```
$ python attackoftheorcs.py
```

Where `python` is either version 3.5 or 2.7.9 (or higher), depending on your environment.

Creating a package

Now that we have modularized the code, let's create a Python package. What is a package? It is a kind of fancy name for a directory where Python modules are located. However, there is more to it than that. For such a directory to be called a package, it must also contain an __init__.py file. This file can be kept empty or you can put some initialization code in this file. To transform the wargame directory as a Python package, we will create an empty __init__ .py file in this directory. The new directory structure is shown in the following screenshot:

Importing from the package

Let's see how to use the functionality from this newly created package. To test this out, create a new file, run_game.py, at the same directory level as the wargame package. The directory structure will appear as follows. Here, mydir is the top-level directory (it can be any name):

Add the following code to the `run_game.py` file:

```
from wargame.attackoftheorcs import AttackOfTheOrcs

game = AttackOfTheOrcs()
game.play()
```

The first line is the new `import` statement. Here, we are importing the `AttackOfTheOrcs` class from the `attackoftheorcs.py` file. If you execute this file in a terminal window, the program might abruptly end with the error traceback shown in the following code:

```
$ python run_game.py
Traceback (most recent call last):
  File "run_game.py", line 2, in <module>
    from wargame.attackoftheorcs import AttackOfTheOrcs
  File "/mydir/wargame/attackoftheorcs.py", line 29, in <module>
    from hut import Hut
ImportError: No module named 'hut'
```

Such an error will occur if the `wargame` directory path is not included in the Python environment. In the error traceback, it is unable to find the `hut.py` file. The file is located at `/mydir/wargame/hut.py`. However, the location `/mydir/wargame` is not in Python's search path. As a result, it cannot find the modules in this directory. There are several ways to fix this. The simplest option is to specify a PYTHONPATH environment variable in the terminal. In the Bash shell of Linux OS, this can be specified as follows:

```
$ export PYTHONPATH=$PYTHONPATH:/mydir/wargame
```

On Windows OS, you can set it from the command prompt, as follows:

```
> set PYTHONPATH=%PYTHONPATH%;C:\mydir\wargame
```

Just replace `/mydir/wargame` with the appropriate path on your system. Another way to fix the problem is to add a `sys.path.append("/mydir/wargame")` statement at the beginning of the code in `run_game.py` before the `import` statement, as shown in the following code:

```
import sys
sys.path.append("/mydir/wargame")
from wargame.attackoftheorcs import AttackOfTheOrcs
```

With both these options, however, you have to specify the full path. Yet another way to handle the problem is to add the following code in the wargame/__init__.py file:

```
import sys
import os
current_path = os.path.dirname(os.path.abspath(__file__))
sys.path.append(current_path)
# optionally print the sys.path for debugging)
#print("in __init__.py sys.path:\n ",sys.path)
```

The current path gives the absolute path to the directory where the __init__.py file is located. With this update, you should be all set to run the game.

Releasing the package on PyPI

The **Python Package Index (PyPI)** (https://pypi.python.org/pypi) is a package distribution mechanism for the Python community. It is the official repository for the third-party packages. By default, the Python package manager, pip, searches this repository to install the packages.

This is the place where we will upload our source distribution and make it generally available to the Python community. The PyPI repository has a devoted **test server** (https://testpypi.python.org/pypi) for developers who are just learning to package their code. As this is a learning activity, we will first deploy our package on the test server.

Prepare the distribution

Let's start by laying out the ground work for the release. We first need to prepare the distribution to be released. The following steps provide a minimal set of instructions to prepare the distribution.

Step 1 – Setting up the package directory

Make a new directory, and call it `testgamepkg` or give it any name you like. In this directory, copy the `wargame` package we created earlier. Now, create the following four empty files in this directory, README, LICENSE.txt, MANIFEST.in, and a `setup.py` file. The directory tree is shown in the following screenshot:

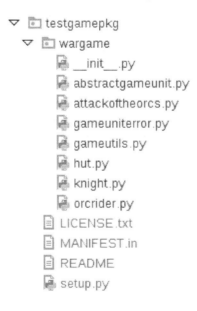

 It is not required to create a new directory, `testgamepkg`. Instead, you can create these four files in the same directory where the `wargame` package is present. All these files can also be found in the supporting material for this chapter.

Next, we will add contents to each of these new files.

Step 2 – Writing the setup.py file

The `setup.py` file is a required file that contains the metadata for the package you want to release. Let's write the following code in this file:

```python
from distutils.core import setup

with open('README') as file:
    readme = file.read()

setup(
    name='some_unique_name',
    version='2.0.0',
    packages=['wargame'],
    url='https://testpypi.python.org/pypi/some_unique_name/',
    license='LICENSE.txt',
    description='my fantasy game',
    long_description=readme,
    author='your_name',
    author_email='your_email'
)
```

The `import` statement on the first line imports the built-in `setup` function. On the next few lines, the contents of the README file are stored in a string called `readme`. Finally, we call the `setup` function with various arguments, as shown in the preceding code snippet.

Out of these arguments, only `name`, `version`, and `packages` are required fields. You can add several other optional metadata arguments to the `setup` function. In the preceding code, we have specified the most common ones.

> The `setup` function takes several optional arguments. See the API reference (`https://docs.python.org/3/distutils/apiref.html`) for details.

In the code, update the `name` field with a unique string. Make sure that the name is not already taken as a PyPI package. The `version` field represents the current version of the package. Earlier in the chapter, we gave the version number 2.0.0 to the modularized code. You can either go with this scheme or use your own versioning convention. The third required field, `packages`, is a list of source packages to be included in the distribution. In this case, it is just the `wargame` package that contains all the code. The string stored in the `long_description` field is used to display the home page for the package on the PyPI website. In the code, we will put the contents of the README file as `long_description`.

Step 3 – Updating the README and LICENSE.txt files

In the `LICENSE.txt` file, simply copy the license description under which you want to release the package. For example, if you are distributing this package under the **MIT License** (`https://opensource.org/licenses/MIT`), copy and paste the MIT License description in this file.

The `README` file is the file where you can add a detailed description of your project. PyPI expects this file to be in the **reStructuredText (RST)** or `.rst` format. More information on this format is available at `http://docutils.sourceforge.net/rst.html`. Here is an example of the `README` file. Note that the new lines before each heading and the one after the keyword `.. code:: python` are important:

```
Attack of the Orcs
==================

Introduction
-------------
This is a command line fantasy war game!

Documentation
--------------
Documentation can be found at...

Example Usage
-------------
Here is an example to import the modules from this package.

.. code:: python

    from wargame.attackoftheorcs import AttackOfTheOrcs
    game = AttackOfTheOrcs()
    game.play()

LICENSE
-------
See LICENSE.txt file.
```

Step 4 – Updating the MANIFEST.in file

By default, `distutils` includes the following files while creating the distribution:

- The `README`, `README.txt`, `setup.py`, or `setup.cfg` files are present in the top-level distribution directory
- All the `*.py` files implied by the packages list in `setup.py`
- All the `test/test*.py` files
- The C source files indicated by `libraries` or `ext_modules` in `setup.py`

But what if you want to include some additional files in your project? For example, we wish to ship `LICENSE.txt` along with the distribution. It won't get included as there is no provision to add it by default. For this, `distutils` looks for a template file called `MANIFEST.in`, where custom rules can be specified for the inclusion of additional files.

Let's edit the `MANIFEST.in` file and make a rule for the inclusion of `LICENSE.txt`. Add the following line to this file and save it:

```
include *.txt
```

Each line in this template represents a command. The preceding line tells Python to include all the `.txt` files in the top-level distribution directory. Thus, `LICENSE.txt` will now get included in the distribution.

All the files are now updated. It is time to build the distribution now!

Step 5 – Build a deployment-ready distribution

Let's create a source distribution. In a terminal window, run the following commands:

```
$ cd testgamepkg
$ python setup.py sdist
```

The `sdist` command creates a distribution with the source files included. Running the second command creates a new `dist` directory containing an archive file. For example, in `setup.py`, if the `name` field is `testgamepkg` and the `version` is `2.0.0`, the archive will be `testgamepkg-2.0.0.tar.gz` on Linux and `testgamepkg-2.0.0.zip` on Windows OS.

Additionally, it creates a MANIFEST file with a list of all the included files in the package. The following screenshot shows the command-line output after running the python setup.py sdist command:

```
[user@hostname testgamepkg]$ ls
LICENSE.txt   MANIFEST.in   README   setup.py   wargame
[user@hostname testgamepkg]$ python3 setup.py sdist
running sdist
running check
reading manifest template 'MANIFEST.in'
writing manifest file 'MANIFEST'
creating testgamepkg-2.0.0
creating testgamepkg-2.0.0/wargame
making hard links in testgamepkg-2.0.0...
hard linking LICENSE.txt -> testgamepkg-2.0.0
hard linking README -> testgamepkg-2.0.0
hard linking setup.py -> testgamepkg-2.0.0
hard linking wargame/__init__.py -> testgamepkg-2.0.0/wargame
hard linking wargame/abstractgameunit.py -> testgamepkg-2.0.0/wa
rgame
hard linking wargame/attackoftheorcs.py -> testgamepkg-2.0.0/war
game
hard linking wargame/gameutils.py -> testgamepkg-2.0.0/wargame
hard linking wargame/hut.py -> testgamepkg-2.0.0/wargame
hard linking wargame/knight.py -> testgamepkg-2.0.0/wargame
hard linking wargame/orcrider.py -> testgamepkg-2.0.0/wargame
creating dist
Creating tar archive
removing 'testgamepkg-2.0.0' (and everything under it)
[user@hostname testgamepkg]$
```

Creating a bdist

The `sdist` command creates a source distribution. The examples in this chapter will only use `sdist`. However, you can also create a built distribution. The simplest way to create a built distribution is `$ python setup.py bdist`. This creates a default built distribution for your platform, such as `dist/testgamepkg-2.0.0.linux-x86_64.tar.gz` on Linux OS. As an exercise, create this distribution and see the contents of the archive. Another way to create a `bdist` is with a Python package called `wheel` (`https://pypi.python.org/pypi/wheel`). It is a built package format, although there is some work involved to use `wheel`. You can try this as yet another exercise. You may need to do the following:

```
$ pip install pip --upgrade
$ pip install wheel
$ pip install setuptools –upgrade
```

Then, add the following `import` statement to `setup.py` file: `import setuptools`. Finally, run the command `$ python setup.py bdist_wheel`. This will create a distribution archive in the `dist` directory with a `.whl` extension.

Uploading the distribution

The distribution is ready for deployment. Let's deploy it now!

Step 1 – Creating an account on PyPI test website

If you do not have an account on the PyPI testing site, create one at `https://testpypi.python.org/pypi?:action=register_form`. Follow the steps on this website to create a new account.

Step 2 – Creating a .pypirc file

This is an important step. Python assumes the default repository for uploading distributions is `https://pypi.python.org/pypi`. However, the PyPI test server has a different address that needs to be specified in a `.pypirc` file (notice the dot at the beginning of the name). This file has a special format. Add the following contents to the `.pypirc` file:

```
[distutils]
index-servers=
pypitest

[pypitest]
```

```
repository = https://testpypi.python.org/pypi
username=<add username>
password=<add password>
```

The file has details of the PyPI test repository under the header `[pypitest]`. In this file, you can store different profiles. Here, `[pypitest]` is a profile that stores the repository URL and your user credentials for the PyPI test repository. This provides a convenient way to specify the account credentials and repository URL while registering or uploading the distribution. The name of the profile can be changed to any other string, as long as the corresponding entry in the `index-servers` variable is updated. For example, you can name it `[test]`. You can also create multiple such profiles if you have multiple accounts on the PyPI or PyPI test websites.

In this file, update the `username` and `password` fields with your actual credentials and save the file. On Linux OS, put this file in the user home directory: `~/.pypirc`. On Windows OS, create it at `C:\Users\user_name\.pypirc`. Replace `user_name` with the actual username.

Step 3 – Register your project

A simple way to register your project is to log in to the test PyPI website and then use the package submission form: `https://testpypi.python.org/pypi?:action=register_form`

Alternatively, the project registration can also be done using the command line. Open a terminal window and type the following commands. Replace the `/path/to/testgamepkg` with the actual path to the directory containing `setup.py`:

```
$ cd /path/to/testgamepkg
```

```
$ python setup.py register -r pypitest
```

The `-r` option for the `register` command is used to specify the URL of the PyPI test repository. Notice that, instead of the URL, we have simply written the profile name, `pypitest`. Alternatively, you can also specify the full URL, as shown in the following command:

```
$ python setup.py register -r  https://testpypi.python.org/pypi
```

The following screenshot shows the output after command execution:

```
[user@hostname testgamepkg]$ ls
dist           MANIFEST      README      wargame
LICENSE.txt  MANIFEST.in   setup.py
[user@hostname testgamepkg]$ python3 setup.py register -r https:
//testpypi.python.org/pypi
running register
running check
Registering testgamepkg to https://testpypi.python.org/pypi
Server response (200): OK
[user@hostname testgamepkg]$ █
```

If you log in to the test PyPI website, a new project with the unique name you have chosen (in this example, it is testgamepkg) will show up.

Step 4 – Uploading the package

Finally, it is time to upload the package. This can be accomplished with the following command:

```
$ python setup.py sdist upload -r pypitest
```

This command does two things. First, it creates the source distribution using the sdist command and then the source distribution is uploaded to the PyPI test repository with the upload command.

> *That's a good point, Sir Foo! In the* Prepare the distribution *section (see* **Step 4 – Updating the MANIFEST.in** *file), we indeed created the distribution using the* `python setup.py sdist` *command.*

At the time this book was written, `setuptools` did not have a provision to upload an existing distribution—the distribution creation and upload need to happen in a single command. The good news is that there is a third-party Python package called `twine` that enables uploading an already created distribution.

This package can be installed using pip:

```
$ pip install twine
```

This will install `twine` at the same location as your Python executable. For example, if Python 3 is accessed as `/usr/bin/python`, then `twine` can be accessed as `/usr/bin/twine`. Now, upload the existing source distribution as:

```
$ twine upload -r pypitest dist/*
Uploading distributions to https://testpypi.python.org/pypi
Uploading testgamepkg-2.0.0.tar.gz
```

The distribution is now available for anyone to download and install on the PyPI test repository! To verify this, visit the package home page on the PyPI test site, `https://testpypi.python.org/pypi/your_package_name`. The home page of `testgamepkg` with a **2.0.2** version is shown in the following screenshot:

Security note

For older versions of Python (before v2.7.9 or v3.2), when you use `python seup.py sdist upload`, a HTTP connection is used to upload the files. What it means is that your user name and password are a security risk if there is a cyber attack! In this case, it is highly recommended to use the `twine` package. It securely uploads the distribution over HTTPS using a verified connection.

For Python 2.7.9+ and 3.2+, HTTPS is the default choice to upload the distribution. But you can still use `twine` for the other advantages as discussed. Visit `https://pypi.python.org/pypi/twine` for more information.

A single command to do it all

Now that we know all the steps, let's combine these three steps, namely registering the project, creating a distribution, and uploading the distribution into a single command.

For this to work, we will make two small changes in `setup.py`, as follows:

1. Change the `name` field to another unique name. This should be different from what you chose while following the earlier steps.

2. Update the `url` field to reflect this new name.

After these changes, run the following command in a terminal window:

```
$ python setup.py register -r pypitest sdist upload -r pypitest
```

This is a combination of three commands executed in a serial manner. The first one, `register -r pypitest`, registers a new project; the second command, `sdist`, creates a source distribution; and finally, the third command, `upload -r pypitest`, submits the distribution to the PyPI test repository!

Installing your own distribution

The distribution is now available for installation using pip. Let's install it ourselves to make sure there are no problems. Run the `pip` command shown in the following code snippet. Replace `testgamepkg` with the distribution name you have uploaded:

```
$ pip install -i https://testpypi.python.org/pypi testgamepkg
```

The `-i` (alternatively, `--index-url`) option specifies the base URL of PyPI. If you don't specify this option, it will default to `https://pypi.python.org/simple`. Here is a sample response when the `install` command is executed:

```
Collecting testgamepkg
Downloading https://testpypi.python.org/packages/source/t/testgamepkg/
testgame
pkg-2.0.0.tar.gz
Installing collected packages: testgamepkg
  Running setup.py install for testgamepkg
Successfully installed testgamepkg-2.0.0
```

Once the package is successfully installed, test it by calling the functionality from that package. For example, start your Python interpreter and write the following code:

```
>>> from wargame.attackoftheorcs import AttackOfTheOrcs
>>> game = AttackOfTheOrcs()
>>> game.play()
```

If you do not see any errors, everything is working as expected! The distribution is now generally available to our users on the PyPI test website.

You are right. We only talked about the open distributions using the Python community repositories! If you want to create a private distribution, you should set up and maintain your own PyPI repository. Let's talk about that next.

Using a private PyPI repository

This section will briefly cover how to setup a private PyPI repository. The discussion will be limited to creating a simple HTTP-based local server. There are several packages that can help you do this. Let's use a popular package called `pypiserver` (`https://pypi.python.org/pypi/pypiserver`). Let's open a terminal window and get ready for action.

Step 1 – Installing pypiserver

First, install the required package:

```
$ pip install pypiserver
```

The `pypi-server` executable sits at the same location that you have the Python executable. For example, if you have `/usr/bin/python`, `pypi-server` will be available as `/usr/bin/pypi-server`.

Step 2 – Building a new source distribution

Go to the directory where you have `setup.py` and all other files. In the discussion earlier, we named it `testgamepkg`:

```
$ cd /path/to/testgamepkg
```

We have already installed `testgamepkg` in an earlier section. To simplify things, in `setup.py` let's change the `name` field to something else. While you are at it, also change the `url` and `version` field. The `setup.py` with these changes is shown in the following screenshot. The changes are highlighted:

```python
from distutils.core import setup
with open('README') as file:
    readme = file.read()
setup(
    name='testpkg_private',
    version='2.0.0',
    packages=['wargame'],
    url='http://localhost:8081/simple',
    license='LICENSE.txt',
    description='test pkg private',
    long_description=readme,
    author='your_name',
    author_email='your_email'
)
```

Now, let's create a new source distribution by the name of testpkg_private. As before, the archive will be created in the dist directory:

```
$ python setup.py sdist
```

Step 3 – Starting a local server

Next, let's start a local server on your computer:

```
$ pypi-server -p 8081 ./dist
```

The -p option is used to specify a port number. You can choose a number other than 8081. The command also takes a directory as an argument. We have specified it as the dist directory. This is where it will search for your private distribution packages.

Welcome to pypiserver!

This is a PyPI compatible package index serving 2 packages.

To use this server with pip, run the the following command:

```
pip install --extra-index-url http://localhost:8081/simple/ PACKAGE [PACKAGE2...]
```

To use this server with easy_install, run the the following command:

```
easy_install -i http://localhost:8081/simple/ PACKAGE
```

The complete list of all packages can be found here or via the simple index.

This instance is running version 1.1.8 of the pypiserver software.

The server will start listening on `http://localhost:8081`. That's it! Open this URL in a browser. It will display a simple web page with instructions, as shown in the preceding screenshot:

Step 4 – Installing the private distribution

The installation instructions at `http://localhost:8081` are self explanatory. You can click on the **simple** link to view all the available packages. It essentially shows the contents of the `dist` directory specified when we started the server. If you want to include any additional packages, you can simply copy those to this directory. The following command installs this private distribution:

```
$ pip install -i http://localhost:8081 testpkg_private
```

This was a quick introduction to setting up a private PyPI repository. For illustration, we just created a local server based on HTTP. In practice, you should set up a secure server with the HTTPS protocol and authenticate users, similar to what the PyPI website does. Also, we had a basic mechanism where the package was copied over to the repository directory. In a real-world situation, you will need to support remote uploads. For further reading, visit the GitHub page of `pypiserver`, `https://github.com/pypiserver/pypiserver`. Some other packages that help set up a private repository include `pyshop` at `https://pypi.python.org/pypi/pyshop` and `djangopypi` at `https://pypi.python.org/pypi/djangopypi`.

Making an incremental release

The package is released but that is not the end of the story. Very soon, you will need to make changes to the code and make the newer version available again. In this section, we will learn how to submit incremental patches to an already deployed distribution.

Packaging and uploading the new version

Preparing for the new release is pretty simple. Just update the version number to, for instance, `2.0.1` in the `setup.py` file. After making this change, run the earlier command that creates a source distribution and uploads the package in one go:

```
$ python setup.py sdist upload -r pypitest
```

The incremental release of v2.0.1 will now be available on the PyPI test repository.

Upgrading the installed version

If the previous version of the package is already installed on your computer, use the `--upgrade` option to update to the latest release version. This step is optional, but it is always good practice to verify the released version is working as expected:

```
$ pip install -i https://testpypi.python.org/pypi testgamepkg --upgrade
```

As we did before, replace the name `testgamepkg` with the package name you have chosen.

Version controlling the code

Let's recap what we have done so far. We started application development with a simple script. Gradually, we redesigned the application, added new features and fixed bugs to transform it into its current state. What if you want to go back to an earlier state of the code, say the code you wrote two days ago? You may want to do this for various reasons. For instance, the latest code might have some bugs that you didn't see two days ago. Imagine another scenario where you are collaborating with your colleagues on a project and you all need to work on the same set of files. How do we accomplish that?

In such situations, a **version control system** (**VCS**) comes to our rescue. It maintains a record of changes you make to the code. The files and directories now have a version associated with them. The VCS enables you to pull a specific version of any file.

There are several version control systems in use. Git, SVN, CVS, and Mercurial are some of the most popular open source VCS. In this book, we will cover some preliminary operational instructions on using Git, a distributed revision control system.

Git resources

Git is a very powerful tool for collaborative development. It is a pretty big topic. This chapter just gives a brief overview of some common use cases. The goal here is to provide a minimal set of instructions to bring our Python application code under version control.

> The following are a few links to the resources that cover Git in a depth well beyond our scope:
> - `https://gitscm.com/documentation`
> - `http://gitref.org`

If you are already familiar with Git, or have used another version control such as SVN, jump directly to the final topic to solve an exercise. Also, the upcoming discussion will primarily focus on using Git from the command line. If you prefer a GUI client, the section *Using GUI clients for Git* will provide some pointers.

Installing Git

Git software can be downloaded from `https://git-scm.com/downloads`. The website provides detailed installation instructions for various operating systems.

With most Linux flavors, it can be simply installed using the package manager of the OS. For example, on Ubuntu, it can be installed from a terminal like this:

```
$ sudo apt-get install git
```

For Windows OS, install using the installer available on the Git website. After the installation, you should be able to access the Git executable from the command line. If it is not available, add the PATH to its executable in your environment variables.

Configuring your identity

Before creating a Git repository and committing any code, you should tell Git who you are:

```
$ git config --global user.name  "YOUR NAME HERE"
$ git config --global user.email YOUR_EMAIL_HERE
```

With this command, any commits you make will automatically be associated with your username and e-mail address.

Basic Git terminology

Let's understand a few frequently used commands in Git. This list is far from being comprehensive. The intention is to just learn the most common Git commands:

- add: This is a keyword used to bring any file or directory under the version control. With the add command, the Git index is updated and the new files are staged for the next commit, along with other changes in the directory.

- commit: This keyword, after making changes to any of the files under version control, can be used to commit the files to the repository to register that change. In other words, Git records a new revision for the file, which also has information on who made those changes. While committing files, you can also add an informative message on what changes were made.

- clone: This keyword, in Git terminology, means copying an original repository into a new one. This cloned repository on your computer can be used as a local or a working repository for your source code. Such a repository keeps a track of all the local changes you make to the contained code.

- push: Suppose you have a central repository that you have shared with your team. It could be located on a remote server. You have cloned this repository on your computer and have made several changes within this repository. Now you want to make these changes available to others. The push command is used to send these changes to the central repository.

- **pull**: You have updated the central repository with the `push` command. Now, if others want to use this code, their cloned repository needs to be synchronized with the central one. The `pull` command can be used to update the cloned repository with the new changes available in the central repository. If any of the files being updated with this command have local modifications, Git will try to merge the changes from the central repository into the local one.

Creating and using a Git repository

Let's set up a Git repository for our application. The steps we are about to follow are represented in the following simplified schematic.

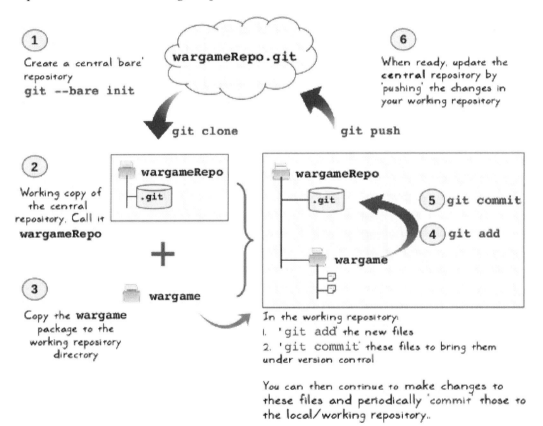

There are many alternatives to bring the code under version control. What is illustrated here is just one such option. For example, you can directly start with `git init` in the existing `wargame` package directory instead of creating a bare repository and then cloning it.

Creating a bare remote repository

First, we will create a **bare** Git repository. It is just a directory that stores the revision history of your project. Note that it does not have any commits or branches. We will use this bare repository as our central or remote repository.

Git uses the concept of remote repository. In this book, we won't really set up a truly remote repository. The remote repository will be just another local directory on your computer. To avoid confusion, we will refer to the remote repository as the central repository in the upcoming discussion. The details of the remote repository and Git branches are stored in the `.git/config` file.

The convention is to add a `.git` extension to the name. On the command line, execute the following commands to initialize a bare repository:

```
$ mkdir wargameRepo.git
$ cd wargameRepo.git
$ git --bare init
```

First, a directory by the name `wargameRepo.git` is created. Inside this directory, the `git --bare init` command initializes a new repository. This command creates a `.git` directory for your project. The dot prefix indicates that it is a hidden directory. The `--bare` option indicates that this is a bare repository.

Clone the repository

As seen earlier, the `clone` command can be used to create a copy of the central repository. Here is the command to do this:

```
$ git clone ~/wargameRepo.git wargameRepo
Cloning into 'wargameRepo'...
warning: You appear to have cloned an empty repository.
done.
```

Here, it clones `wargameRepo.git` as `wargameRepo` (a new directory). This assumes that you do not have any directory by this name. You can now use the cloned repository, `wargameRepo`, as your working copy. This repository has the full working tree. In this case, however, there is nothing in there except the `.git` folder. Next, we will add files and directories to this working tree.

Copying the code to the cloned repository

After cloning, copy the `wargame` package created earlier into the cloned repository. The directory structure after this operation is shown here:

Staging the code and committing

Just copying the code into the repository doesn't mean it is version controlled. To do this, open the command prompt and go to the `wargameRepo` directory using the `cd` command.

```
$ cd wargameRepo
```

Now, run the following command. Notice the dot in the command. This assumes that `git` is recognized as a command in your terminal window. If it isn't, you need to update the `PATH` environment variable or just specify the full path to this executable.

```
$ git add   .
```

This tells Git to stage everything in the current directory for a commit. In this case, it will add the `wargame` directory and all files inside it. If you run the `git status` command, it will show all the new files prepared for the initial commit (whenever that happens). The next step is to actually commit the files within our working repository:

```
[user@hostname wargameRepo]$ ls
wargame
[user@hostname wargameRepo]$ git commit -m "initial commit of wargame app"
[master (root-commit) 104d2b7] initial commit of wargame app
 7 files changed, 430 insertions(+)
 create mode 100644 wargame/__init__.py
 create mode 100644 wargame/abstractgameunit.py
 create mode 100644 wargame/attackoftheorcs.py
 create mode 100644 wargame/gameutils.py
 create mode 100644 wargame/hut.py
 create mode 100644 wargame/knight.py
 create mode 100644 wargame/orcrider.py
```

The `-m` argument in the `git commit` command is used to specify an informative message on what the commit is all about. The messages after this command are shown in the response received from Git after this command.

Pushing the changes to the central repository

This step is useful, especially when you are co-developing the code with other developers. In such a scenario, there will be a central repository, which we created earlier with the `--bare` option. To make your changes available to others, you need to push those to the central repository. As mentioned in a side note earlier, the central repository in this case is just another Git directory on your computer.

We started with an empty repository. For the initial push into the central repository, execute the following command:

```
$ git push origin master
```

What is `origin` here? Recall that our cloned repository, `wargameRepo`, originated from the central repository, `wargameRepo.git`. The `origin` is simply the URL pointing to your central repository. The second argument, `master`, is the Git branch name where the changes will be pushed. The default branch is called master. You can create different branches as well. We will limit this discussion to the default branch. The `.git/config` file stores details about the origin and branches in your local repository.

To summarize, the command mentioned earlier pushes the master branch in your working repository to the new master branch in your central repository (`origin/master`).

After the initial push, if you make any changes to the code, you first need to commit those in the working repository:

```
$ git commit -m "some changes to files" foo.py
```

Assuming that you continue to work on the same branch (master), for any subsequent push to the central repository, simply execute the following command:

```
$ git push
```

This will update the master branch of the central repository with your changes. With this, you are all set to share your code with other developers using the central repository. If you want to get changes made by other developers, you can use `$ git pull` to fetch those changes and merge them with your working copy. We did not discuss the other Git features, such as tagging your code, creating branches, resolving conflicts, and so on. It is recommended you read the Git documentation, `https://git-scm.com/doc`, to better understand these concepts.

Using GUI clients for Git

The earlier section exclusively discussed how to use Git from the command line. These commands can also be accessed through a **graphical user interface** (**GUI**). There are many GUI clients available for Git, for instance, **gitk** on Linux (`http://gitk.sourceforge.net/`) or **Github Desktop**, available for Mac and Windows 7 or later (`https://desktop.github.com/`). The free Python IDEs, such as the community edition of PyCharm, provide an easy-to-use GUI integration for Git and other version control systems. PyCharm provides a context menu integration for Git commands. For example, right-clicking on a file in the IDE will give you a context menu option to add or commit the file to a repository.

Exercise

We released the distribution to the PyPI test repository as it was just a toy problem. For more serious stuff, you should deploy the package to the PyPI main repository, `https://pypi.python.org/pypi`. As an exercise, deploy a package on the main PyPI server. The process is similar to what we discussed earlier.

- Create a new account on the PyPI website. Note that you need to create a separate account; the test PyPI account won't work here.

- In the `.pypirc` file, create a new profile to store credentials for the main server. See the following illustration for an inspiration:

```
[distutils]
index-servers=
pypitest
pypimain

[pypimain]
```

```
repository = https://pypi.python.org/pypi
username=<add PyPI main username>
password=<add PyPI main password>

[pypitest]
repository = https://testpypi.python.org/pypi
username=<add username>
password=<add password>
```

- Appropriately, update the `url` field in `setup.py`.
- Follow the other steps in package creation and release. Remember to specify the main repository everywhere, instead of the test repository. For example:

  ```
  $ python setup.py register -r pypimain
  ```

  ```
  $ python setup.py sdist upload -r pypimain
  ```

- See what happens if you do not specify the `-r` option Which repository would it default to?

Summary

This chapter introduced you to some key aspects of application development in general and Python application development in particular. The chapter started with an introduction to different versioning conventions. It demonstrated how to create Python modules and packages.

With step-by-step instructions, the chapter demonstrated how to prepare a distribution (also called a package), deploy it on the PyPI test server, and install this deployed package using pip. Additionally, it also showed you how to make incremental releases and set up a private Python distribution. Finally, the chapter provided an overview of version control using Git.

Coding standards are a set of guidelines that you should follow while developing the code. Complying with these standards can have a significant impact on the code readability and the life of the code. In the next chapter, you will learn another important aspect of software development, code documentation, and best practices.

4
Documentation and Best Practices

So far, the focus was on developing the code and getting the first release out the door. We have not talked about another vital aspect of application development, the documentation and coding standards. Although the code base is still quite manageable, before it is too late, we should learn techniques to improve code readability. In this chapter, we will cover the following topics:

- Understanding the basics of the **reStructuredText** (**RST**) format and how to use it for writing docstrings

- Learning how to create HTML documentation for the code using the **Sphinx** document generator

- Covering some important coding standards for writing the Python code

- Using **Pylint** to evaluate how well we are doing in following these guidelines

As you can guess from the preceding topics, we are taking a short break from coding to learn these very important concepts.

If you are well aware of the code, you might find documentation unnecessary. But imagine you are assigned a different project that has a big code base with very little documentation. How will you feel? Of course, you will have to review the code anyway to get familiar with it. But your productivity will take a blow if it is not well documented. The time you spend understanding such code also depends on how well it has been written. This is where the coding standard aspect comes into the picture.

In summary, never ignore coding standards and documentation. Make sure you follow these guidelines while the code is being developed. It is also important to maintain the documentation and not to over document. Let's start by learning techniques to create good documentation for a Python project.

Documenting the code

There are, broadly, three levels of documentation. At the top, you have project- or **distribution-level documentation**. It is intended to give high-level information on a project, such as installation instructions, licensing terms, and so on. In *Chapter 3, Modularize, Package, Deploy!*, you already had a flavor of this documentation. We created the README and LICENSE files to go along with the distribution. Additionally, you can add more files to make the documentation comprehensive, such as INSTALL, TODO, RELEASENOTES, CREDITS, and so on.

The second level is the **API-level documentation**. It summarizes how a function, method, class, or module should be used. Python docstrings, which we will learn next, are used to generate API-level documentation.

The third level of documentation is in the form of **code comments**. Such comments help explain how a piece of code works.

Sphinx is a document generation tool for Python that is used to create project- and API-level documentations. In this chapter, we will use Sphinx to create API-level documentation from the docstrings. But, before jumping into this topic, let's first understand what docstrings in Python are.

Python Enhancement Proposals (PEPs) provide a way to propose and document various design standards for the Python language. There are several PEPs, and each one is identified by a permanent number. For example, *PEP 8*, *PEP 257*, *PEP 287*, and so on.

PEP 257 documents the guidelines to write docstrings, whereas *PEP 287* provides information on the reStructuredText docstring format (more on the reStructuredText format later in the chapter).

The purpose of this chapter is not to repeat what is already documented by these PEPs. We will refer to these guidelines whenever appropriate in the sections to follow. For a comprehensive understanding of these and other PEPs, check out https://www.python.org/dev/peps.

Docstrings

A docstring or document string is a string literal used to describe a class, method, function, or module. The purpose of a docstring is to briefly describe features of the code. It is different than a comment that elaborates details on the internal working of a piece of code. It can be accessed using the built-in attribute, __doc__. Let's write an example to illustrate this concept. Open the Python interpreter and write the following trivial function:

```
>>> def get_number():
...      return 10
...
>>>
```

Let's see what the __doc__ attribute for this function stores:

```
>>> get_number.__doc__
>>>
```

The __doc__ attribute for the function is an empty string as we have not written any documentation for this function. Now let's write a docstring for the function and print this attribute again:

```
>>> def get_number():
...      """Return a special number"""
...      return 10
...
>>> get_number.__doc__
'Return a special number'
```

The __doc__ attribute now shows the docstring for the function. As can be seen, a docstring is represented differently than a comment. It is surrounded by triple double quotes (recommended style), """Return a special number""", or triple single quotes, '''Return a special number''', and is written as the first statement of that class, method, function, or module.

PEP 257

The simple example shown in the previous code is that of a single-line docstring. Similarly, you can have multi-line docstrings. Review the PEP 257 convention (`https://www.python.org/dev/peps/pep-0257`) for further details.

To generate effective documentation using Sphinx, the docstring should be written in a markup language known as reStructuredText. Let's understand the basics of this format next.

Introduction to reStructuredText

reStructuredText (RST), defines a simple markup syntax, mainly for Python documentation. It is a part of the Python documentation processing system called **docutils** (`http://docutils.sourceforge.net/index.html`).

RST

Does this sound familiar? In *Chapter 3, Modularize, Package, Deploy,* without much elaboration, we created a README file with the RST format. In that chapter, refer to the section *Prepare the distribution* for more information. This section will give you a bare minimum introduction to the RST syntax. For further reading, comprehensive documentation is available at `http://docutils.sourceforge.net/rst.html`.

Let's review some of the most frequently used features of RST.

Section headings

To distinguish a section title from the rest of the text, it is decorated with an underline created using any one of the non-alpha numeric characters, such as ~~~~, ====, ----, or ####. The decorated underline should be of the same length (or longer) as the heading text, as shown in the following example header:

```
1. Introduction
---------------
```

Here, dashes (---) are used to decorate the heading. Suppose this is considered as the *Heading 1* style in the document; any subsequent use of this decorator will result in the same style. In the following screenshot, the RST syntax is shown in the left column; the right column shows how it will be displayed in a browser:

```
1.  Introduction                    RST Syntax
------------------
This is a command line fantasy war game!

1.1 Intro A
~~~~~~~~~~~~~~~~
1.1.1 Inside Intro A
.....................

2.  Documentation
------------------
Documentation can be found at..

2.1 Documentation A
~~~~~~~~~~~~~~~~~~~~~~
```

Web browser

1. Introduction

This is a command line fantasy war game!

1.1 Intro A

1.1.1 Inside Intro A

2. Documentation

Documentation can be found at..

2.1 Documentation A

Try it yourself!

You can use online RST editors, such as `http://rst.ninjs.org`, to quickly test how your RST file will be processed.

Paragraphs

To create a paragraph, simply write one. When done, leave at least one blank line at the end of it. Also, if you indent a paragraph in the RST file, it will appear as an indented block in the browser. Here is the RST syntax to write two paragraphs:

```
para1. Just write the sentences in the para
and end it by adding one or more blank line.



    para2 . blah blah blah.
    ...more stuff in paragraph 2 See how it gets appended..
```

As an exercise, use any online RST editor and see how it will appear in a web browser.

Text styles

You can apply a different text style inside a paragraph or to the body text. Decorate the text with double asterisks to make it appear bold, for example, `**bold_text**`. Similarly, a single asterisk decoration, `*italics_text*`, is used for *italics* style.

Code snippets

RST provides various directives to process formatted document blocks. The `code-block` directive is specified with syntax, for example, `.. code-block::`. Note that there is a space between the word `code-block` and the two preceding dots. The `code-block` directive can be specified along with the code language to construct a literal block. In the sample RST shown next, we have specified Python as the code language:

```
.. code-block:: python

    from wargame.attackoftheorcs import AttackOfTheOrcs
    game = AttackOfTheOrcs()
    game.play()
```

The argument to the `code-block` directive is specified as `python`. It tells the document generator that it is Python syntax. Additionally, note that there should be a blank line after the directive before writing the actual code. You can also use the `code` directive, `.. code::`, to represent a piece of code. For the syntax highlighting, a Python package called **Pygments** is required. We'll talk more on this later, when we learn about the Sphinx document generator.

Mathematical equations

The `math` directive is used to write mathematical equation. Note that you need to leave a blank space before and after the mathematical equation block. The following syntax (the left column) is one way to represent a mathematical formula. The right column shows how it will be displayed in a web browser:

RST Syntax	Web browser
Some text before a cubic equation.	Some text before a cubic equation.
`.. math::` `    ax^3 + bx^2 + cx + d = 0`	$ax^3 + bx^2 + cx + d = 0$
Some text after the equation.	Some text after the equation.

Bullets and numbering

Bullets can be added using any of the following characters: *, +, or -. It is required to have at least one blank line, immediately before the first bullet and immediately after the last bullet item:

```
Text before the bullet points. A blank line follows...

* First bullet item
  Some continuation text for first bullet,
  Note that its alignment should match the bullet it is part of.
* second bullet item
* last bullet item

Text after the bullets. Again needs a blank line after the last
bullet.
```

Similarly, you can specify a numbered list, as follows:

```
Text before the enumerated list. A blank line follows...

1. item 1
2. item 2
   some continuation stuff in item 2
3. item 3

Text after the enumerated lust. Again needs a blank line after the
last item.
```

> **Key things to remember**
>
> The RST syntax requires you to leave blank lines between different style blocks. For example, when you write a code snippet, a mathematical equation, or a paragraph, you need one blank line before and after these documentation blocks. RST is indentation sensitive.

Docstrings using RST

To generate nice-looking documentation for our application, we need to first write docstrings in the RST format. The *PEP 287* proposes guidelines to write docstrings using the RST format. For a comprehensive description, check out https://www.python.org/dev/peps/pep-0287. Here, we will discuss some of the most important things to remember when you write docstrings. To illustrate the concept, let's write a docstring for the wargame/hut.py module. The documentation is also provided in the supplementary code for the chapter.

The following code screenshot has a sample class-level docstring for the Hut class:

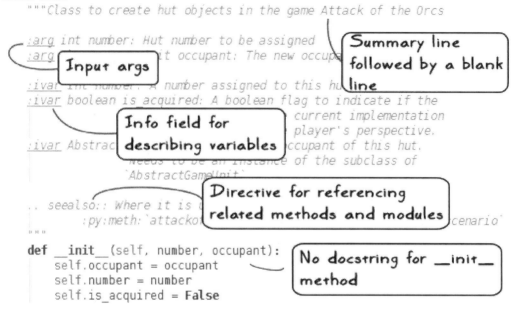

Let's review this syntax now:

- The documentation standard recommends a one-line summary separated by a blank line before the next descriptive block.

- The :arg fields describe the input arguments for this class, as given in the __init__ method. You can also use the :param field for this.

- The :ivar field is used to describe the instance variables for the class. You can, optionally, specify the type of the instance variable on the same line, for example:

  ```
  :ivar int number: A number assigned to this hut.
  :ivar AbstractGameUnit occupant: The occupant of...
  ```

  When Sphinx generates the HTML documentation, the instance variable type will be displayed next to its name. It will also try to create a link to that type.

- The .. seealso:: field directive is used to reference anything related to this class that you feel is important.

- The :py:meth: field is used for cross-referencing methods. Note that the method name should be bound by the back quotes (symbol `).

- Observe that we have not written any docstring for the __init__ method. The guidelines suggest that you either write a docstring for the class or for its __init__ method. For simplicity, let's follow the style just illustrated, where the docstring is written at the class level.

>
> When Sphinx generates the documentation, by default, it ignores the docstring for the __init__ method. You can change this default behavior using the autodoc-skip-member event inside conf.py. For more information, check out http://sphinx-doc.org/ext/autodoc.html#skipping-members.

Sphinx-generated HTML documentation for the Hut class will appear as shown in the following screenshot. You will learn how to create such documentation shortly!

wargame.hut module

class wargame.hut.**Hut**(*number, occupant*)

    Bases: **object**

    Class to create hut objects in the game Attack of the Orcs

Parameters:	• **number** (*int*) – Hut number to be assigned
	• **occupant** (*AbstractGameUnit*) – The new occupant of the Hut
Variables:	• **number** (*int*) – A number assigned to this hut
	• **is_acquired** (*boolean*) – A boolean flag to indicate if the hut is acquired. In the current implementation this is viewed from the players perspective.
	• **occupant** (*AbstractGameUnit*) – The occupant of this hut. Needs to be an instance of a subclass of AbstractGameUnit

See also:
Where it is used –
attackoftheorcs.AttackOfTheOrcs.setup_game_scenario()

What was just presented should serve as a basic example. There is a lot more that you can do with RST and Sphinx. The following table lists some of the most commonly used features (directives, information fields, and syntax) to write docstrings. Use these fields in the same way as illustrated in the preceding example. For comprehensive documentation, visit the Sphinx website (http://sphinx-doc.org).

Information field or directive	Description
`:param`	Parameter description.
`:arg`	Used to describe input arguments.
`:key`	Keyword description.
`:type`	Type of the parameter or argument, for example, `int`, `string`, and so on. You can also use the alternate syntax, for example: `:param type param_name: description`
`:ivar` or `:var`	Any variable description. Generally used for instance variables.
`:vartype`	Variable type description.
• `:py:meth:` • `:py:func:` • `:py:class:` • `:py:attr:`	Syntax to cross-reference a Python method, function, class, or attribute receptively. For example, `:py:meth:`MyClassA.method_a`` will be shown as `MyClassA.method_a()`.
`.. code::`	Any code samples can be included here. The section under this directive is processed as a code block by the Sphinx document generator.
`.. todo::`	Use this directive to list the TODO items.
`.. note::`	Document anything worthy of mentioning using the notes directive.
`.. warning::`	Directive to write warnings in the docstring. The warning block will be generally rendered with a light red background.
`.. seealso::`	Use this directive to reference anything (a method, a function, and so on) related to the code for which you are writing the docstring.

Docstring formatting styles

In this chapter, we will only use the default RST format to write the docstrings. Various projects follow their own convention to write docstrings. Many of these styles are compatible with the Sphinx document generator.

The *Google Python Style Guide* (https://google.github.io/styleguide/ pyguide.html) will be briefly discussed here. This style is widely used because of the simplicity it offers. It will become obvious when you see the following code screenshot. It is the same docstring we wrote for the Hut class, rewritten using the *Google Python Style Guide*:

```
class Hut:
    """Class to create hut objects in the game Attack of the Orcs

    Args:
        number (int): Hut number to be assigned
        occupant(AbstractGameUnit): The new occupant of the Hut

    Attributes:
        number (int): A number assigned to this hut
        is_acquired (boolean): A boolean flag to indicate if the
                               hut is acquired. In the current implementation
                               this is viewed from the player's perspective.
        occupant (AbstractGameUnit): The occupant of this hut.
                               Needs to be an instance of the subclass of
                               `AbstractGameUnit`.

    .. seealso:: Where it is used --
        :py:meth:`attackoftheorcs.AttackOfTheOrcs.setup_game_scenario`
    """
```

Google Python Style Guide example

For this to work with Sphinx, you need to install **napoleon**, an extension for Sphinx. It is essentially a pre-processor that parses and converts the Google style docstrings into the RST format. Check out https://pypi.python.org/pypi/sphinxcontrib-napoleon/ for installation instructions for napoleon. Examples on the Google Python documentation style can be found on the napoleon documentation page, http://sphinxcontrib-napoleon.readthedocs.org.

> The **Numpy** style of documentation is another popular style used within the Python community. It is also supported by the napoleon extension. Check out http://sphinxcontrib-napoleon.readthedocs.org for further details.

Automatically creating docstring stubs

This is bit of an advanced topic, mainly because it needs some background in using command-line tools such as **patch**.

In many situations, you do not even have the basic docstrings written for the functions, methods, and classes. Or, you might be following a Google docstring style but now you would like to switch to a different one, say a basic RST style. The open source tool **pyment** is meant for such scenarios. It can be used to create or update docstrings and also to convert between some common formatting styles, such as RST, Google docstring, and **numpydoc**.

> Read it again...the tool's name is "pyment" and not "payment" (not to be confused with the Python package Pygment). This tool is available on GitHub (https://github.com/dadadel/pyment). It was not available on the PyPi website at the time this chapter was written. So you might not be able to install it using the pip $pip install pyment command.

As pyment is not available using pip, the installation instructions are different. Follow the install instructions on the GitHub project homepage (https://github.com/dadadel/pyment). The alternative install instructions, which do not require the use of Git, are provided here:

1. Download the ZIP archive of pyment from the project homepage.
2. Extract this ZIP file to some folder, for example, pyment-master.
3. Open the command prompt and execute the following commands:

```
$ cd  pyment-master
$ python setup.py install
```

The last command should install pyment in the same directory where you have the Python executable. Depending on where your Python is installed, you may need to execute the preceding command as an administrator. After the installation, run this tool from the command line as follows:

```
$ pyment hut.py
```

This generates a patch file called hut.py.patch where the basic docstring stubs are written.

> Here, it is important to note that pyment will only create a basic docstring stub. It is our responsibility to fill in the blanks. Put another way, we should further improve these docstrings by writing the appropriate summary of the function or method—a one-liner on what each input argument (if any) does and so on.

Next, you are expected to merge this patch with the main file, hut.py. On Linux, use the following patch command (check out https://en.wikipedia.org/wiki/ Patch_(Unix) for more details) to merge the generated docstrings with the main file:

```
$ patch hut.py hut.py.patch
patching file hut.py
```

Windows users

The patch command described here is a Unix command. On Windows, patching a file might not be straightforward. Here are a few options that can be used to apply a patch:

- **Gnu utilities for win32**: This will also install a bunch of other utility tools commonly seen on the Unix platform. Use the patch.exe executable to apply patches. You can check out these utilities at (http://unxutils.sourceforge.net).
- **python-patch**: Check out this cross-platform Python utility at https://github.com/techtonik/python-patch.
- **TortoiseMerge**: It is a GUI tool used to apply patches (https://tortoisesvn.net/docs/release/ TortoiseMerge_en/tmerge-dug.html).

With this, the hut.py module should show the basic docstring stubs. We have developed a basic understanding on creating docstrings. Let's take the documentation to the next level using Sphinx.

Generating documentation with Sphinx

Sphinx is the *de facto* standard document generation tool for Python. Do not confuse it with a docstring. A docstring is something you write to summarize the behavior of an object. For example, a class docstring typically lists instance variables and public methods depending on your project's documentation guideline.

Sphinx uses such docstrings, or any RST file, to create nice-looking documentation. It can generate documentation in various output formats, such as HTML, PDF, and so on. Let's follow a step-by-step approach to generate API documentation in HTML format with Sphinx.

Step 1 – Installing Sphinx using pip

Sphinx can be installed using pip, as shown in the following command line:

```
$ pip install Sphinx
```

 pip is the package manager used to install Python packages. Refer to *Chapter 1, Developing Simple Applications* for more information on pip.

This creates four executable scripts, `sphinx-autogen`, `sphinx-apidoc`, `sphinx-build`, and `sphinx-quickstart`.

 On Linux, these executable are placed at the same location as your Python executable. For instance, if Python is available as `/usr/bin/python`, Sphinx executables can be accessed from the same location. On Windows OS, the Sphinx executables are put in the `Scripts` directory. It is the same directory where you have `pip.exe`. Refer to *Chapter 1, Developing Simple Applications* for further details.

For syntax highlighting the code, Sphinx uses a tool called **Pygments** (http://pygments.org). Install this package using pip, if it is not already provided in your Python distribution:

```
$ pip install pygments
```

Step 2 – cd to the source directory

In *Chapter 3, Modularize, Package, Deploy*, we created a Python package by the name of `wargame`, containing all the modules. Open a terminal window and `cd` to this directory. The directory contents are shown in the following screenshot of the terminal window:

```
  File   Edit   View   Search   Terminal   Help
[user@hostname ~]$ cd /home/book/wargame_distribution/wargame
[user@hostname wargame]$ ls -1
abstractgameunit.py
attackoftheorcs.py
gameuniterror.py
gameutils.py
hut.py
__init__.py
knight.py
orcrider.py
[user@hostname wargame]$ █
```

Step 3 – Running sphinx-quickstart

As the name suggests, this script will get you started with Sphinx. It sets up a directory where the documentation files will be placed and also creates a default configuration file, conf.py. Run the following command:

```
$ sphinx-quickstart
```

When you run this tool, it will ask you several questions to complete the basic setup. Choose the default answers for most of the questions by pressing the *return* key on Mac or *Enter* key for other systems. We will customize the answers for a few questions, shown next. The first prompt asks for the directory to place the documentation in. We will create a new directory called docs for this purpose:

```
> Root path for the documentation [.]: docs


> Separate source and build directories (y/n) [n]: y


> Project name: wargame


> Author name(s): Your_Name


> Project version: 2.0.0


Please indicate if you want to use one of the following Sphinx
extensions:
> autodoc: automatically insert docstrings from modules (y/n) [n]: y
```

The last answer enables the `autodoc` extension of Sphinx. This extension will help us create the documentation from the docstrings created earlier. Leave the rest of the questions with the default answers. In the end, `sphinx-quickstart` prints the following summary information:

```
Creating file docs/source/conf.py.
Creating file docs/source/index.rst.
Creating file docs/Makefile.
Creating file docs/make.bat.

Finished: An initial directory structure has been created.

You should now populate your master file docs/source/index.rst and create other documentatio
n
source files. Use the Makefile to build the docs, like so:
    make builder
where "builder" is one of the supported builders, e.g. html, latex or linkcheck.
```

The directory structure created by this script is shown in the next screenshot:

```
[user@hostname wargame]$ ls
abstractgameunit.py   docs                  gameutils.py    __init__.py   orcrider.py
attackoftheorcs.py    gameuniterror.py  hut.py          knight.py
[user@hostname wargame]$ ls -1 ./docs/
build
make.bat
Makefile
source
```

The generated `Makefile` (Linux/Mac) and `make.bat` (Windows OS) will be used in the final section of this topic, *Step 6 – Building the documentation*. The `docs/source` directory is where we need to put all the RST files (or the documentation source files). By default, it creates an empty `index.rst` file. It also contains a file, `conf.py`, which will be discussed next.

Step 4 – Updating conf.py

The `sphinx-quickstart` script creates a build configuration file, `conf.py`. Here, it is located at `docs/source/conf.py`. This is the file where all the customization for Sphinx is defined. For example, you can specify which Sphinx extensions to use while generating the documentation. In the previous step, we enabled the `autodoc` extension to include the documentation from docstrings. It is represented in `conf.py` as:

```
extensions = [   'sphinx.ext.autodoc', ]
```

To take care of some warnings related to the . . todo:: directive, add the following to the extensions list (you can also specify this during sphinx-quickstart):

```
extensions = [   'sphinx.ext.autodoc', 'sphinx.ext.todo', ]
```

We just need to make a small change in this file. As our source code is not in the docs directory, we will need to add an appropriate path to avoid import errors while generating the documentation. Uncomment the following line of code. You should find this line immediately after the import statements:

```
#sys.path.insert(0, os.path.abspath('.'))
```

You also need specify the full path to the directory containing the wargame package on your system. An example is shown in the following code:

```
sys.path.insert(0,
  os.path.abspath('/home/book/wargame_distribution')
)
```

Step 5 – Running sphinx-apidoc

Now, it is time to create the documentation source files (RST files) using the sphinx-apidoc tool. This tool uses the autodoc extension to extract the documentation from the docstrings. The syntax is as follows:

```
$ sphinx-apidoc [options] -o <outputdir> <sourcedir> [pathnames …]
```

In the terminal window, run the following commands (make sure you are in the docs directory, using cd, before running the following command):

```
$ sphinx-apidoc  -o source/ ../
```

The -o argument specifies the output directory where the generated RST files will be placed. In this case, the output directory is the directory by the name of source. This is a counterintuitive name, but remember that the source directory is where we keep the documentation source files. In the next step, these files will be used to create the final output (such as HTML files). The second argument represents the directory path where we have the Python code. In this case, the directory path is specified relative to the current working directory. Alternatively, you can also specify the full path, for example:

```
$ sphinx-apidoc  -o source/  /home/book/wargame_distribution
```

The command-line output after running this tool is shown next:

```
[user@hostname docs]$ ls
build   make.bat  Makefile   source
[user@hostname docs]$ sphinx-apidoc  -o source/ ../
Creating file source/setup.rst.
Creating file source/wargame.rst.
Creating file source/modules.rst.
[user@hostname docs]$ nedit source/wargame.rst
[user@hostname docs]$ 
```

 As an exercise, review the auto-generated file, source/wargame.rst. It contains the automodule directive of the autodoc extension. For further details, refer to the Sphinx documentation (http://sphinx-doc.org/ext/autodoc.html).

Step 6 – Building the documentation

The previous step created all the raw material we will need to create nice-looking documentation! There are two ways to create HTML documentation. The first option makes use of the sphinx-build tool and the other option uses the Makefile we created earlier. Let's discuss these options next.

Using sphinx-build

The sphinx-build tool makes it trivial to generate the final documentation. Run the following command while it is still in the docs directory:

```
$ sphinx-build source build
```

The first argument is the source directory where we have all the RST files, and the second argument is the directory where the final HTML documentation will be created. Open the `docs/build/index.html` file in a web browser and navigate through the links to view the documentation!

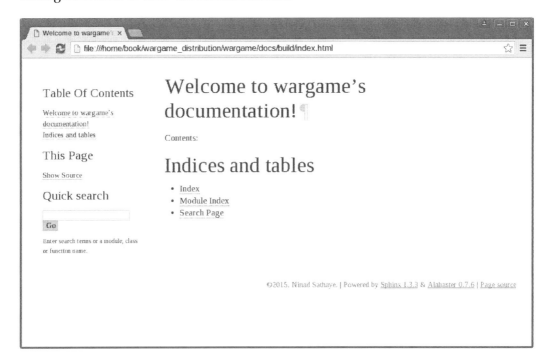

Using Makefile

An alternative to `sphinx-build` is to use the `Makefile` (or `make.bat`) created in *Step 3 – Running sphinx-quickstart*. On Linux, type the following commands (first move to the `docs/source` directory using `cd`):

```
$ cd /home/book/wargame_distribution/wargame/docs/source
$ make html
```

The last command creates HTML documentation in the `docs/build` directory. If you are using Windows OS, use `make.bat`, for example:

```
> make.bat  html
```

Now that you have learned how to write good documentation, let's proceed further and see what guidelines should you follow while writing your Python code.

Python coding standards

Coding standards serve as guidelines to write good quality code. Complying with these standards can have a significant impact on code readability, and in general on the life of the code.

PEP 8 Style Guide for Python Code

The *PEP 8* convention provides a style guide for writing Python code. If you are working on a project that follows its own set of coding conventions, rather than enforcing the *PEP 8* standards, you should adhere to the project-specific conventions. What matters the most is consistency. For any new project, you are strongly recommended to use the *PEP 8* style guide. In this section, we will cover a bare minimum set of guidelines that you should be aware of. For a comprehensive overview, check out `https://www.python.org/dev/peps/pep-0008`.

The following table lists some of the important guidelines documented in *PEP 8* to write Python code:

PEP 8 Style Guide For Python Code	Details
Use four spaces per indentation level	This can be set as a preference in most Python editors.
Use spaces instead of tabs for indenting	Mixed use of tabs and spaces is not allowed in Python 3. Most editors have an option to convert tabs to spaces.
Limit maximum line length to 79 characters	This may vary across projects. Some projects follow a limit of 80 characters. The illustrations in this book use an 80-column limit. Most editors will give you an option to draw a line at a specified column that serves as a visual indication.
Put all `import` statements at the top of the file	Don't put `import` statements inside the class or function bodies. Bring those out and put them at the top.

One `import` statement per line	An exception to this guideline is that, if you are importing multiple objects from a single module, it is OK to use a single import for all. The following imports are acceptable:
	
	`import os`
	`import sys`
	`from numpy import trapz, polyfit`

PEP 8 Style Guide For Python Code	Details
Module names	Try to keep these short. They should be all lowercase. For example: `attackoftheorcs.py`
Class names	Use **UpperCamelCase** with the first letter of every word capitalized. For example: `class AttackOfTheOrcs:`
Function and method names	These should be in all lowercase; use underscores if it improves readability. For example: `def show_game_mission(self):` Avoid the following style: `showGameMission` (**lowerCamelCase**). Use such names only if you are working on a project that uses this convention. This might surprise you if you are coming from a different programming background, such as C++. Using underscores in the method and function names is the Pythonic way.

Comparing with None	Always compare a variable against None like this:
	
	`if my_var is None:`
	`    # do something`
	
	Or like this:
	
	`if my_var is not None:`
	`    # do something else.`
	
	Never compare it like this:
	
	`if my_var == None OR my_var != None`

PEP 8 Style Guide For Python Code	Details
Exceptions: • When catching an exception, specify the exception type instead of just using the bare `except` clause. • Use the `Exception` class to derive exceptions instead of using the `BaseException` class. • Avoid writing a lot of code inside a single `try` clause; doing so makes it difficult to isolate the bugs.	Refer to *Chapter 2, Dealing with Exceptions,* which discusses some of these guidelines.
Public and non-public attributes: • Non-public attributes should have a leading underscore. • When in doubt, make attributes non-public.	As discussed in *Chapter 1, Developing Simple Applications,* Python does not enforce any rule to make non-public attributes inaccessible to the outside world. However, a good practice is to refrain from using non-public attributes outside the scope. If you are unsure whether it should be scoped as public or non-public, as a starter, make it non-public. Later, change it to a public attribute if necessary. Refer to *Chapter 5, Unit Testing and Refactoring,* where we discuss the testing strategies for a non-public method, `_occupy_huts`.

As mentioned earlier, this is just a representative sample of the comprehensive *PEP 8* guidelines. Read the *PEP 8* documentation for further details.

Code analysis – How well are we doing?

In this section, we will talk about tools that help to detect coding standard violations.

Good to have you back, Sir Foo! You've been awfully quiet, hope you are following along. You have raised a valid concern. Developers might get overwhelmed while trying to adhere to so many guidelines. Initially, it could appear like a challenge but practice should make you perfect. That said, there is still a likelihood that you will forget a guideline. Luckily, there are tools available that not only detect coding standard violations, but also inspect the code for errors. Some tools also try to reformat the code to adhere to coding standards. Let's learn that next.

Code analysis using IDE

Some popular Python **integrated development environments (IDEs)** were listed
in *Chapter 1, Developing Simple Applications*. Before looking at any of the inspection
tools discussed next, start with your IDE. Many IDEs come well equipped with code
inspection and reformatting tools. For example, PyCharm Community Edition has
excellent support for code inspections. The following screenshot shows some options
offered under the **Code** menu:

Comment with Line Comment	Ctrl+Slash
Comment with Block Comment	Ctrl+Shift+Slash
Reformat Code	Ctrl+Alt+L
Auto-Indent Lines	Ctrl+Alt+I
Optimize Imports	Ctrl+Alt+O
Rearrange Code	
Move Statement Down	Ctrl+Shift+Down
Move Statement Up	Ctrl+Shift+Up
Move Line Down	Alt+Shift+Down
Move Line Up	Alt+Shift+Up
Inspect Code	
Code Cleanup	
Run Inspection by Name...	Ctrl+Alt+Shift+I
Configure Current File Analysis...	Ctrl+Alt+Shift+H
View Offline Inspection Results...	

Using an IDE with a good code analysis tool has a major advantage. It can help
you detect the problems as you write the code. The tool can continuously monitor
the code for common coding violations and show a visual indication of the error or
warning next to the code. Typically, this indication appears just how a spellchecker
shows spelling mistakes in a word processor. These timely indications help
immensely in addressing common coding mistakes right when they occur.

Pylint

Pylint is a tool that inspects the code for errors and also warns you about coding standard violations. It is integrated with several IDEs (check out `http://docs.pylint.org/ide-integration` for a list of IDEs and editors where Pylint is either available or can be installed as a plugin). We will see how to use Pylint as a command-line tool. First, install it using pip—depending on your Python installation, you might need administrative access in order to install it:

```
$ pip install pylint
```

This installs `pylint` (or `pylint.exe` on Windows) at the same location where you have Python executable. Now, you should be able to use this tool from the command line. On Linux, the syntax is as follows:

```
$ pylint module_name.py
```

Where `module_name.py` is the file you want to check for errors and coding style problems. When you run `pylint` from the command line, it prints a detailed report of the analysis. This report has information on coding style, warnings, errors, and refactoring needs. In the end, it rates your code on a scale out of 10.

You can also customize the default settings to fit to your project needs. This is done using a configuration file. On Linux, run the following command in a terminal:

```
$ pylint --generate-rcfile > ~/.pylintrc
```

This creates a default template for your Pylint configuration and saves it in your `$HOME` directory (`~/.pylintrc`). Even on Windows OS, this file can be created in your user's home directory Alternatively, you can specify the `PYLINTRC` environment variable, which holds the complete path to the file.

Pylint in action

It is time for some action. Run the Pylint code analysis on the `wargame/hut.py` file. Recall that in an earlier section, *Docstrings using RST*, we added a class-level docstring. That's pretty much the documentation we have for this file. Pylint will not like this so be prepared to get beaten up!

```
$ cd wargame
$ pylint hut.py
```

The last command prints a detailed report on the command line. Let's see what we have got. The following screenshot shows the final report—the code has been rated **5.00** out of **10** points:

```
File  Edit  View  Search  Terminal  Help

Messages
--------


+----------------------------+-------------+
|message id                  |occurrences  |
+============================+=============+
|missing-docstring           |3            |
+----------------------------+-------------+
|wrong-import-position       |1            |
+----------------------------+-------------+
|pointless-string-statement  |1            |
+----------------------------+-------------+
|import-error                |1            |
+----------------------------+-------------+



Global evaluation
-----------------
Your code has been rated at 5.00/10 (previous run: 5.00/10, +0.00)
```

That's pretty bad! Let's look at where we can improve by reviewing the report Pylint has generated. In the report, it complains about an `import` error. Well, there is nothing wrong with the imports. Clearly, it is missing the Python directory PATH. This can be fixed by editing the `.pythonrc` file. Look for a commented line that reads `init-hook` (it should appear near the beginning of the file). Uncomment it and write the following code:

```
init-hook='import sys; sys.path.append("/path/to/wargame/")'
```

Replace /path/to/wargame with the actual path on your system to the wargame directory. With this change, rerun Pylint on this file. The new evaluation is shown next:

File   Edit   View   Search   Terminal   Help

```
Messages
--------

+----------------------------+------------+
|message id                  |occurrences |
+============================+============+
|missing-docstring           |3           |
+----------------------------+------------+
|wrong-import-position       |1           |
+----------------------------+------------+
|pointless-string-statement  |1           |
+----------------------------+------------+


Global evaluation
-----------------

Your code has been rated at 7.50/10 (previous run: 5.00/10, +2.50)
```

Not bad! Just fixing the import error has already improved the score by **2.50** points. Let's review the generated report one more time. At the beginning of the report, Pylint lists all the issues present in the file. In this case, it complains about missing docstrings for the module and the methods of the class. The other thing it is not happy about is the import statement, from __future__ import print_function, as the first line of the module.

PEP 236 convention

Although the __future__ import statement must appear as the first line, the exception to this rule is a module docstring. A module docstring can be written before writing a __future__ import statement. Review the *PEP 236* convention (https://www.python.org/dev/peps/pep-0236) for more information.

We can easily fix both these issues. A reworked module docstring along with the rearranged __future__ import statement is shown in the following code screenshot:

```
"""wargame.hut

This module contains the Hut class implementation.

This module is compatible with Python 3.5.x. It contains
supporting code for the book, Learning Python Application Development,
Packt Publishing.

:copyright: 2016, Ninad Sathaye

:license: The MIT License (MIT) . See LICENSE file for further details.
"""


from __future__ import print_function
from gameutils import print_bold


class Hut:
    """Class to create hut objects in the game Attack of the Orcs
```

Let's see how are we doing by running Pylint again after this change:

```
File   Edit   View   Search   Terminal   Help

Messages by category
--------------------

+-------------+--------+---------+------------+
|type         |number  |previous |difference  |
+=============+========+=========+============+
|convention   |0       |4        |-4.00       |
+-------------+--------+---------+------------+
|refactor     |0       |0        |=           |
+-------------+--------+---------+------------+
|warning      |0       |1        |-1.00       |
+-------------+--------+---------+------------+
|error        |0       |0        |=           |
+-------------+--------+---------+------------+


Global evaluation
-----------------
Your code has been rated at 10.00/10 (previous run: 7.50/10, +2.50)
```

Yey! We have got full points for this module! Follow the similar process to improve the rest of the code. As an exercise, add the docstrings for the class methods. You can also download `wargame/hut.py` from the supplementary material for this chapter, which already has all the docstrings written.

PEP8 and AutoPEP8

pep8 is another tool that inspects the code to check whether it confirms to the *PEP 8* coding style guide. It can be installed using pip as follows:

```
$ pip install pep8
```

To know how to use pep8, visit the project page (`https://pypi.python.org/pypi/pep8`). There is another handy tool called **autopep8** that will automatically reformat the code to confirm to the style recommended by *PEP 8* guidelines. This tool can also be installed using pip:

```
$ pip install autopep8
```

Note that this tool requires pep8 to be installed. Check out `https://pypi.python.org/pypi/autopep8` for more information and usage examples.

Exercise

In this chapter, you learned how to document code, use Sphinx to generate documentation, and analyze the code using tools such as Pylint. Here is an exercise that covers these three aspects:

- Download the code illustrated in *Chapter 3*, *Modularize, Package, Deploy* (you can also use your own Python code instead).

- Write docstrings for this code (be sure to write docstrings at module, class, and method/function levels). You can use the default RST format to write the docstring or choose the *Google Python Style Guide*.

- Generate an HTML documentation using Sphinx.

- Run code analysis, using Pylint or any other tool, to fix coding errors and style problems.

The supporting code for this chapter is already documented to an extent. You can use this code as a reference and also try to improve the existing documentation further.

Summary

You learned how to document the code using the RST format. The chapter introduced the Sphinx document generator that was used to create an HTML documentation for our application code. You also learned about some important Python coding standards that helped improve readability. Finally, we saw how to check our application code for errors and style violations using code analysis.

In an ideal world, you wish your code fully confirms to the coding convention. Often, that is not the case for various reasons, ranging from new team members to tight project deadlines. Sometimes, to make it compliant with the coding standards, you will need to refactor it at a later stage. While doing so, you will also need to make sure no functionality gets broken. This is accomplished by writing unit tests. We will study these inter-related aspects in the next chapter.

5

Unit Testing and Refactoring

Here is a quick recap of what you have learned so far. You developed a command-line application using the OOP approach, and then learned techniques to make your code robust by handling exceptions. You modularized the code, prepared a distribution, and released it to a broader audience. Finally, you learned about coding standards and documentation.

So far, we have not paid much attention to testing the application. We relied solely on manual testing, where some features were tested by playing the game. The task of manual testing becomes increasingly difficult with the complexity of the application. Soon you will be overwhelmed, and the bugs will start to creep in. While manual testing may not be avoided completely, we need an automated way to make sure the features work as expected. In this chapter, you will do the following:

- Learn about unittest, the unit testing framework in Python
- Write some unit tests for our application
- See how to use the mock library in unit tests
- Learn how to measure the effectiveness of unit tests (code coverage)
- Understand what is code refactoring, why, when, and how to do it
- Come back to the unit testing discussion after doing some code refactoring

This is how the chapter is organized

The chapter starts with a game scenario, where a bug slips through to production and stays hidden until a user discovers it. This scenario underlines the need for automated testing, and then leads into a discussion on unit testing framework in Python. You will be introduced to the unittest framework and the mock library in Python. The chapter will demonstrate the use of these libraries by writing a few unit tests for our project.

Moving ahead, it shows an example where it is difficult to write a unit test without refactoring the code first (see *Refactoring preamble*). This is where we take a detour, learn the basics of refactoring, refactor the code, and then develop the last unit test.

Important housekeeping notes

These notes will be useful in case you haven't read the earlier chapters. Otherwise, just move on to the next heading. Like every other chapter, this one has its own set of Python source files. The source code can be downloaded from the *Packt Publishing* website. Just follow the instructions mentioned in this book's *Preface*.

This is the last chapter that depends on the code developed in the earlier chapters. Starting with *Chapter 6*, *Design Patterns*, we will have independent, simplified examples to demonstrate various concepts. That said, everything will be tied back to the same high fantasy theme.

Why test?

Did you play the game developed so far? If not, just try playing it once. During the combat with the enemy, the following can be observed. For each attack, either Sir Foo or the enemy sustains injuries. This is indicated by the reduced hit points. For example, in the sample game output shown next, `Sir Foo` gets hit in the first attack turn, whereas the enemy is injured in the next two attack turns.

```
Health: Sir Foo: 40
Current occupants: ['enemy', 'friend', 'friend', 'enemy', 'friend']
Choose a hut number to enter (1-5): 1
Entering hut 1... Enemy sighted!
Health: Sir Foo: 40 Health: enemy-1: 30
...continue attack? (y/n): y
ATTACK! Health: Sir Foo: 27   Health: enemy-1: 30
...continue attack? (y/n): y
ATTACK! Health: Sir Foo: 27   Health: enemy-1: 16
...continue attack? (y/n): y
ATTACK! Health: Sir Foo: 27   Health: enemy-1: 2
...continue attack? (y/n): █
```

A new feature was requested

A user requested an enhancement to the combat scenario:

"During combat, the program asks whether you want to continue attacking the enemy. In each attack move, one of the warriors, the player or the enemy, gets injured. Can you make it more interesting? What if both the warriors escape unhurt sometimes?"

I can't imagine the enemy escaping unhurt even after my fierce attack! Do not entertain this feature request... what say you?

It will benefit you as well Sir Foo! We will go ahead and implement this minor enhancement. Despite Sir Foo's stiff opposition, you rushed to implement this new feature.

You implemented this feature

Recall that the `gameutils.weighted_random_selection` function randomly selects an element from `weighted_list`. The list is populated such that, for approximately 30% of the time, the unique identifier of `obj1` gets selected, and for the rest of the time, the unique identifier representing `obj2` gets chosen. Put another way, the chance of Sir Foo (`obj1`) getting injured is approximately 30%, and that of the enemy (`obj2`) is nearly 70%.

To add the likelihood that no one gets hurt, you changed the composition of `weighted_list` by adding a new element, `None`. The new chances of injury to the warriors are as follows:

- The chances of the enemy (`obj2`) getting hurt are ~ 60%
- The chances of Sir Foo (`obj1`) getting hurt are ~30%
- Both escaping unhurt (`None`) are ~ 10%

The following is the `weighted_random_selection` function before and after the aforementioned change:

```python
def weighted_random_selection(obj1, obj2):
    weighted_list = 3 * [id(obj1)] + 7 * [id(obj2)]
    selection = random.choice(weighted_list)

    if selection == id(obj1):
        return obj1

    return obj2
```

> Original function

```python
def weighted_random_selection(obj1, obj2):
    weighted_list = 3 * [id(obj1)] + 6 * [id(obj2)] + 1*[None]
    selection = random.choice(weighted_list)

    if selection == id(obj1):
        return obj1
    elif selection == id(obj2):
        return obj2
    else:
        return None
```

> An additional random choice 'None' added to the selection algorithm

That was easy, wasn't it? You played the game once to make sure nothing is broken. It looked all fine. Without any delay, you released a new version.

But something wasn't right...

However, soon after release, user complaints started pouring in. This was unexpected. Your commit introduced a new bug!

Calm down Sir Foo! You are still in war mode! Relax and take a deep breath. We will address this issue soon.

So what went wrong? There is no problem with the function you wrote. It is behaving as intended. However, you forgot to make some changes to the code that calls `weighted_random_selection`. As a result, the following uncaught exception is seen:

```
Health: Sir Foo: 40
Current occupants: ['unoccupied', 'friend', 'unoccupied', 'enemy', 'enemy']
Choose a hut number to enter (1-5): 4
Entering hut 4... Enemy sighted!
Health: Sir Foo: 40 Health: enemy-4: 30
...continue attack? (y/n): y
Traceback (most recent call last):
  File "attackoftheorcs.py", line 188, in <module>
    game.play()
  File "attackoftheorcs.py", line 172, in play
    self.player.acquire_hut(self.huts[idx-1])
  File "/home/ch/wargame/knight.py", line 87, in acquire_hut
    self.attack(hut.occupant)
  File "/home/ch/wargame/abstractgameunit.py", line 74, in attack
    injured_unit.health_meter = max(injured_unit.health_meter - injury, 0)
AttributeError: 'NoneType' object has no attribute 'health_meter'
```

The error traceback points to the `AbstractGameUnit.attack` method. This method calls the `weighted_random_selection` function to randomly select an injured unit. The problem occurs when `injured_unit` is None. The trouble-causing line of code is shown in the following code snippet:

```
def attack(self, enemy):                              returns 'None'
    """Attack the enemy unit..."""
    injured_unit = weighted_random_selection(self, enemy)
    injury = random.randint(10, 15)
    injured_unit.health_meter = max(injured_unit.health_meter - injury, 0)
    print("ATTACK! ", end='')            results in unhandled
    self.show_health(end='  ')           exception when this is 'None'
    enemy.show_health(end='  ')
```

It required thorough testing

You had done basic testing by running the game once. But then why didn't you notice this problem? The chances that the function returns None are slim. For example, for every 10 calls to the function `weighted_random_selection`, the value None would be on average returned only once. In this case, the testing you did was not enough to reproduce the problem.

This is just one of the scenarios where thorough testing is required. At the same time, it is prone to human error because of the random nature of the output. If you had some automated means to test this functionality, the bug could have been easily avoided.

So let's learn how to create automated tests in Python using the unittest framework. After you know how to write a unit test, we will come back and write a unit test for the `weighted_random_selection` function that was discussed here.

Unit testing

In unit testing, you tinker with a code fragment within the application. The main task is to verify that this piece of code continues to work as expected throughout the life of the application. This is accomplished by writing a test for that functionality.

A unit test can be better explained with an example. Consider a trivial function that returns the sum of two numbers. In a unit test, you invoke this function by passing two numbers as arguments, and then verify the value returned by the function is indeed the sum of the given numbers.

There are many frameworks available for writing unit tests. The examples in this chapter will be based on the built-in unit testing framework called unittest. See the heading *Other unit testing tools*, which gives a very short overview of alternative unit testing tools and frameworks.

Python unittest framework

The `unittest` module provides the functionality to automate tests. Before we implement any tests for our application, let's first start with the terminology.

Basic terminology

- **Test case**: When you write a unit test, it is referred to as a test case. `TestCase` is the superclass for creating different test cases.

- **Test suite**: When you group together various test cases, it becomes a test suite. A test suite may also represent a collection of other test suites. `unittest.TestSuite` provides a superclass for creating a suite. The `TestSuite` does not define any unit tests, but it just accumulates the tests or other test suites. This is a major difference between `TestSuite` and `TestCase`.

- **Test fixtures**: These are preparatory methods for the smooth running of the unit tests. For example, `TestCase.setUp` is called just before executing a test case. It can be used to feed the required data to the test cases. Similarly, `TestCase.tearDown` method is called immediately after the test execution. Such methods could be used in combination, for instance to start and stop a service consumed by a unit test.

- **Test runner**: The runner helps execute a test case or a test suite. It also provides a way to represent the results after running the tests. For example, the results can be displayed on the command line or in some graphical form. The basic implementation is provided by the `unittest.TextTestRunner` class.

Creating tests with unittest.TestCase

To understand the basics of constructing and running the tests, let's write a trivial program. Observe the following code:

```python
import unittest

class MyUnitTests(unittest.TestCase):
    def setUp(self):
        print("In setUp..")

    def tearDown(self):
        print("Tearing Down the test.")
        print("~"*10)

    def test_2(self):
        print("in test_2")
        self.assertEqual(1+1, 2)

    def test_1(self):
        print("in test_1")
        self.assertTrue(1+1 == 2)

    def will_not_be_called(self):
        print("this method will not be called automatically")

if __name__ == '__main__':
    unittest.main()
```

> Inherited methods of TestCase

> Methods with prefix 'test' are recognized as test cases by the test runner

> By default this is not identified as a test method

> Load and run the tests

As mentioned earlier, the `setUp` and `tearDown` methods are known as fixtures. `MyUnitTests.setUp()` is called before executing each test. This allows the initialization of some common variables before the test gets executed. The `MyUnitTests.tearDown()` method is called after every test.

When the `unittest.main()` program is invoked, the tests defined in the `MyUnitTests` class are run one after the other. This program can also accept a test runner as an optional argument (not used in this example). By default, the program loads and runs only the methods that have names starting with `test`. In the `MyUnitTests` class, the tests defined in the `test_1` and `test_2` methods will be executed as shown in the following command-line output:

```
[user@hostname ch5]$ python testcasedemo.py
In setUp..
in test_1                      First test
Tearing Down the test.
~~~~~~~~~~~
.In setUp..
in test_2                      Second test
Tearing Down the test.
~~~~~~~~~~~
.
------------------------------------------------------------
Ran 2 tests in 0.001s       All is well. No problems found
                            while running these tests
OK  ←
```

Now that we know how the test cases are executed, let's review one of the methods, which is as follows:

```
def test_2(self):
    print("in test_2")
    self.assertEqual(1+1, 2)
```

The `assertEqual` method is a built-in method of the `TestCase` class. It essentially checks whether the two input arguments are equal, otherwise an assertion error is raised. The test illustrated in the preceding code fragment will pass. Let's review a test that would fail:

```
def test_2(self):
    print("in test_2")
    self.assertEqual(1+1, 3)
```

Obviously, `1+1 != 3`, so we would expect the test to fail, as shown in the following command-line output. For a failed test, it also prints the letter `F` in the output:

```
[user@hostname ch5]$ python testcasedemo.py
In setUp..
in test_1
Tearing Down the test.
~~~~~~~~~~
.In setUp..
in test_2
Tearing Down the test.
~~~~~~~~~~
F
=====================================================================
FAIL: test_2 (__main__.MyUnitTests)
---------------------------------------------------------------------
Traceback (most recent call last):
  File "testcasedemo.py", line 14, in test_2
    self.assertEqual(1+1, 3)
AssertionError: 2 != 3


---------------------------------------------------------------------
Ran 2 tests in 0.002s

FAILED (failures=1)
```

Similarly, the `unittest.TestCase` class defines a bunch of convenient methods. For example, the `assertTrue` and `assertFalse` methods verify a condition. Another method, `assertRaises`, is used to check whether a certain exception is raised by the code.

Controlling test execution

Is there a way to run only selected test cases? One way is to use Python **decorators** for the tests you want to ignore. Let's add this decorator to both the test cases from the previous example:

```
@unittest.skip("Skipping test_2")
def test_2(self):
    print("in test_2")
    self.assertEqual(1+1, 3)

@unittest.skip("Skipping test_1")
def test_1(self):
    print("in test_1")
    self.assertTrue(1+1 == 2)
```

Essentially, none of the test cases would be run. The output, after running the code, indicates that these tests have been skipped. For each skipped test, it prints s in the output:

```
[user@hostname ch5]$ python testcasedemo.py
ss
----------------------------------------------------------------
Ran 2 tests in 0.000s

OK (skipped=2)
```

> There are two more decorators not covered here, namely skipIf
> and skipUnless. These decorators are used for the condition-based
> skipping of the test. See the following documentation page for details:
> https://docs.python.org/3/library/unittest.html.

Sometimes, you do expect a few test cases to fail. For example, a test may fail due to a difference between a development versus a production environment, or due to the presence or absence of expected database content. Such expected failures can be tagged with another decorator. We know that test_2 fails, so let's add the decorator for this test:

```
@unittest.expectedFailure
def test_2(self):
    print("in test_2")
    self.assertEqual(1+1, 3)

@unittest.skip("Skipping test_1")
def test_1(self):
    print("in test_1")
    self.assertTrue(1+1 == 2)
```

For each anticipated failure, it prints x in the output. At the end, it summarizes how many tests were expected to fail:

```
[user@hostname ch5]$ python testcasedemo.py
sIn setUp..
in test_2
Tearing Down the test.
~~~~~~~~~~
x
-----------------------------------------------------------------
Ran 2 tests in 0.002s

OK (skipped=1, expected failures=1)
```

Using unittest.TestSuite

Refer to the testsuitedemo.py file in the supporting code bundle for this chapter. The module contains two classes, namely MyUnitTestA and MyUnitTestB. Each of these inherit from unittest.TestCase, and define some trivial methods as unit tests.

In *Chapter 3, Modularize, Package, Deploy!* we created a separate module for each class. Here, the testsuitedemo.py module contains two classes. As an exercise, you can put these classes in separate modules.

The following code snippets show these classes. For compactness, the code comments are omitted here:

```python
import unittest

class MyUnitTestA(unittest.TestCase):
    def test_a2(self):
        print("MyUnitTestA.test_a2")
        self.assertNotEqual(1 + 1, 3)

    def test_a1(self):
        print("MyUnitTestA.test_a1")
        self.assertTrue(1 + 1 == 2)

    def not_called_by_default(self):
        print("MyUnitTestA: This method will not be called by default")

class MyUnitTestB(unittest.TestCase):
    def test_b2(self):
        print("MyUnitTestB.test_b2")
        self.assertNotEqual( 4*4 , 15)

    def test_b1(self):
        print("MyUnitTestB.test_b1")
        self.assertTrue(4 + 4 == 8)

    def not_called_by_default(self):
        print("MyUnitTestB: This method will not be called by default")
```

The `makeSuite` function of the `unittest` module can be used to create an instance of `TestSuite`:

```python
suite_a = unittest.makeSuite(MyUnitTestA)
```

The preceding line of code will construct a test suite using all the unit tests defined in the `MyUnitTestA` class. Only the method names starting with `test*` are added to the test suite. In this example, these methods are `test_a2` and `test_a1`. The third method, `not_called_by_default`, will not be automatically considered as a unit test.

 Non-test methods (such as `not_called_by_default` in this example), are often useful for sharing code between the tests.

Let's see how to include such methods in the test suite. The code snippet that follows shows a function `suite()` defined in this module:

```
def suite():
    """Return a composite testsuite that aggregates two testsuits.

    These sub-testsuites, in turn, aggragate all the tests in classes
    `MyUnitTestA` and `MyUnitTestB`.
    :return: Instance of `unittest.Testsuite`
    """
    print("Inside suite()...")

    # Create a test suite by collecting all test cases defined
    # in MyUnitTestA. By default it only looks for methods starting
    # with test*
    suite_a = unittest.makeSuite(MyUnitTestA)

    # Similarly, create suite_b  using testcases from MyUnitTestB
    suite_b = unittest.makeSuite(MyUnitTestB)

    # Add a new testcase to suite_b.
    suite_b.addTest(MyUnitTestB("not_called_by_default"))

    # Return a composite test suite containing suite_a and suite_b
    return unittest.TestSuite((suite_a, suite_b))
```

Let's review the preceding code snippet:

- This function creates two instances of `TestSuite`, namely `suite_a` and `suite_b`.
- The `MyUnitTest.not_called_by_default` method is added as a test case in the test suite using the `addTest` method.
- The function returns a new `TestSuite` object. It takes a Python tuple as an argument. In this example, the tuple includes the two instances of `TestSuite` created before.

The last part of this module is the execution code:

```
if __name__ == '__main__':
    # Run the tests.
    unittest.main(defaultTest='suite')
```

Running the `testsuitedemo.py` module produces the following output. Observe that it has also executed the test defined in `MyUnitTestB.not_called_by_default`:

```
[user@hostname ch5]$ python testsuitedemo.py
Inside suite()...
MyUnitTestA.test_a1
.MyUnitTestA.test_a2
.MyUnitTestB.test_b1
.MyUnitTestB.test_b2
.MyUnitTestB: This method will not be called by default
.
----------------------------------------------------------------
Ran 5 tests in 0.000s

OK
```

 Test suites are also very convenient for grouping test cases, depending on their runtime. For example, you can group together fast-running tests and slow-running tests, and give the test runner script a command-line option to choose which one to run.

Writing unit tests for the application

It is time to write some unit tests for the application. We will make a new subclass of `unittest.TestCase` to hold all the unit tests.

Setting up a test package

As a first step, let's create a new package for holding the test cases. Create a new directory called `test` at the same level where you have the rest of the code. Next, create two new files inside this `test` directory, as shown here:

The `test_wargame.py` module is where new unit tests will be created. To recognize the directory as a Python package, add an empty `__init__.py` file.

 If you haven't already, read *Chapter 3, Modularize, Package, Deploy!* for details on creating a Python package.

Creating a new class for unit testing

The `test_wargame.py` file can also be found in the supporting code. It has all the code to be discussed next. In the following discussion, it is assumed that you will code from scratch to an empty file.

Create a new subclass of `unittest.TestCase`, and call it `TestWarGame` or any name you like. The class is shown here:

```python
import unittest
from knight import Knight
from orcrider import OrcRider
from abstractgameunit import AbstractGameUnit
from gameutils import weighted_random_selection
from hut import Hut
from attackoftheorcs import AttackOfTheOrcs

class TestWarGame(unittest.TestCase):
    """This class contains unit tests for the game Attack of The Orcs."""

    def setUp(self):
        """Overrides the setUp fixture of the superclass."""
        self.knight = Knight()
        self.enemy = OrcRider()

    def test_injured_unit_selection(self):
        """Unit test to verify working of weighted_random_selection()"""
        pass # To be implemented!

if __name__ == '__main__':
    unittest.main()
```

We start by making the necessary imports. Recall that the setUp() fixture is called immediately before running the unit tests. Inside setUp, instances of the Knight and OrcRider classes are created, and are then used in the unit test we are about to write: test_injured_unit_selection. As seen before, the call to unittest.main() will automatically execute methods whose names start with test. In this example, it will run test_injured_unit_selection().

You can write the same code without using fixtures as well. Simply create the required instances inside the test you are writing. As you will see next, the test_injured_unit_selection() unit test uses the objects created in setUp(). Alternatively, you can create those instances locally, inside the test, like so:

```python
def test_injured_unit_selection(self):
    knight = Knight()
    enemy = OrcRider()
    # rest of the test code...
```

First unit test – Injured unit selection

Let's go back to the scenario we discussed under the section *Why test?* Recall that you changed the behavior of the `weighted_random_selection` function so that it can also return `None` (nobody injured). This new feature broke the program, and the application terminated because of an uncaught exception.

The test we are about to write will verify the original behavior of this function. The original behavior was to select either Sir Foo (the `Knight` instance) or the enemy (the `OrcRider` instance) as the injured unit. The unit test we are about to write will verify exactly that. Observe the following code:

```python
def test_injured_unit_selection(self):
    """Unit test to verify if the injured unit is
    an instance of class AbstractGameUnit
    """
    for i in range(100):
        injured_unit = weighted_random_selection(self.knight,
                                                  self.enemy)
        self.assertIsInstance(
            injured_unit,
            AbstractGameUnit,
            "Injured unit must be an instance of AbstractGameUnit")
```

With this preceding function, the chance of `self.enemy` getting injured is approximately 70%, and that of `self.knight` (Sir Foo) is nearly 30%. The top-level `for` loop just ensures it is called `100` times to account for the random nature of the function return value. `TestCase.assertInstance()` raises an assertion error if `injured_unit` is not an instance of `Knight` or `OrcRider`. Let's run this test now.

Running the first unit test

In a terminal window, run this test from the top-level `wargame` directory:

```
$ cd wargame
$ python -m unittest test.test_wargame
```

`-m` is a built-in command line option in Python. It allows you to run a library module as a script. In this case, it will run the `unittest` module as a script. The argument `test.test_wargame` represents the file `test/test_wargame.py`. The `unittest` script will run the tests defined in this module.

If the old behavior of `weighted_random_selection` is left unchanged, the test will pass. However, if you implement the new behavior where the function could also return `None`, it will fail by raising an `AssertionError`, as shown next:

```
[user@hostname wargame]$ python -m unittest test.test_wargame
F
=====================================================================
FAIL: test_injured_unit_selection (test.test_wargame.TestWarGame)
Unit test to check if the function ..
---------------------------------------------------------------------
Traceback (most recent call last):
  File "/home/bookuser/wargame/test/test_wargame.py", line 72, in test_
injured_unit_selection
    "Injured unit must be an instance of AbstractGameUnit")
AssertionError: None is not an instance of <class 'abstractgameunit.Abs
tractGameUnit'> : Injured unit must be an instance of AbstractGameUnit


---------------------------------------------------------------------
Ran 1 test in 0.001s

FAILED (failures=1)
```

 There is no need to run the `for` loop `100` times. Just make sure to call the function at least 10 times. As an exercise, update the test to verify further details. For example, verify that the function returns the `Knight` instance approximately 30% of the time, and so on.

Second unit test – Acquiring the hut

Let's pick another functionality for testing. This time, it is a method from the `Hut` class:

```python
def acquire(self, new_occupant):
    self.occupant = new_occupant
    self.is_acquired = True
    print_bold("GOOD JOB! Hut %d acquired" % self.number)
```

In this method, what do you think we can test? The method serves the following purposes: (a) It updates the occupant information, and (b) It sets the `is_acquired` flag to `True`.

Redesign exercise:

In this application, we assume everything from the context of the player. For example, the is_acquired flag of the Hut instance is from the point of view of the player. If it is set to True, it means the hut is acquired by the player and not the enemy. This is already prone to bugs. Imagine an OrcRider instance calling this method! You can add assertions to make sure it accepts only the Knight instance. As an exercise, remove the dependence on the is_acquired flag from the code.

When writing a test, we will ensure that the new occupant is the same object as the one passed as an argument to the method.

Good question Sir Foo. Why write this test if the method is already working fine? Keep in mind the scenario we discussed earlier. An intentional change in the functionality caused us so much trouble. Why wait for such a bug to show up?

Today, this code is behaving as expected. The unit test is meant for tomorrow. Imagine multiple developers contributing to this application. As a result, more code would get added, and someone may inadvertently introduce code that will break the intended functionality of this method. In such a scenario, how do you ensure that the fundamental behavior remains unchanged? A unit test will notice such changes.

*A future requirement might even change the fundamental behavior of the method. This was illustrated in the scenario under the heading **Why Test?** When that happens, the unit test you wrote would obviously fail. You do expect it to fail now, and that would make it imperative to update the test to match the new requirement.*

In short, a unit test will make sure that accidental changes to the code are captured right away, and don't become your nightmare, such as when someone reports a bug and you learn the hard way that it was caused by a silly mistake in the code you wrote a few months ago.

Let's write a new method in the same class, `TestWarGame`:

```python
def test_acquire_hut(self):
    """Unittest to verify hut occupant after it is acquired

    Unit test to ensure that when hut is 'acquired', the
    `hut.occupant` is updated to the `Knight` instance
    """
    print("\nCalling test_hut.test_acquire_hut..")
    hut   = Hut(4, None)
    hut.acquire(self.knight)
    self.assertIs(hut.occupant, self.knight)
```

In the preceding code, we first create an instance of `Hut`. In the second line, this hut is acquired by `self.knight`. The `TestCase.assertIs` checks whether the object representing the hut's occupant is the same as `self.knight`, otherwise an `AssertionError` is raised.

Running only the second test

If we execute the following command, it would run all the tests defined in the
`test_wargame.py` module:

```
$ cd wargame
$ python -m unittest test.test_wargame
```

What if you just want to run `test_acquire_hut`? Assuming you are already inside
the `wargame` directory, here is a command to accomplish this:

```
$ python -m unittest test.test_wargame.TestWarGame.test_acquire_hut
```

This command-line argument can be read as `package_name.module_name.class_name.method_name`.

The output after running this test is shown here:

```
[user@hostname wargame]$ python -m unittest \
> test.test_wargame.TestWarGame.test_acquire_hut
GOOD JOB! Hut 4 acquired
.
-----------------------------------------------------------------
Ran 1 test in 0.000s

OK
```

Creating individual test modules

The last unit test we wrote was meant for testing the functionality in the `Hut` class. We
created this as a method of the `TestWarGame` class in the `test_wargame.py` module.

Do we have to put all the tests for the application inside a single module? No! You
can, optionally, create individual test modules for each class.

> For large applications, it is often convenient to have separate test modules
> at the class level or the package level. Choose a strategy that best suits
> your project. If it makes sense, you can also create a test class that clubs
> together some common functionality in your application.

Let's rework the previous example. We will create a new module, test_hut.py, as a home for a new class, TestHut. The source code is also available in the supplementary material for this chapter—see wargame/test/test_hut.py. Next, we will move the TestWarGame.test_acquire_hut method into this class. This is shown here:

```python
from knight import Knight
from hut import Hut

class TestHut(unittest.TestCase):
    """Contains unit tests for the game Attack of The Orcs."""
    def setUp(self):
        """Called just before the calling each  unit test"""
        self.knight = Knight()

    def test_acquire_hut(self):
        """Unittest to verify hut occupant after it is acquired"""
        print("\nCalling test_hut.test_acquire_hut..")
        hut = Hut(4, None)
        hut.acquire(self.knight)
        self.assertIs(hut.occupant, self.knight)

if __name__ == '__main__':
    unittest.main()
```

The syntax to execute the unit test is similar to the one used before:

```
$ cd wargame
$ python -m unittest test.test_hut
```

Batch executing unit tests

If your test directory contains multiple test modules, how do you run all the tests at once inside the directory? One option is to write a script listing commands to execute the unit tests one after the other. The unittest module, however, provides a discover option to batch execute the tests on the command line:

```
$ python -m unittest discover
```

The following command-line output shows the batch execution of two test modules inside the `test` directory:

```
[user@hostname wargame]$ ls -1 test | cat
__init__.py
test_hut.py              ──────test modules
test_wargame.py
[user@hostname wargame]$ python -m unittest discover ./test/

Calling test_hut.test_acquire_hut..
GOOD JOB! Hut 4 acquired

Calling test_wargame.test_injured_unit_selection..

-------------------------------------------------------------------
Ran 2 tests in 0.001s

OK
```

Unit tests using mock library

The two tests we wrote earlier were pretty straightforward to implement. Often, it is not trivial to write a test for verifying the functionality. The reasons could vary. In some scenarios, the code is required to be refactored in order to access the functionality you would like to test. In another scenario, the code might have dependencies that require you to write a lot more code than necessary. It is also possible that the functionality to be tested needs time consuming preparatory work such as crunching some numbers. This adds to the total test execution time. We will now learn how to write a unit test in such situations using the mock library. Before working on the actual code, let's understand what functionality this library provides.

Quick introduction to mock

The mock library provides a flexible way to create dummy objects that can be used to replace some parts in the program that you are testing.

Mock is available in the Python standard library (v3.3 onwards) as `unittest.mock`. If you are using a prior distribution, install it using this command:

`$ pip install mock`

Visit `https://pypi.python.org/pypi/mock` for further information.

With a mock object, you can focus on the main functionality to be tested without worrying much about the things on which this functionality depends. It provides a way to decouple the supporting chunks of code from the functionality being tested. This can be better explained with an example. Refer to the following cartoon:

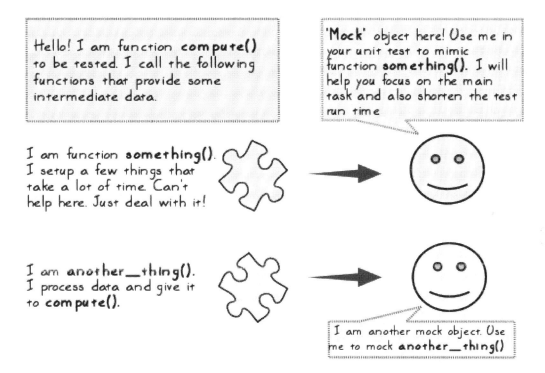

Imagine you are writing a unit test for a function called `compute()` that does a lot of scientific computations. Within this function, you are calling other supporting functions that process some data. This is a time-consuming operation. If you know what information is being provided by the supporting functions, you can define their behavior using mock objects.

Let's mock!

It's time for some action. Open your Python interpreter, and start writing the following code. It is assumed that the mock module is already available. If it isn't, install it using pip, as suggested earlier. First, import the Mock class as follows:

```
>>> from unittest.mock import Mock
```

Next, create a Mock object:

```
>>> mockObj = Mock()
```

The object type and its unique ID can be found as follows:

```
>>> mockObj
<Mock id='140524045365320'>
```

Moving on, type the following code in the Python interpreter:

```
>>> mockObj.foo
```

Good observation! Apologies for using your name here...that was unintentional. In the developer world, people just love your name! So the question is, would it really give an attribute error? Try it yourself!

Executing this last line of code will print an output similar to the following:

```
>>> mockObj.foo
<Mock name='mockObj.foo' id='140524032172664'>
```

This is the interesting part! It did not complain about the missing attribute; instead, it created a new mock object. You can access any arbitrary attribute of this object as if it was already defined. It will create and return a new `Mock` object representing that attribute. Here, `foo` is also called a child mock of `mockObj`.

Let's see how to make use of this feature. `Mock.mock_calls` can be used to track all the calls of a mock object along with its child mocks. The results are returned as a Python list. Write the following line of code in the Python interpreter:

```
>>> mockObj.mock_calls
[]
```

Here, it returns an empty Python list, as we have not called the `mockObj` or its child mocks.

Next, let's see how this list gets populated. The `Mock` objects are callable. Write the following code to call `mockObj.foo`:

```
>>> mockObj.foo()
<Mock name='mockObj.foo()' id='140524032173280'>
```

We will create and call another new child mock like so:

```
>>> mockObj.foo2(return_value = 20)
<Mock name='mock.foo2()' id='140271893632056'>
```

Now, let's invoke `mockObj.mock_calls` one more time:

```
>>> test_call_list = mockObj.mock_calls
>>> test_call_list
[call.foo(), call.foo2(return_value=20)]
```

The returned list now contains two objects, namely `call.foo()` and `call.foo2()`. These are the helper objects provided by `unittest.mock.call`.

How do we use this information? When you write a unit test, you can use this list to make assertions on which objects are invoked and in what order. To understand this concept better, we will write a simple unit test in the next section.

Using Mock objects in a unit test

Let's write a unit test for the compute method of a class, MyClassA. The class is shown next. You can also download the wargame/test/mockdemo.py file from the supporting code bundle:

```python
import unittest
from unittest.mock import Mock, call

class MyClassA:
    """Class for mock demo"""
    def foo(self):
        """Return a number"""
        # Assume it does some lengthy computation here (not shown)
        return 100

    def foo2(self, num):
        """Return another number"""
        # Assume it does some lengthy computation here (not shown)
        return num + 200

    def compute(self):
        """Demonstrate use of mock objects"""
        x1 = self.foo()
        x2 = self.foo2(x1)
        print("x1 = %d, x2 = %d"%(x1, x2))
        result = x1 + x2
        print("In MyClassA.compute, result = x1 + x2 = ", result)
        return result
```

This is a trivial example. The compute method depends on the values returned by two methods, foo and foo2. It uses these values to compute and return the result. In this example, the methods foo and foo2 are simple.

Imagine a scenario where the aforementioned methods perform tasks that take a very long time. Now, to write a unit test that verifies the functionality of the compute method, you would need to check the final value of result. Naturally, it would take a long time to finish because of the time spent in foo and foo2. If you know the expected outcome of these methods, you can simply replace them with Mock objects in the test. We can do this because foo and foo2 are assumed to be the supporting functions, and the main functionality to be tested is the value of result.

The Mock objects would behave as if they are the original methods, and return the output you need. But in reality, we bypass the time consuming computations. In this illustration, we already know that foo is expected to return a value of 100. The return value of the foo2 method depends on the input argument x.

Looking at the compute method, we can easily deduce that the return value of `foo2` would be `100 + 200 = 300`. So let's write a unit test that mocks these method calls. The code is shown here:

```python
class TestA(unittest.TestCase):
    """Write test cases for methods from class MyClassA"""

    def test_compute(self):
        """Unit test for MyClassA.compute"""
        a = MyClassA()

        # Create a mock object and mock methods of MyClassA
        mockObj = Mock()
        a.foo = mockObj.foo
        a.foo2 = mockObj.foo2

        # Assuming you know the return values, set those for the mocks
        a.foo.return_value = 100
        a.foo2.return_value = 300

        # Run the computation. Calls to foo and foo2 in compute method are
        # now replaced with mock object calls that return the desired value.
        result = a.compute()

        # Verify the results
        self.assertEqual(result, 400)

        # Get info on how the mock objects are actually called by compute.
        test_call_list = mockObj.mock_calls
        print("test_call_list =", test_call_list)

        # Compare it against some reference calling order
        reference_call_list = [call.foo(), call.foo2()]
        self.assertEqual(test_call_list, reference_call_list)

if __name__ == '__main__':
    unittest.main()
```

Let's review the method in the preceding code snippet

- The `a.foo` and `a.foo2` methods are now represented by new `Mock` objects, `mockObj.foo` and `mockObj.foo2`, respectively. Inside `a.compute()`, the `self.foo()` and `self.foo2()` calls are now mocked with these new objects.

- The test verifies the value of the parameter result. This is done by calling `TestCase.assertEqual`.

- The test also verifies which objects are called and the order in which they are called. As seen before, `test_call_list` is used to track all the calls to `mockObj` and its child mocks. This list is compared with some reference list that stores the expected calling order of the objects. In this example, `reference_call_list` stores this information. It expects the `foo` and `foo2` methods be called in that order. In future, if someone tweaks this order in `MyClassA.compute`, this test would help catch the change.

The MagicMock class:

`MagicMock` is a subclass of `Mock`. It essentially provides all the functionality that you would expect from a `Mock` class. Additionally, it provides default implementation for many of the magic methods in Python. A magic method is a special method whose name has double underscores as both prefix and suffix. Some examples of magic methods include `__init__`, `__iter__`, `__len__`, and so on. In the illustrations, you can use `MagicMock` instead of the `Mock` class. For further details, go to the following page: `https://docs.python.org/3/library/unittest.mock.html`.

Working with patches

Under the previous heading, we covered some basics of the `Mock` class. The mock library provides another important functionality in the form of patch decorators. Patching is a mechanism that allows you to change the behavior of an object temporarily within a test. This is a broad topic. In this book, we will limit our discussion to creating patches using `unittest.mock.patch`.

Patches can be invoked in four different ways, namely `patch`, `patch.object`, `patch.dict`, and `patch.multiple`. For further information, see the documentation at `https://docs.python.org/3/library/unittest.mock.html`.

The `patch` decorator function takes `target` as the required argument, followed by a long list of optional arguments. Only one of the optional arguments (`new`) is shown here. Refer to the unittest documentation for information on other optional arguments:

```
patch(target, new=DEFAULT)
```

- In the preceding function, the `target` argument is the thing you would like to patch. It can be any function, class method, or an object.

- The `target` is imported, and should be represented by a string, which resembles a typical `import` statement (without the keyword `import`).

- For example, if you want to patch a method inside a test case, the `target` should be represented like so: `pkg.module.myclass.mymethod`.

- If this method is in the same file where you are creating the patch (for example, the method and its test are in the same Python file), then `target` should be written as: `__main__.myclass.mymethod`.

Among the optional arguments, we will only discuss and use `new`. The `new` argument tells which object would replace the `target`. It can be any class or a `Mock` object. This can be better understood with an example. See the following line of code:

```
patch('__main__.MyClassA.foo', new=Mock(return_value=500))
```

The first argument is `target`. It is a method `foo` of `MyClassA`, whose behavior needs to be changed temporarily within a test. Put another way, this is the method (or `target`) that needs to be patched. The `new` argument specifies the object that would replace this method. In other words, the `target` is patched with the `new` object. If you do not specify the `new` argument, the `target` would be automatically patched with a `MagicMock` object.

Using patch in a unit test

To demonstrate the use of a `patch` decorator, we will use the example discussed under the heading *Using Mock objects in a unit test*. Before reading the following discussion, review the `MyClassA.compute` method. It was illustrated in the aforementioned heading, and the code can also be found in the file `wargame/test/mockdemo.py`. The following is a unit test written for `MyClassA.compute` using patch:

```python
def test_compute_with_patch(self):
    """Unit test for MyClassA.compute using mock.patch"""
    print("Running test_compute_with_patch...")
    with unittest.mock.patch('__main__.MyClassA.foo',
                    new = Mock(return_value = 500)):
        a = MyClassA()
        result = a.compute()

        # Verify the results. The test is expected to fail since we
        # are using a return value of 500 using MyClassA.foo!
        self.assertEqual(result, 400)
```

In the preceding unit test:

- `patch` is a context processor invoked using the with statement.

- The `with` keyword cleans up the resources used after the code execution.

- The method `MyClassA.foo` gets replaced with a `Mock` object created by the optional argument new.

- In other words, the call `self.foo()` in `MyClassA.compute()` is replaced with `return_value` of this `Mock` object. At runtime, the expression x = `self.foo()` becomes x = `500` without actually invoking the method foo.

> Would the test in the earlier illustration pass? For that, review the code in the `MyClassA.compute` method. The `Mock` object created by the new argument returns a value of `500`. In the unit test, if the result is not `400`, it raises an assertion error. So, this test is expected to fail.

What happens if you do not specify the `new` argument? As mentioned earlier, `target` would automatically get replaced with a new `MagicMock` object. Here is another way you can write the same test. As an exercise, run this test, and print `foo_patch.__class__` to find out which class it belongs to:

```python
def test_compute_with_patch_alternate(self):
    """Unit test for MyClassA.compute, using mock.patch

    .. note:: This uses `mock.patch` but does not use the `new` arg
    """
    print("Running test_compute_with_patch_alternate...")
    mockObj = Mock()
    with unittest.mock.patch('__main__.MyClassA.foo') as foo_patch:
        foo_patch.return_value = 500
        a = MyClassA()
        result = a.compute()

        # Verify the results. The test is expected to fail since we
        # are using a return value of 500 using MyClassA.foo!
        self.assertEqual(result, 400)
```

With this introduction to the mock library, let's write a unit test for a method in our application using the `patch` decorator.

Third unit test – The play method

In this section, we will use the mock library to write a unit test for
`AttackOfTheOrcs.play`. Let's review the method first. You can also find the source
code in the `wargame/attackoftheorcs.py` file:

```python
def play(self):
    """Workhorse method to play the game...."""
    # Create a Knight instance, create huts and preoccupy them with
    # a game character instance (or leave empty)
    self.setup_game_scenario()

    # Initial setup is done, now the main play logic.
    acquired_hut_counter = 0
    while acquired_hut_counter < 5:
        idx = self._process_user_choice()
        self.player.acquire_hut(self.huts[idx-1])

        if self.player.health_meter <= 0:
            print_bold("YOU LOSE  :(  Better luck next time")
            break

        if self.huts[idx-1].is_acquired:
            acquired_hut_counter += 1

    if acquired_hut_counter == 5:
        print_bold("Congratulations! YOU WIN!!!")
```

This preceding method does many things. It starts by creating some necessary
objects such as the player and huts. Then the program runs until all the huts are
acquired by the player or the player loses the combat. Observe the code closely. It
depends on a user input for selecting a hut. This is not the only user input it needs.
The call to the `Knight.acquire_hut` method would again ask the user whether to
continue the attack.

In an automated test, you cannot expect someone to enter the hut number, and other inputs to continue the execution. So how do we write a unit test for this method? This is where we can use `patch` decorators to mimic the user input:

What should we test here? We should test the overall functioning of the method. There are a couple of thing to test here:

- The winning or losing criterion. The player is declared a winner when all the huts are acquired.
- For this to happen, the player must also be in good health, meaning the value of `player.health_meter` should be greater than zero.

Thus, the winner is declared only when both these conditions are true. Similarly, there will be a losing criterion that you can easily determine. For precise control, you should also write separate unit tests for individual methods invoked within the `play` method. For example, there should be a separate test to verify the working of `Knight.acquire_huts`.

Let's write a test to verify the overall functionality. This test will use `patch` to handle the user input. As before, you can find this test in the `wargame/test/test_wargame.py` module. The following code snippet shows the `TestWarGame.test_play` method in this module. At the beginning of the module, the mock library is imported like so:

```
from unittest import mock
```

The rest of the code in this module will not be discussed here. Review the aforementioned file for further details:

```
def test_play(self):
    """Unit test to verify AttackOfTheOrc
    """
    game = AttackOfTheOrcs()
    self.hut_selection_counter = 0
    with mock.patch('builtins.input', new = self.user_input_processor):
        game.play()
        # Create a list that collects information on whether the
        # huts are acquired. It is a boolean list
        acquired_hut_list = [ h.is_acquired for h in game.huts]

        # Player wins if all huts are acquired AND the player health
        # is grater than 0.
        if all(acquired_hut_list):
            # All the huts are acquired (winning criteria).
            # check the player's health!
            self.assertTrue(game.player.health_meter > 0)
        else:
            # This is the losing criteria., Player health can not be
            # positive when he/she loses.
            self.assertFalse(game.player.health_meter > 0)
```

The patch target is the built-in 'input' function. Replace it with our custom method

The important part in the preceding code is `mock.patch`. Our first goal is to make sure that the user input is properly handled. Recall that in Python 3, the user input is handled by the built-in function `input()`. So, we need to patch this function with something that would simulate the user input. In other words, replace the `builtins.input` function with the handling function represented by the `new` argument.

The `self.hut_selection_counter` attribute is used as a simple counter to simulate the user input. The rest of the code implements the logic to verify that the winning and losing criteria are honored. The `acquired_hut_list` is generated using list comprehension. More on list comprehension later when we talk about the performance improvements. The `all` function returns `True` if all the list elements are `True`.

If you are using Python 2.7.9, try replacing `builtins.input` with `__builtin__.raw_input`. However, this technique does not seem to work well, as it will still prompt you while running the test! With Python 3.5, this is not a problem. As said elsewhere, before Python 3.3, mock was not a built-in module (`unittest.mock`). So for Python 2.7.9, you may need to install mock as `pip install mock`, and make appropriate changes to the `import` statement.

Next, we will review the `user_input_processor` that patches the built-in `input` function:

```python
def user_input_processor(self, prompt):
    """Simulate user input based on user prompt

    :param prompt: The question asked to the user
    :return: The simulated user input
    """

    # The prompt can be either of the following:
    # 1. "choose a hut number to enter (1-5):"
    # 2. "...continue attack? (y/n):"

    # Check if some keywords exist in the prompt
    if 'hut' in prompt.lower():
        # 'The prompt contains 'hut'..should be asking for a hut number.
        self.hut_selection_counter += 1
        assert self.hut_selection_counter <= 5
        return self.hut_selection_counter
    elif 'attack' in prompt.lower():
        # This prompt should be asking permission to continue attack
        return 'y'
    else:
        raise Exception("Got an unexpected prompt!", prompt)
```

It takes user `prompt` as an argument, and returns an answer (user input) to that prompt. For example, when prompted to enter the hut number, it increments `self.hut_selection_counter` by 1, and returns the updated value. This attribute is initialized to 0 in the `test_play` method. To better understand this code, add some `print` statements to these two methods, and execute the test as follows:

```
$ cd wargame
$ python -m unittest test.test_wargame.TestWarGame.test_play
```

The output on executing the test is shown in the following screenshot. Notice that it does not print the user prompts such as Continue attack?(y/n) in the command-line output:

```
[user@hostname wargame]$ python -m unittest test.test_wargame.TestWarGame.test_play
Mission:
  1. Fight with the enemy.
  2. Bring all the huts in the village under your control
----------------------------------------------------------

Health: Sir Foo: 40
Current occupants: ['friend', 'friend', 'unoccupied', 'friend', 'enemy']
Entering hut 1... Friend sighted!
GOOD JOB! Hut 1 acquired
Current occupants: ['ACQUIRED', 'friend', 'unoccupied', 'friend', 'enemy']
Entering hut 2... Friend sighted!
GOOD JOB! Hut 2 acquired
Current occupants: ['ACQUIRED', 'ACQUIRED', 'unoccupied', 'friend', 'enemy']
Entering hut 3... Hut is unoccupied
GOOD JOB! Hut 3 acquired
Current occupants: ['ACQUIRED', 'ACQUIRED', 'ACQUIRED', 'friend', 'enemy']
Entering hut 4... Friend sighted!
GOOD JOB! Hut 4 acquired
Current occupants: ['ACQUIRED', 'ACQUIRED', 'ACQUIRED', 'ACQUIRED', 'enemy']
Entering hut 5... Enemy sighted!
Health: Sir Foo: 40 Health: 5: 30 ATTACK! Health: Sir Foo: 25  Health: 5: 30  ATTACK!
Health: Sir Foo: 25  Health: 5: 15  ATTACK! Health: Sir Foo: 25  Health: 5: 2  ATTACK!
 Health: Sir Foo: 25  Health: 5: 0
GOOD JOB! Hut 5 acquired
Congratulations! YOU WIN!!!

----------------------------------------------------------
Ran 1 test in 0.001s

OK
```

Is your code covered?

Is there a way to check how well you are doing as far as testing is concerned? How much code is covered by the unit tests? For this, you need a Python package called coverage. It can be installed using pip as follows:

```
$ pip install coverage
```

The preceding command creates an executable called coverage at the same location as your Python installation. In Linux, if Python 3 is installed in /usr/bin/, coverage will be available at the same location as /use/bin/coverage. In Windows OS, it will be available in the Scripts directory, at the same location as pip.exe. Run the coverage command as follows:

```
$ cd wargame
$ coverage run -m test.test_wargame && coverage report
```

This command is a combination of two commands separated by `&&` and executed one after the other. The first command runs the tests: `coverage run -m test.test_wargame`. This is similar to how we run the unit tests. The `run` option runs a Python program, and measures the code execution. As noted before, the `-m` option instructs `coverage` to consider the next argument as an importable Python module instead of treating it as a script. This is why we specify the next argument as `test.test_wargame` (just like an `import` statement) instead of writing `test/test_wargame.py`.

The second command, `coverage report`, generates the report indicating the test coverage. Here is how the coverage report is presented after running this command. For ease of illustration, the output pertaining to the execution of the test cases (the first command) is not shown in the following screenshot:

```
. .
-----------------------------------------------------------------------
Ran 4 tests in 0.002s

OK
Name                     Stmts   Miss   Cover
------------------------------------------------
abstractgameunit.py         39      4    90%
attackoftheorcs.py          79     20    75%
gameuniterror.py            12      8    33%
gameutils.py                19      7    63%
hut.py                      19      0   100%
knight.py                   41      7    83%
orcrider.py                 12      1    92%
test/__init__.py             5      0   100%
test/test_wargame.py        55     12    78%
------------------------------------------------
TOTAL                      281     59    79%
[user@hostname wargame]$ ▊
```

To see a different coverage report, try disabling some tests in `test_wargame.py`, and rerun the `coverage` command noted earlier.

Resolving import errors, if any

Read this section only if you encounter any import errors while executing the coverage. If you run `coverage` as instructed, you are unlikely to encounter any import errors such as no module named `knight`. In other words, run the test from the top-level directory `wargame`, and make sure to run it as a module (the `-m` option) instead of a script. If you run `coverage` in the following way, you would likely see import errors:

```
$ cd wargame/test
$ coverage run test_wargame.py && coverage report
```

In the preceding case, it is unable to find the right PATH for the modules from the `wargame` directory. Make sure that both `wargame` and `test` directories are in your `sys.path`. One quick and dirty hack is to add the following code to `test_wargame.py`. Assuming you are running coverage from within the `test` directory, add the following code before the `import` statements, such as `from knight import Knight`:

```
import sys
# Append the directory one level up to the sys.path .
# Alternatively specify the full path to that dir.
sys.path.append('../')
```

Other unit testing tools

In this chapter, we have exclusively used the built-in `unittest` framework for writing the tests. There are several other tools available for unit testing that were not discussed. The purpose of this section is only to introduce you to the other unit testing tools available out there besides the built-in `unittest` module. For instance, there are tools such as nose or pytest that make it easier to write the unit tests to a large extent. Let's briefly review some of these unit testing tools.

Doctest

This is a built-in module, which looks for text that resembles Python code written in an interpreter. Here is a trivial example that shows a docstring with an example usage of the function:

```
def add_nums(a, b):
    """Return sum of two numbers

    Example usage:
    .. doctest::

    >>> add_nums(10, 20)
    30
    """
    return (a + b)
```

Doctest identifies such code, and runs it to check if it really does what it says. This is quite an effective way to verify the correctness of the code examples you write in the documentation and/or in the docstrings. While this is very useful, it is worth noting here that the extensive code samples in the docstring could be distracting. See `https://docs.python.org/3/library/doctest.html#module-doctest` for further details.

Nose

Nose is a popular third-party tool that simplifies writing and running unit tests. Install it using pip as follows:

$ pip install nose

Nose extends `unittest`. One of the advantages of using this tool is it doesn't require you to write tests as inherited class methods of `unittest.TestCase`. You can even write tests as separate functions. Let's write a simple test, and run it with `nosetests`. Create the following function in a file called `test_nose.py`:

```
def test_a():
    assert( 1 == 1)
```

Run this test from the command line as follows:

```
$ nosetests test_nose.py
```

That's all. It will run the test. Obviously, this test will pass. As can be seen, we did not need to put the test inside the subclass of `unittest.TestCase`. The function name needs to contain `test` or `Test`, since we are using the default nose configuration. Try renaming the function so that it does not have the word `test`. For example, name it `foo_a`. If you run `nosetests` again, it will exclude this function. To consider function names that do not have the word `test`, use the command-line option `--tests` like so:

```
$ nosetests --tests foo_a test_nose.py
```

See `https://nose.readthedocs.org` to learn how to use nose effectively.

Pytest

Pytest is yet another popular tool that simplifies writing unit tests. It can be installed using `pip` as follows:

```
$ pip install pytest
```

You can run the same test we wrote for nose. Let's save the following code in a file, `test_pytest.py`:

```
def test_a():
    assert( 1 == 1)
```

Run the preceding test from the command line as follows:

```
$ py.test test_pytest.py
```

See `http://pytest.org/` to find out more about this tool.

Refactoring preamble

Let's write one more unit test for the game. This time we will focus our attention on the main class `AttackOfTheOrcs`. When the `play` method is called, the first thing it does is to randomly occupy the five huts. We will write a test to verify that there are exactly five huts. Another thing to test is that the hut occupant must be an instance of the class `AbstractGameUnit`, or should be of the type `None`.

The `_occupy_hut` method has the related code. But this necessitates writing a test for a non-public method (or call it protected or private).

What you say is right! Although Python does not restrict you from calling methods that start with an underscore, we should be nice to others, and try to avoid calling such methods.

So how do we handle this situation? Here is a list of the available options:

1. In the test, create an instance of `AttackOfThOrcs`, and directly call the protected method.

2. Transform this method into a `public` method (remove the underscore prefix from the name).

3. Call the `play` method, which then calls `_occupy_huts`.

4. Refactor the `play` method, and wrap the `_occupy_huts` into a `public` method that could be tested.

We already have a moral conflict with the first option, as `_occupy_huts` is a non-public method. The second option suggests turning it into a `public` method. That is possible, but if this method is not supposed to be called from outside for any reason, we should avoid such a change. We will keep this option in mind, and look for some other alternative.

The third option needs to call the `play` method. We have already done that in the last example using the patch decorator. Although possible, it is inefficient to run a large block of code for testing a small functionality. Let's leave that option aside for now. The fourth option suggests refactoring the code. Let's discuss it further.

 In the simple application that we have developed, there is no harm in changing `_occupy_huts` to a `public` method! We could simply rename it `occupy_huts` (no underscore prefix), then update the calling code, and happily write a test! In fact, renaming is also a form of refactoring that will be covered next. In the real world, however, you may not have the luxury to transform a protected method to a public one. Keeping this situation in mind, we will refactor the code to illustrate one way of making the code test friendly.

Take a detour – Refactor for testability

Step 4 in the previous section needs us to refactor the play method before writing the test. This refactoring will improve our ability to write cleaner tests. So what is refactoring? How is it performed? The good news is that you have already done a form of refactoring in *Chapter 1*, *Developing Simple Applications* while transforming the initial command-line script into a set of functions. Let's take a detour and learn some refactoring techniques. We will then come back with the refactored code, and develop the final unit test for our application.

Refactoring

You have already come across the word refactoring in earlier chapters, and might have wondered what it means. An explanation is in order.

Just look around. Peep inside your closet or open your desk drawer. On day one, everything looks tidy and manageable. The drawer is meant to store all your important financial documents. Things begin to accumulate over time, and the drawer is now stuffed with not just with financial documents, but anything varying from scribbled notes, office documents, to greeting cards. Very soon, you cannot find that important document you need right now. You spend a lot of time digging out what you need.

The golden moment finally arrives. You begin the cleanup operation! Several things are found to be useless, and are thrown away. A few other things are still useful, such as tickets to a football game next week. You move this stuff to a different drawer where it really belongs. You also find several papers laying around belonging to a single category: house maintenance bills. You put these papers together inside a single folder. Finally, with all this rearrangement and cleanup, your drawer breathes the new day one!

What is refactoring?

Refactoring is something very similar to your desk drawer. The application code is analogous to the drawer filled with documents. As the code evolves, both the good and bad stuff creeps in. From outside, the behavior of the drawer remains the same. You can still put documents (code) in it, and business goes on as usual. In the absence of refactoring, someday it reaches a tipping point, and becomes non-accommodating to new documents.

 With refactoring, you make internal changes to your code without affecting its external behavior.

Why refactor?

The short answer is, do it if you wish your code a long and healthy life! Timely refactoring is important to keep the code maintainable and extensible. You could rather spend more time working on a cool new feature than burning the midnight oil to fix a petty issue—a bug that could have been fixed within minutes had the code been properly maintained.

 Refactoring should be more of a habit than an obligation.

When to refactor?

So when do we refactor the code? You have to seek the optimal balance. If you realize it too late in the development life cycle, it affects productivity, as you would need to spend a considerable amount of time doing the code cleanup. Many times, the project deadline makes you turn your back on refactoring. Unfortunately, the user-visible part of the software wins over the internal cleanup. You only think of the immediate deliverable, and overlook the fact that refactoring will only help you deliver the product faster.

One strategy is to review the code at fixed intervals, and allocate some time for refactoring. If you are following a **Scrum** methodology, you can devote a sprint to some smaller refactoring projects. Such maintenance sprint will pay off in the long run. If you are staring at a big legacy code that needs immediate refactoring for survival, the required changes could be disruptive. In such situations, consider breaking it down into smaller problems, and use the other strategy discussed in the next paragraph.

Agile development methodology

This is often tied to a set of non-traditional software development methods for managing a project. In this method, you define targets achievable in a short time duration. There are regular checkpoints known as sprints or iterations. The end of a sprint should result in an incremental and releasable version of the product. This is useful in complex projects, where it is tough to plan the complete project, or predict what to expect next because of the dynamic nature of the project. The methodology adopts an incremental and iterative approach to handle this task. For further reading, see the following wiki page: `https://en.wikipedia.org/wiki/Agile_software_development`.

Scrum

It is a product development methodology. It is a framework based on the agile development methodology for managing complex systems. It implements an incremental and iterative (sprints) strategy for product development. The following is the link to the wiki for further details: `https://en.wikipedia.org/wiki/Scrum_(software_development)`.

Another strategy is to take up the refactoring task immediately after a major release. The customers just got what they were asking for. In the absence of any show-stopper bugs, you would typically find some free work cycles during this period. It is a good time for the next release planning and working on code refactoring tasks. This will vary from project to project. It depends on how actively the application is being developed, its size, architecture, and so on.

How to refactor?

Now that we have seen what refactoring means, let's see how to do it. The first task is to identify the piece of trouble-making code, and then restructure it. The restructuring should not affect the external behavior of the code. At the same time, it should help make the developer's life easy by simplifying the internal machinery (the code). We will discuss some of the most commonly performed refactoring operations. To help understand these operations, we will use the UML-like representative blocks wherever appropriate.

 Unified Modeling Language (UML) representation. See `http://www.uml.org`.

Renaming

Imagine a developer introducing a new feature in the game *Attack of the Orcs*. Each hut has a secret box. Whenever a unit acquires a hut, the contents of the box are revealed to the new owner as a print statement. This developer has introduced a new method called `showStuff()` in the class `Hut`. However, the name used here is not intuitive. It is not clear whether it shows what is inside the box, or whether it gives some information about some other stuff in the hut. Renaming such methods is one of the simplest forms of code refactoring. You could rename it to something verbose, such as `show_box_contents` or `reveal_box_contents`. However, make sure you perform the renaming task thoroughly by renaming all the method calls as well.

 Coding standards:

This example brings forward an interesting topic, the Python coding standards. In case you have jumped straight to this chapter, read *Chapter 4, Documentation and Best Practices* that talks about the coding standards! These standards basically provide a coding style guide for Python programmers. Following these standards and defining your own guidelines for the project would help reduce such renaming tasks.

Extracting

In *Chapter 1, Developing Simple Applications* we had a single script representing the game. We identified pieces of code that could be written as individual functions. The name of each function was chosen such that it represented what the function body was supposed to do. This is shown in the following code snippets:

```
if __name__ == '__main__':                    Before function extraction
    keep_playing = 'y'
    occupants = ['enemy', 'friend', 'unoccupied']
    # Print the game mission
    width = 72
    dotted_line = '-' * width
    print(dotted_line)
    print("\033[1m" + "Attack of The Orcs v0.0.1:" + "\033[0m")
    msg = (
        "The war between humans and their arch enemies, Orcs, was in the "
        "offing. Sir Foo, one of the brave knights guarding the southern "
        "plains began a long journey towards the east through an unknown "
        "dense forest. On his way, he spotted a small isolated settlement."
        " Tired and hoping to replenish his food stock, he decided to take"
        " a detour. As he approached the village, he saw five huts. There "
        "was no one to be seen around. Hesitantly, he  decided to enter..")

    print(textwrap.fill(msg, width=width))
```

```
def show_theme_message(dotted_line, width):    After function extraction
    """Print the game theme in the terminal window"""
    print(dotted_line)
    print("\033[1m" + "Attack of The Orcs v0.0.1:" + "\033[0m")
    msg = (
        "The war between humans and their arch enemies, Orcs, was in the "
        "offing. Sir Foo, one of the brave knights guarding the southern "
        "plains began a long journey towards the east through an unknown "
        "dense forest. On his way, he spotted a small isolated settlement."
        " Tired and hoping to replenish his food stock, he decided to take"
        " a detour. As he approached the village, he saw five huts. There "
        "was no one to be seen around. Hesitantly, he  decided to enter..")

    print(textwrap.fill(msg, width=width))

if __name__ == '__main__':
    keep_playing = 'y'
    occupants = ['enemy', 'friend', 'unoccupied']
    # Print the game mission
    width = 72
    dotted_line = '-' * width
    show_theme_message(dotted_line, width)
```

This refactoring operation is called function extraction. Likewise, you can group together relevant code fragments to extract a method within a class or extract a new class.

Moving

In *Chapter 3, Modularize, Package, Deploy!* we did yet another type of refactoring operation. Can you guess what it was? The application code was contained within a single file. We modularized it by moving each class to its own file, and updating the referenced code.

Imagine you have a method of Class A, which is used mostly by various features in Class B. Depending on the nature of the problem, see if this method better fits in Class B than in the existing Class A. If it does, moving this method to Class B could be an option.

Pushing down

There is a new feature request. This time it is coming from Sir Foo!

The `Knight` and `OrcRider` are mounted units riding a horse and a wild boar-like creature respectively. You introduced a new method, `unmount`, in the superclass `AbstractGameUnit`. It gives them the ability to get off the animal they are riding:

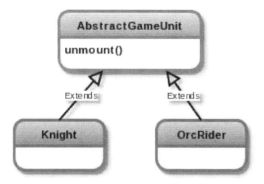

However, you have now introduced several other imaginary characters in the game. For a majority of the characters, the method has become irrelevant. Now it makes sense to push down the `unmount` method in the inheritance hierarchy to the subclasses where it is relevant. This is shown in the diagram that follows. The `unmount` method is moved to the subclasses `Knight` and `OrcRider`:

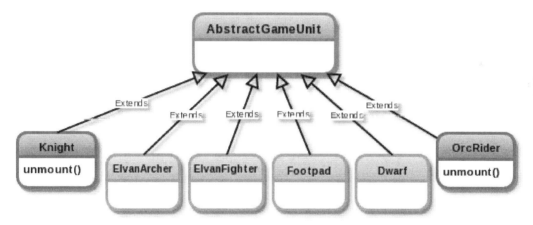

While pulling up (see the next heading) or pushing down type of refactoring simplifies things, it may not always serve its purpose. The unmount method was intended just as an illustration. The horse is associated with movement. One option is to define a move behavior here. For example, move using a horse, move using a wild boar, and so on. Another alternative is to define the unit types as mounted or unmounted. Refer to *Chapter 6, Design Patterns* on design patterns, which shows an elegant way to handle a similar situation.

Pulling up

It is the opposite of pushing down, where we use the inheritance principle. A subclass defines some functionality. The exact same method is defined in other subclasses. This method can be pulled up and defined in the superclass to make it available to all the subclasses.

Refactoring tools for Python

There are tools that automate certain types of refactoring. For example, if you want to rename a method, the tool will rename it, and automatically update all the references to the method in the code. Here is a partial list of such tools:

- **Use a Python IDE**: Assuming you are using an IDE for Python application development, the most convenient option is to use the built-in features of the IDE to refactor the code. IDEs such as PyCharm provide a menu item for refactoring, and support the most frequently performed refactoring operations, like the ones discussed in previous sections.

- **Rope**: Rope is an open source library for refactoring Python code. If you are a fan of editors such as vim or emacs, plugins are available to integrate the refactoring feature in the editor. The library can be installed using pip. For more information, see the GitHub page `https://github.com/python-rope`.

- **Bicycle repair man**: This is another refactoring tool available for Python. The library can be installed using pip. Visit `https://pypi.python.org/pypi/bicyclerepair` for more information.

Unit testing revisited

Here is a quick recap of where we left the discussion on unit testing. The intention was to write a unit test for the functionality found in the non-public method, `AttackOfTheOrcs._occupy_huts`. One straightforward option was to call this method directly from the unit test. However, calling a non-public method is not considered best practice, so we started looking for alternatives. Another option was to refactor `AttackOfTheOrcs.play`, and use an extracted `public` method in the unit test. At this point, we took a detour from unit testing and learned the basics of refactoring. Now it is time to refactor `AttackOfTheOrcs.play` using the techniques we have just learned.

Refactoring for testability

The source code for the game *Attack of the Orcs* gives enough opportunity for refactoring. The `play` method is shown next. The code comments are omitted for the sake of illustration:

```python
def play(self):
    """Workhorse method to play the game...."""
    self.player = Knight()
    self._occupy_huts()
    self.show_game_mission()
    self.player.show_health(bold=True)

    # Initial setup is done, now the main play logic.
    acquired_hut_counter = 0
    while acquired_hut_counter < 5:
        idx = self._process_user_choice()
        self.player.acquire_hut(self.huts[idx-1])

        if self.player.health_meter <= 0:
            print_bold("YOU LOSE  :(  Better luck next time")
            break

        if self.huts[idx-1].is_acquired:
            acquired_hut_counter += 1

    if acquired_hut_counter == 5:
        print_bold("Congratulations! YOU WIN!!!")
```

Before refactoring

The first part of the preceding code does some preparatory work to create the objects needed. It creates the `Knight` and the `Hut` instances, along with the objects that represent the hut occupants. Additionally, it prints some information on the game. As an initial refactoring, we will extract a new `public` method, as shown here:

```python
def setup_game_scenario(self):
    """Create player and huts and then randomly pre-occupy huts..."""
    self.player = Knight()
    self._occupy_huts()
    self.show_game_mission()
    self.player.show_health(bold=True)

def play(self):
    """Workhorse method to play the game...."""
    # Create a Knight instance, create huts and preoccupy them with
    # a game character instance (or leave empty)
    self.setup_game_scenario()

    # Initial setup is done, now the main play logic.
    acquired_hut_counter = 0
    while acquired_hut_counter < 5:
        idx = self._process_user_choice()
        self.player.acquire_hut(self.huts[idx-1])

        if self.player.health_meter <= 0:
            print_bold("YOU LOSE  :(  Better luck next time")
            break

        if self.huts[idx-1].is_acquired:
            acquired_hut_counter += 1

    if acquired_hut_counter == 5:
        print_bold("Congratulations! YOU WIN!!!")
```

After refactoring

The new method primarily improves code readability, and also makes it simpler to write a test.

As noted in the *Refactoring preamble* section, this is a toy problem. The refactoring strategy used here is to extract a new method for improved readability and testability. You could refactor this by some other means as well. For example, the setup code creates things such as the player and huts. May be you should also rename _occupy_huts to `create_huts`? Choices may vary, and so do the refactoring strategies. More than answering the question what is the best strategy to refactor here, this section mainly serves as an example of how refactoring could help simplify the task of writing a unit test.

This basic refactoring of the `play` method will enable writing a unit test for the `setup_game_scenario` method, which in turn, will help test the functionality in `_occupy_huts`.

Fourth unit test – setup_game_scenario

As discussed in the *Refactoring preamble* section, this test will verify the following things: (a) there are exactly five huts, and (b) the hut occupant is an instance of `AbstractGameUnit`, or of the type `None`.

This test is shown next. You can also find this test in the supporting code along with the other tests. See the `wargame/test/test_wargame.py` file. The code comments should make it self-explanatory:

```python
def test_occupy_huts(self):
    """Unittest to verify number of huts and the occupants...."""
    game = AttackOfTheOrcs()
    game.setup_game_scenario()

    # Verify that only 5 huts are created.
    self.assertEqual(len(game.huts), 5)

    # Huts occupant must be an instance of a Knight or OrcRider
    #   or it could be set to None.
    for hut in game.huts:
        assert((hut.occupant is None) or
                isinstance(hut.occupant, AbstractGameUnit))
```

Run the preceding unit test as follows:

```
$ cd wargame
$ python -m unittest test.test_wargame.TestWarGame.test_occupy_huts
```

Exercise

Some exercises have already been suggested in various sections of this chapter. Try those exercises. For example, split the unit tests so that you have separate modules for testing functionality from different classes. Add more unit tests to improve the code coverage. Also, try running `nosetests` on the tests that we have already written.

Refactoring and redesign exercise

There are several low-hanging fruits for refactoring! Review the `AttackOfTheOrcs._occupy_huts` method. It creates hut objects, and puts an occupant in each of them. As the first step, you can rename it `create_huts`. The code in this method could be better written. It uses `if...else` conditions to decide which occupant to create. Although it works in this simple application, if you add other types of occupant (elves, dwarfs, wizards, and so on) it will become a maintenance headache.

What could we do here? One strategy is to let the `Hut` class manage the creation of the `occupant` object. The hut could ask a factory to randomly create an occupant. You will learn about the factory pattern in *Chapter 6, Design Patterns*. Since we are looking at this as a refactoring problem, you could try the following:

- Change the signature of `Hut.__init__` so that you can optionally specify the `occupant`.

- Inside the `Hut` class, create an `occupant` (if not already available) by calling a new utility function, `create_unit`. You will need to write this new utility function (the solution is not provided). The function should not be a method of the class `Hut`.

Summary

The chapter started by emphasizing the need for testing. It introduced you to the unit testing framework in Python. You learned how to write and execute unit tests. The next topic served as an introduction to Python mock library. The chapter demonstrated the use of `Mock` objects in unit tests. Next, it showed an example where it was difficult to write a unit test without refactoring the code first. At this point, you learned the basics of refactoring, refactored the code, and then developed a unit test for this example.

During development, you often encounter a recurring problem. Often, a general solution (or a recipe) exists that works for this problem. This is often referred to as a design pattern. In the next chapter, we will review a few commonly used design patterns in Python.

6
Design Patterns

This chapter will introduce you to some commonly used design patterns. Here is how the chapter is organized:

- We will start with a quick introduction to design patterns, followed by a discussion on some Python language features that help to simplify their implementation.

- Next, with the help of a fantasy game theme, we will discuss the following design patterns:

    ° Strategy pattern

    ° Simple and abstract factory pattern

    ° Adapter pattern

- For each pattern, a simple game scenario will demonstrate a practical problem. We will see how the design pattern can help solve this problem.

- We will also implement each of these patterns using a Pythonic approach.

There are several known design patterns out there. As outlined earlier, we will discuss only a few. The idea is not to present a new cookbook on patterns, but just to show you how design patterns help solve some commonly encountered problems, and how to implement them in Python. Beyond this book, you can explore other traditional design patterns and try adding a Pythonic flavor to them.

By the way, you are about to get introduced to some new game characters. So get ready to learn design patterns with Sir Foo and friends!

Introduction to design patterns

Let's say that during application development, you stumble upon a problem that pops up again and again. Frustrated, you ask your co-developers or a community for help. Guess what, you are not alone. Many have encountered a similar problem in their code. Luckily, you get a response from someone who has found a solution. This solution seemed to have worked reliably on similar problems. You change your problematic code so that it conforms to the suggested design, and voila! Your problem is resolved!

What we just discussed is a software design pattern. A software design pattern is a tried and tested solution or a strategy that helps us solve a commonly encountered problem in the code. Let's start with the broad categories of design patterns followed by some important design principles.

The Gang of Four book:

Before beginning any discussion on the design patterns in Python, it is worth noting that there is an excellent book you may want on your bookshelf, *Design Patterns: Elements of Reusable Object-Oriented Software*, by Erich Gamma, Richard Helm, Ralph Johnson, and John Vlissides. These four authors are commonly referred to as the **Gang of Four** (**GoF**). Their book illustrates design patterns using C++ and Smalltalk examples. If you have a background in programming languages such as C++ or Java, this might be of more interest to you. As you will see in this chapter, some high-level language features in Python make many design patterns much simpler to implement. The GoF book is still a great reference, and will help you understand the core concepts behind the design patterns.

Classification of patterns

Software design patterns can be broadly classified into four categories, namely behavioral patterns, creational patterns, structural patterns, and concurrency patterns. In this book, we will limit our discussion to just three design patterns. We will see one example each of behavioral, creational, and structural patterns. The concurrency patterns are not covered here, as it is an advanced topic, beyond the scope of this book. For an in-depth understanding of other design patterns, you can grab a book on design patterns, such as the GoF book mentioned earlier. With this in mind, let's briefly talk about each of these categories next.

Behavioral patterns

The behavioral design patterns try to simplify how different objects communicate with each other. While doing so, these patterns help keep these objects loosely coupled or less dependent on each other. The following is a partial list of behavioral design patterns: chain of responsibility, command, strategy, observer, iterator, visitor pattern, and many more. In this chapter, we will see how to implement the strategy pattern in Python.

Creational patterns

These patterns are all about instance creation mechanisms. These design patterns show a better way to create objects depending on the situation you are dealing with.

Here is a list of the major creational design patterns: abstract factory, factory method, builder, prototype, and singleton pattern. We will discuss the abstract factory pattern in this chapter.

Structural patterns

The structural design patterns typically deal with the relationship between the components, such as objects or classes, so that it is easier to make these entities work together in a larger and more complex system. Some examples of structural design patterns include adapter, composite, decorator, facade, flyweight, proxy pattern, and so on. In this chapter, we will see a Pythonic implementation of the adapter pattern.

Concurrency patterns

In a nutshell, concurrency means simultaneously performing multiple things. Concurrency enables your application to execute one task (for example, updating a database) while it is also working on something else (such as responding to a user query). Concurrency design patterns, in general, deal with the multi-threaded programming paradigm. The following is a partial list of concurrency patterns: active object, balking, monitor object, double-checked locking, and so on. As mentioned before, we will not talk about any of the concurrency patterns in this book. That said, *Chapter 9, Improving Performance – Part two, NumPy and Parallelization* will introduce you to some aspects of multi-threaded programming in Python. Visit the wiki for more information at `https://en.wikipedia.org/wiki/Concurrency_pattern`.

Python language and design patterns

Thanks to the high-level built-in language features in Python, many of the formal design patterns are easy to implement. In some cases, the patterns appear so natural to the language that it becomes tough to realize them as formal design patterns. For example, an iterator pattern can be realized by using any iterable object, such as lists, dictionaries, and so on. Let's quickly review such language features or paradigms in this section. It is not an exhaustive list, but we will cover some important aspects.

The idioms that you are about to read (first-class functions, closures, and so on) might sound onerous. But do not get overwhelmed by these terms! If you are a Python programmer, it is very likely that you have already used many of these features knowingly or unknowingly. If these idioms mean nothing to you at the moment, skip ahead to the next section where we fast forward to an imaginary game scenario. In the upcoming discussion, we will use some of these language features. You can then come back to this section whenever you need a handy reference.

First-class functions

There is a programming idiom called **first-class citizens**. In Python, any function, a class, a class method, or an object, all qualify as first-class citizens. On each of these entities, you can freely perform operations that are typically supported on other entities.

For example, you can assign a function to a variable as if you are assigning a value to that variable. Likewise, you can pass this function as an argument, or get it as a return value of some other function. Any programming language that supports such operations on functions is said to have first-class functions. The following is a simple piece of code that illustrates what we can accomplish with a first-class function in Python. In this example, a function, test, is assigned to a variable, x. After the assignment, the function can be called either x() or as test():

```
>>> def test():
...     print("inside test function")
...
>>> x = test
>>> x()
inside test function
>>> x
<function test at 0x7fca460efbf8>
```

Here is another example that illustrates the first-class function feature. It shows how we can pass the same function, `test`, as an argument to another function, called `some_function`:

```
>>> def some_function(y):
...     y()
...
>>> some_function(test)
inside test function
```

Let's see what we can do with the other first-class entity, Python classes.

Classes as first-class objects

Just like functions, Python classes are first-class citizens. They can be passed around as an argument, assigned to variables, or returned from a function. Here is an example where a class, `Foo`, is assigned to a variable `bar`. After this assignment, you can use `bar` to create an instance of `Foo`:

```
>>> class Foo:
...     def say_hi(self):
...         print("hi!")
...
>>> bar = Foo
>>> z = bar()
>>> z.say_hi()
hi!
```

 We will not be using closures in this chapter. It is a bit of an advanced topic that is included for completeness. You can optionally skip the next section.

Closures

Take any function in Python that defines some local variables. You can use these variables inside the function, but those can not be accessed by the outside world (unless you return it from the function). In some sense, the functions can be considered as closed. When the function executes, it uses these local variables; when the function is done, the local variables go out of scope. Their job is done, that's the end of the story. Now what if you want a function that keeps its local environment at the time it was created?

We want some way to wrap this function along with its local environment. It could be better explained with the following example:

```python
def initial_number(x):
    print("1. Initial number "
          "(orig environment during function creation): {}".format(x))

    def modified_number(y):
        print(" x: {}, y: {} , x+y: {} ".format(x,y,x+y))
        return x+y

    return modified_number

if __name__ == '__main__':
    foo = initial_number(100)
    print("2. Now calling this function with "
          "its original environment loaded:")
    foo(1)
    foo(5)
```

In the preceding example:

- `modified_number` is a nested function within the function `initial_number`.
- This nested function uses a local variable, x, which is in the scope of the top-level function.
- In the main program, we create `foo`, which is the return value of `initial_number`. But look at the return value of the `initial_number` function. It returns the nested function, `modified_number`.
- What this means is that the `foo` variable becomes the nested function, `modified_number`.

What did we achieve here? We accomplished two things—first, it enabled access to a nested function from the main program, and second, the nested function still has the original working environment we used while instantiating `initial_number`. In this example, the working environment refers to the x argument with a value of 100, passed to this function. The following is the program output:

```
1. Initial number (orig environment during function creation): 100
2. Now calling this function with its original environment loaded:
 x: 100, y: 1 , x+y: 101
 x: 100, y: 5 , x+y: 105
```

Observe that the value of x remains unchanged. Any subsequent calls to `foo` retain this original local environment, which is used by the nested function `modified_number`. Likewise, you can create another instance of `initial_number` with a different value of x. This is called a closure in Python. Closures can be used to realize design patterns such as the observer pattern.

Miscellaneous features

Let's review some built-in functions and decorators that would come in handy while implementing some design patterns. Again, it is not a complete list, but enough to aid us in the upcoming discussion on design patterns.

Class method

A class method (`@classmethod`) is something that you can call without the need to create an instance of that class. Unlike a regular instance method, which takes the instance of the class (`self`) as its first argument, a class method takes the class as its first argument. The decorator `@classmethod` is just one convenient way to create a class method. We will see how to use a class method in the discussion on simple factory.

Abstract method

The `@abstractmethod` decorator is used to indicate that the given method is abstract and must be reimplemented in subclasses. Recall that we have already used this to implement `AbstractGameUnit.info()` as an abstract method using this decorator. See the *Abstract base classes in Python* section in *Chapter 1, Developing Simple Applications* for further details. In this chapter, we won't be using this decorator.

The __getattr__ method

Python automatically calls the __getattr__ method when you try to access an instance attribute that is not already defined in your class. You can implement __getattr__ in your class, and use it to add special handling code for all such undefined attributes. The use of this method will be later illustrated in the adapter pattern.

Duck typing

The term **duck typing** is often exemplified as, *if it swims and quacks like a duck, then we will treat that object as a duck*. Let's see what this means with a simple example. We have a class, Knight, with the methods move and attack, as follows:

```
class Knight:
    def move(self):
        pass
    def attack(self):
        pass
```

A function takes an instance of Knight as an argument, and calls these methods like so:

```
def do_something(a_thing):
    a_thing.move()
    a_thing.attack()
```

However, the function does not check whether the input argument is really an instance of the Knight class. As long as the object has the move and attack methods, it will not complain. Thus, in duck typing, the language does not make any verification of the object. The only thing it cares about is whether or not it can call certain attributes using that object. One advantage of duck typing is code reusability. You can reuse the do_something function in some other code by passing an object of a different class.

For example, imagine a Lion class that implements the move and attack methods. You would like to reuse the aforementioned do_something function in some other project that is already using this class:

```
class Lion:
    def move(self):
        pass
    def jump(self):
        pass
    def roar(self):
        pass
```

The do_something function will work just fine as long as the input object has the move and attack methods defined. How does this all translate to a design pattern discussion? Other programming languages, such as Java, define a formal interface in the code to implement certain design patterns, such as the abstract factory pattern. In C++, an abstract base class is defined with pure virtual functions. In Python, we have an option to use duck typing instead of implementing an interface or an abstract base class. For clarity on the design pattern itself, you may still want to document such an abstract base class or interface.

In Python, we could still use Java-style interfaces. The **Zope** web framework (not covered in this book) is a good example. Visit the following link for more information: `https://docs.zope.org/ zope.interface/README.html`. Also, see a note in the abstract factory discussion later that shows how to enforce an interface in Python.

Duck typing offers a lot of freedom to programmers, so much freedom that it has the potential to introduce bugs that are difficult to notice just by looking at the code. But such errors can be detected with extensive unit testing. Another way to reduce such problems is to enforce strict coding standards and documentation. For example, you can create some custom coding standards that can avoid confusion arising due to duck typing.

With this basic introduction to some key language features, let's move on and discuss how to implement some design patterns, and what problems they address.

Structure of the rest of the chapter

Before diving into the discussion on design patterns and their implementation, let's first lay out a strategy for the rest of the discussion. As mentioned before, we will review the strategy pattern, the simple and abstract factory patterns, and the adapter pattern. The discussion on design patterns will be roughly structured as follows:

- Start with a formal definition of the pattern
- Present an imaginary scenario where a new feature is requested
- Talk about the problem encountered in introducing this new feature
- Make an attempt to solve this problem, quickly realizing that we need to rethink the design
- The solution(s) to the problem using the design pattern

For a few design patterns, we will discuss two approaches to solving the problem. A traditional approach that resembles the one followed in languages like C++, and the other, the Pythonic approach.

 Skip the traditional solution if you are interested only in the Pythonic approach.

The following is a list of files from the supporting code bundle that will be reviewed:

```
abstractfactory_pythonic.py
adapterpattern_multiple_methods.py
adapterpattern.py
simplefactory_pythonic_alternatesolution.py
simplefactory_pythonic.py
simplefactory_traditional.py
strategypattern_pythonic.py
strategypattern_traditional.py
```

It is also worth noting that we will not be developing a full-fledged game application. The idea is to use this game theme as an aid to understanding some design patterns. The code used in this chapter is quite simple. While most of the code is illustrated in the upcoming discussion, you can also download and review the source from the supplementary code bundle for this chapter.

Fast forward – Attack of the Orcs v6.0.0

Let's fast forward to a future imaginary version of the game!

This imaginary version is one of the most downloaded open source Python applications. Now you have a team of developers helping you with application development. The game has evolved quite a bit. It is no longer a simple application where you gain control of a hut by defeating the enemy. It is now a turn-based fantasy game, where the player and the enemy take turns attacking each other, or use that turn to move towards or away from the opponent.

You have introduced several new game missions, and have redesigned and refactored the code to accommodate the new requirements. In the most recent version, you have the following game characters: Knight, Orc Rider, and Elf Rider.

 An **Elf** is an imaginary supernatural mythical being. Read the *The theme of the book* section in *Chapter 1, Developing Simple Applications* for some references on Elves.

Each game character in this version has an ability to attack the enemy, move towards or away from the enemy, or get healed inside a hut. Let's not worry about the actual logic that implements these features in the application. We shall rather focus on the high-level design of the application. The following pseudo-UML diagram shows various classes and a few of their public methods:

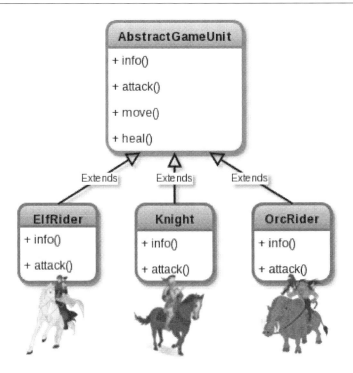

 As indicated in *Chapter 1, Developing Simple Applications*, we will loosely follow the UML representation. We referred to it as a pseudo-UML schematic. An explanation for the convention used here is in order. Each class in the schematics is represented by a rounded rectangle. It shows the class name followed by its attributes. The plus sign (+) before the attribute indicates it is public. A protected or private method is generally represented with a negative sign (-). For ease of illustration, only a few relevant public attributes will be listed.

As illustrated in the class diagram, all the game characters inherit from a common superclass, AbstractGameUnit. Each of the subclasses has its own implementation of info() and attack(). In other words, each subclass has its own way of attacking the enemy. Further assume that in the aforementioned version, all the subclasses use a common move() method defined in the superclass. This could be better imagined if you see the game instructions in action.

See the following screenshot that shows how the player will be prompted to perform a move:

```
[user@hostname v6.0.0]$ python attackoftheorcs.py
Mission:
  1.Defeat all the enemy units in 20 turns.
TIPS:
  1. This is an open battle. Enemy units could be present anywhere.
  2. Use the 'huts' to get 'healed' but watch out for hiding enemies!
  3. You will get automatic help from your army during your turn.
  ---------------------------------------------------------------------
Health: Sir Foo: 40
Friendly units under your command: 6, Enemies to defeat: 10, Huts: 4

Surroundings:
        1. East : A HUT (reachable in 2 turns)
        2. West : An ENEMY (you are facing the enemy right now!)
        3. North: A FRIEND (reachable in 1 turn)
        4. South: A FENCE you CAN NOT cross!

Move(M) or Attack(A)? M

You have decided to move...

Select direction East/West/North/South: South

You CAN NOT move South. There is a FENCE! Try again

Select a direction to move:█
```

> **Cool! I want to play this new game scenario. Where is the source code?**
>
> The intention here is not to develop the full game logic. This is an imaginary scenario that is used just to highlight some commonly encountered problems in application development. With this scenario, we will see how design patterns could help tackle such problems. No code has been provided to actually "play" this new game. The supporting code illustrates how to implement various design patterns discussed here.

As can be seen from the command-line output, it gives the player a choice to move in one of four directions. It also indicates what lies ahead in each direction. In this particular case, the player decides to go South, but this movement is restricted by a fence.

Strategy pattern

A strategy design pattern is a behavioral pattern that is used to represent a family of algorithms. An algorithm within such a family is represented as a strategy object. The pattern enables easy switching between different strategies (algorithms) of a particular family. This is generally useful when you want to switch to a different strategy at runtime. We will revisit this definition towards the end of the discussion on strategy pattern.

Strategy scenario – The jump feature

There is a high priority feature request. Rather, it is a complaint. The users just hate the movement restriction imposed by the fence. Now even Sir Foo has joined the protest...

Rather than removing the fence from the scenario, how about a new feature that enables units to jump over the fence or any similar obstacle?

You have introduced a new method, `jump()`, in the superclass `AbstractGameUnit`. All the classes inherit this method, as shown in the following class diagram:

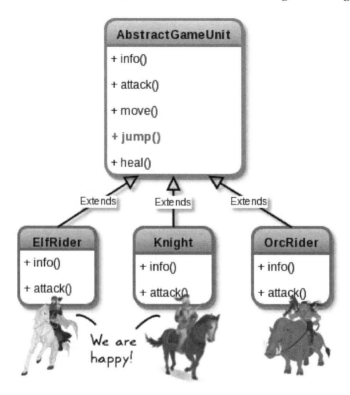

The fence no longer prevents the player from moving around. The new jump option enables crossing the fence without any problem. That was easy, wasn't it? Everyone is happy (especially Sir Foo)!

Strategy – The problem

Let's fast forward to a few more major releases of the application.

You have introduced two new imaginary characters to the game, a Dwarf and a Fairy, offering unique skills. For example, the Fairy has powers to heal nearby injured units in your army, and the Dwarf units offer a solid line of defense against enemy attack. With this, the number of application downloads per week has now reached a new high. However, there is a new problem that the users have reported. Let's hear it from The Great Dwarf:

Do you see the problem here? The jump feature has an unwanted side effect. It allows even a Fairy or a Dwarf to jump over the fence. The Knight, ElfRider, and OrcRider are all mounted units. It is easier to imagine these units jumping over the fence. However, it is not intuitive to think this way for a game character like a Dwarf. We encounter this issue because all the classes use the default implementation of the `AbstractGameUnit.jump` method. This is shown in the following class diagram:

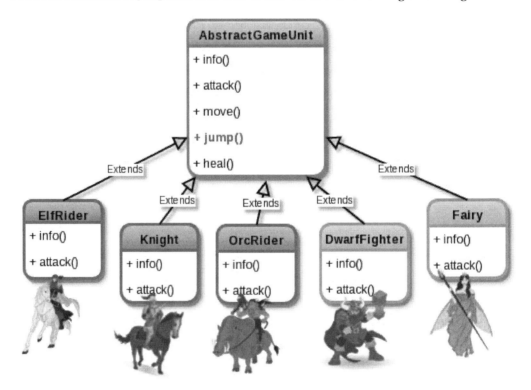

Strategy – Attempted solution

The Dwarf and Fairy game units should not have the jump feature. So what can we do here? The Fairy has something to say:

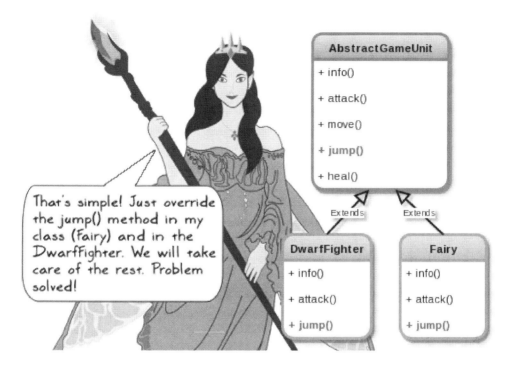

Using inheritance is certainly one approach. You can override the jump method and make it a no operation inside the new classes. However, in the next release, you are planning to introduce a number of new characters that are not supposed to jump, or need to jump differently. Some of the new classes are represented in the following class diagram. All of these need to override and implement their own logic.

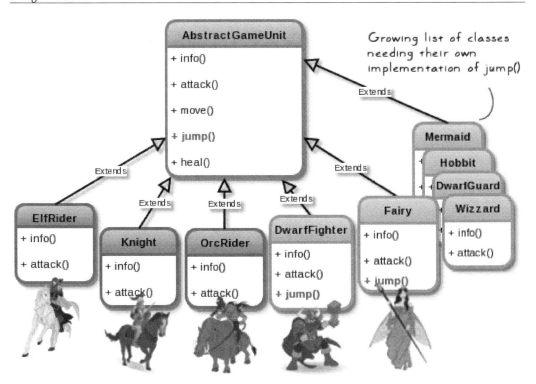

The jump feature is just one of the many things where you will see this problem. We don't even need to look beyond what we already have. In the preceding diagram, look at the move and attack methods. Do you see the same problem brewing?

The game characters are evolving. They have their own rules to move. For example, a Knight riding a horse may cross a river in two turns, whereas a DwarfFighter would need 10 turns for the same task.

Similarly, each unit has its signature style for attacking the enemy. An old Wizard in your army can cast magical spells on the enemy. The ElfRider character attacks twice in a single turn using a bow and arrows. The DwarfFighter character uses a hammer to attack, and so on.

If we continue to use the inheritance principle here, it would soon become a maintenance nightmare. Why so? This is because each class that you write is responsible for implementing and maintaining its own logic for its move, jump, and attack abilities. Initially, you may see this as a trivial issue, where overriding the functionality in the subclasses just works. But with a growing number of character types and their ever-growing set of abilities (move, jump, swim, defend, hide, regenerate, and so on), this will turn out to be a daunting task. The code might also get repeated across classes.

Every small change to the logic will require you to update the corresponding methods in all the classes. It could also invite new bugs if you miss out a few methods during the update process. We need to rethink the design to accommodate future requirements easily. Let's do that next.

Strategy – Rethinking the design

What can we do in such situations? Observe that the implementation code defining these abilities varies across subclasses. In this example, the `DwarfFighter` cannot jump whereas a `Knight` jumps using a horse.

The first question to ask is why do these classes carry the burden of defining abilities? Can this be outsourced to a different class or a function? We will redesign the `AbstractGameUnit` class (and its subclasses) so that the various abilities are now handled by objects dedicated to those tasks. In other words, we will use object composition to take this load off `AbstractGameUnit` and its subclasses.

 Recall that in *Chapter 1, Developing Simple Applications*, we used object composition in the `Hut` class where its `occupant` was represented by a different object. Object composition allows you to represent a complex object by putting together simple objects. Just say it out loud, a Knight has-the ability to move, a Knight has the ability to jump, and so on. Each of these abilities will be represented by separate objects.

How do we implement this new design? We will discuss two approaches to solving this problem. The first one is more of a classical approach that resembles the one typically followed in other languages, such as C++. If you have such a development background, this approach will look more familiar. The second approach is more Pythonic. It uses first-class functions, a language feature in Python. This second approach will make the whole problem appear trivial. If you are not interested in the traditional approach, skip ahead to the Pythonic solution for the strategy pattern.

Strategy solution 1 – Traditional approach

In the preceding section, we decided to create dedicated objects to represent abilities such as jump. Let's draw a class diagram that explains this better:

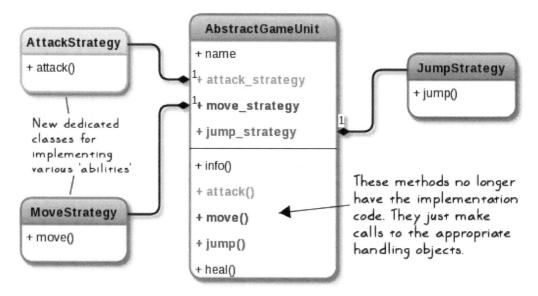

Here is a more verbose description of what is represented in the preceding diagram:

- Three new classes, AttackStrategy, MoveStrategy, and JumpStrategy, now handle the logic for the attack, move, and jump methods respectively.

- The class AbstractGameUnit is now composed of the instances of these classes, namely attack_strategy, move_strategy, and jump_strategy.

- The AbstractGameUnit.jump method just calls jump_strategy.jump(). A similar implementation for the move and attack methods is followed.

As the game characters need their on-jump implementation, we will create subclasses of JumpStrategy. For example, a subclass CanNotJump can be used for game units that are unable to jump. This is illustrated in the following class diagram:

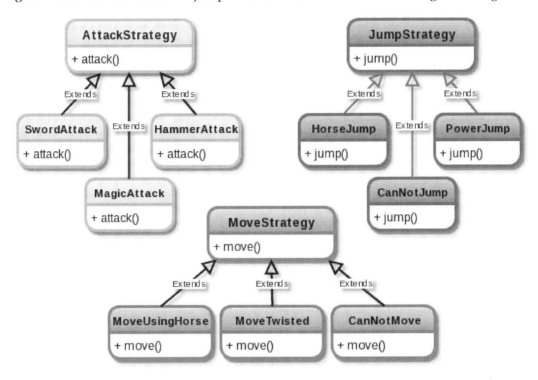

Revisiting the strategy pattern definition:

We started the discussion on strategy pattern with a definition. This design pattern represents a family of algorithms. Take a closer look at the preceding class diagram. The JumpStrategy and its subclasses represent a family of algorithms. Functionality defined in each of these classes is equivalent to an algorithm or a strategy. These classes are part of the same family, because the execution of any of the algorithms is related to a jump. As an example, the PowerJump class defines an algorithm different from the HorseJump class. Likewise, MoveStrategy defines a family of algorithms for movement, and AttackStrategy for attacking the enemy. There is one last missing piece to complete the strategy pattern. We need a way to dynamically switch between algorithm families. Let's see how to implement this next.

Let's review the new class, JumpStrategy. It now defines the jump behavior that was earlier defined in AbstractGameUnit. The overall logic is represented by the following schematic diagram and the code fragments. For easier understanding, we will only discuss the methods related to the jump ability:

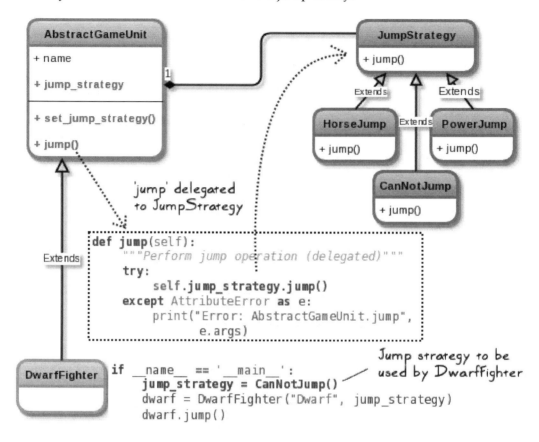

Thus, we have a family of algorithms represented by JumpStrategy and its subclasses. Here is the related code fragment that shows the classes AbstractGameUnit and DwarfFighter. The supporting file, strategypattern_traditional.py, contains this code:

```python
from abc import ABCMeta, abstractmethod

class AbstractGameUnit(metaclass=ABCMeta):
    def __init__(self, name, jump_object=None):
        self.jump_strategy = None
        self.name = name
        self.set_jump_strategy(jump_object)

    def set_jump_strategy(self, jump_object = None):
        """Set the object that defines the jump strategy(algorithm)"""
        if isinstance(jump_object, JumpStrategy):
            self.jump_strategy = jump_object
        else:
            self.jump_strategy = JumpStrategy()

    def jump(self):
        """Perform jump operation (delegated)"""
        try:
            self.jump_strategy.jump()
        except AttributeError as e:
            print("Error: AbstractGameUnit.jump:", e.args)

    @abstractmethod
    def info(self):
        pass


class DwarfFighter(AbstractGameUnit):
    def info(self):
        print("I am a great dwarf of the eastern foo mountain!")
```

The instance variable `self.jump_strategy` is used to represent a strategy or an algorithm for the jump behavior. The subclasses of `AbstractGameUnit` get to choose any jump strategy from the family of algorithms defined by the `JumpStrategy` class and its subclasses. For example, the `DwarfFighter` subclass can use the algorithm defined in the `CanNotJump` class as its jump strategy, and so on. The `AbstractGameUnit.jump` method is now an API method for the calling code. This method relies on the strategy object for the actual jump implementation. It simply calls the corresponding method of that strategy object, as shown in the preceding class diagram.

The subclass `DwarfFighter` in this simple example just overrides the abstract method `info`. You may include some additional customization to this class. Now let's look at the family of algorithms for the jump feature:

```python
class JumpStrategy:
    """Set up the object that defines the jump strategy."""
    def jump(self):
        print("--> JumpStrategy.jump: Default jump")

class CanNotJump(JumpStrategy):
    def jump(self):
        print("--> CanNotJump.jump: I can not jump")

class PowerJump(JumpStrategy):
    def jump(self):
        print("--> PowerJump.jump: I can jump 100 feet from the ground!")

class HorseJump(JumpStrategy):
    def jump(self):
        print("--> HorseJump.jump: Jumping my horse.")
```

As mentioned earlier, the purpose is not to develop a full-fledged game application, but just to understand the important concepts in application development. In this trivial example, we just print an informative message to illustrate the concept. In a practical implementation, these are the classes where your algorithms need to be defined. Finally, let's review the calling code that instantiates a game character, and dynamically sets up different jump strategies:

```python
if __name__ == '__main__':
    jump_strategy = CanNotJump()
    dwarf = DwarfFighter("Dwarf", jump_strategy)
    print("\n{STRATEGY-I} Dwarf trying to jump:")
    dwarf.jump()
    print("-"*56)

    # Optionally change the jump strategy later
    print("\n{STRATEGY-II} Dwarf given a 'magic potion' to jump:")
    dwarf.set_jump_strategy(PowerJump())
    dwarf.jump()
    print("-"*56)
```

We start by creating `jump_strategy`, an object that defines how the unit should jump. In this case, it is passed as an argument to the `__init__` method for `DwarfFighter`. Alternatively, you could also define a default strategy object in this class, as we know the default behavior for this class (the unit cannot jump). You can then call `set_jump_strategy` to switch to a different jump algorithm, as illustrated in the code fragment. Here is the output of this program:

```
[user@hostname ch6]$ python strategypattern_traditional.py

{STRATEGY-I} Dwarf trying to jump:
--> CanNotJump.jump: I can not jump
--------------------------------------------------------

{STRATEGY-II} Dwarf given a 'magic potion' to jump:
--> PowerJump.jump: I can jump 100 feet from the ground!
--------------------------------------------------------
```

Strategy solution 2 – Pythonic approach

What we discussed in the last section was more of a traditional approach, typically followed in programming languages such as C++. Given the flexibility that the Python language offers, there is no real need to define the various strategy classes as illustrated in the previous solution. We will exploit first-class functions, the language feature discussed earlier. Let's look at the revised code. You can also find this code in the `strategypattern_pythonic.py` file in the code bundle:

```python
from abc import ABCMeta, abstractmethod
from collections import Callable

class AbstractGameUnit(metaclass=ABCMeta):
    def __init__(self, name, jump_strategy):
        assert(isinstance(jump_strategy,  Callable))
        self.name = name
        self.jump = jump_strategy

    @abstractmethod
    def info(self):
        pass

class DwarfFighter(AbstractGameUnit):
    def info(self):
        print("I am a great dwarf of the eastern foo mountain!")

def can_not_jump():
    print("--> CanNotJump.jump: I can not jump")

def power_jump():
    print("--> PowerJump.jump: I can jump 100 feet from the ground!")

def horse_jump():
    print("--> HorseJump.jump: Jumping my horse.")
```

Make sure jump_strategy is a function

Assign the function jump_strategy to the variable self.jump. (See the calling code)

Simple functions defining various jump strategies

In the preceding code, we have used the Python language feature that supports assigning a function (`jump_strategy`) to a variable (`self.jump`). Why do we do this? It will become clear when we review the next code fragment. Before that, let's quickly discuss the preceding code snippet.

What exactly do we accomplish with the following assert statement?

```
assert(isinstance(jump_strategy, Callable))
```

This statement is from `AbstractGameUnit.__init__` method in the earlier code snippet. Before assigning the function to a variable, we need to make sure that it is indeed a function. The assertion prevents further execution of the code if this condition is not met. The idea is simple. You want to make sure that `jump_strategy` is a callable object. Any callable object defines a built-in `__call__`() method. The `collections.abc.Callable` class is an abstract base class for all the classes that provide a built-in `__call__`() method. In the `assert` statement, we check whether `jump_strategy` is an instance of this `Callable` class. For Python 2.7.9, this class should be imported directly as `collections.Callable`.

As before, let's review the code fragment that instantiates a game character (`dwarf`), and dynamically sets up different jump strategies:

```python
if __name__ == '__main__':
    dwarf = DwarfFighter("Dwarf", can_not_jump)
    print("\n{STRATEGY-I} Dwarf trying to jump:")
    dwarf.jump()
    print("-"*56)

    # Optionally change the jump strategy later
    print("\n{STRATEGY-II} Dwarf given a 'magic potion' to jump:")
    dwarf.jump = power_jump
    dwarf.jump()
    print("-"*56)
```

Compare this code with the first approach discussed earlier. There is a difference. In the previous solution, while instantiating `DwarfFighter`, we passed an instance of the class `CanNotJump` that deals with the jump behavior. Here, we pass the function `can_not_jump` as an argument, just like any simple variable. To dynamically change the `jump` algorithm, we just assign `dwarf.jump` to `power_jump`, as shown. Now when we call `dwarf.jump()`, it actually executes the code in the `power_jump()` function.

Remarks on the Pythonic way:

What we just saw was a cool Pythonic way that made things very easy. If you are coming from a C++ or Java programming background, at first you might feel uncomfortable with the freedom that Python offers. For example, there could be situations where a programmer mistakenly treats a function argument as a simple variable, leading to potential bugs. But this should not stop you from using this excellent language feature. To avoid such problems, you should document the code well so that the purpose of each input argument is clear.

Simple factory

A simple factory is generally not viewed as a formal design pattern, but you will find it quite useful in your day-to-day programming. The understanding we gain at the end of this section will be helpful in the discussion on a more formal pattern called abstract factory design pattern. Let's start with the definition of a simple factory.

A factory encapsulates the instance creation piece. The client code doesn't need to know the logic of instance creation. It just knows that whenever it needs an object of a specific type, the factory is the go-to place. Any class, or function, or class method that is used to construct such objects is often referred to as a factory. A simple factory is something you will use quite often. It is typically considered a better object-oriented technique than a formal design pattern.

Simple factory scenario – The recruit feature

Recall that we had fast-forwarded the game to an imaginary future version called Attack of the Orcs v6.0.0. This version introduced another much-anticipated feature that enabled recruiting new units to fight against the enemy.

Here is the initial version of the `recruit` method of a new class, `Kingdom`. Other methods are not shown. Let's assume those exist. Further assume that the player or the enemy is allowed to recruit any of the following game characters: `ElfRider`, `Knight`, `DwarfFighter`, `OrcRider`, and `OrcKnight`:

```
class Kingdom:
    def recruit(self, unit_type):
        unit = None
        if unit_type == 'ElfRider':
            unit = ElfRider()
        elif unit_type == 'Knight':
            unit = Knight()
        elif unit_type == "DwarfFighter":
            unit = DwarfFighter()
        elif unit_type == 'OrcRider':
            unit = OrcRider()
        elif unit_type == 'OrcKnight':
            unit = OrcKnight()

        self.pay_gold(unit)
        self.update_records(unit)
        return unit
```

The recruit method has the logic to create a game unit based on user input (the if..else block). Once the character is created, Kingdom pays for the hiring fees (pay_gold), and a central database is updated to reflect the new addition to the army (update_records).

Simple factory – The problem

As expected, users liked this feature, and now want the ability to recruit even more unit types. Let's see what Sir Foo has to say:

Let's add new recruit types, and to avoid Sir Foo's wrath, remove OrcKnight:

```python
class Kingdom:
    def recruit(self, unit_type):
        unit = None
        if unit_type == 'ElfRider':
            unit = ElfRider()
        elif unit_type == 'Knight':
            unit = Knight()
        elif unit_type == "DwarfFighter":
            unit = DwarfFighter()
        elif unit_type == 'OrcRider':
            unit = OrcRider()
        # OrcKnight to be removed in the next release:
        # elif unit_type == 'OrcKnight':
        #     unit = OrcKnight()
        elif unit_type == 'Fairy':
            unit = Fairy()
        elif unit_type == 'Wizard':
            unit = Wizard()
        elif unit_type == 'ElfLord':
            unit = ElfLord()
        elif unit_type == 'OrcFighter':
            unit = OrcFighter()

        self.pay_gold(unit)
        self.update_records(unit)
        return unit
```

As can be seen in the preceding code snippet, this is already becoming difficult to maintain. Tomorrow, you may decide to support even more units, or remove some of the existing ones. How do we handle this problem? Let's see that next.

Simple factory – Rethinking the design

What can we say about that big if..else block in the recruit method? It is subject to change. The rest of the code in the method is just the bookkeeping (for example, updating records) and remains unchanged. What if we take out the variable piece of code and give it a new home? It will take the load off the recruit method so that you don't need to open it for editing every time there is a change in the requirements. The next question to ask is where do we put this code?

Yes Fairy, that is an option. You can create a new method in the `Kingdom` class, and dump all this object creation code in there.

But imagine a game scenario where there is a grand galactic army, represented by a `GalacticArmy` class. This class needs a way to recruit or get various game characters. It is not at all related to the `Kingdom` class. Thus, we won't be able to reuse the object creation code in `Kingdom.recruit`.

Let's free the `Kingdom` class of the responsibility for creating new units. Once again, we will use the object composition principle. Let there be a new class (or even a function) that encapsulates the instance creation piece. We will call this a simple factory. The client code (the `Kingdom` or `GalacticArmy` class in this discussion) can now use this factory to get specific types of objects.

Simple factory solution 1 – Traditional approach

It is now time to implement the simple factory. Let's review a traditional approach first.

> This is the bare minimum code, without any exception handling. The purpose is just to illustrate a simple factory using a style that somewhat resembles a C++ implementation. You can make it more robust as an exercise. The code can be found in the `simplefactory_traditional.py` file. This example is written as a single module for ease of understanding. Ideally, you should refactor this, and put classes in their own modules.

Take a look at the following reworked code. We start with the new class, `UnitFactory`, which encapsulates the object creation piece:

```python
class UnitFactory:
    def create_unit(self, unit_type):
        unit = None

        if unit_type == 'ElfRider':
            unit = ElfRider()
        elif unit_type == 'Knight':
            unit = Knight()
        elif unit_type == "DwarfFighter":
            unit = DwarfFighter()
        elif unit_type == 'OrcRider':
            unit = OrcRider()
        elif unit_type == 'Fairy':
            unit = Fairy()
        elif unit_type == 'Wizard':
            unit = Wizard()
        elif unit_type == 'ElfLord':
            unit = ElfLord()
        elif unit_type == 'OrcFighter':
            unit = OrcFighter()

        return unit
```

In the preceding code, we have refactored out the big `if..else` clause in the `Kingdom.recruit` method discussed earlier, and put it in the `create_unit` method of the `UnitFactory` class. The `create_unit` method only has a single responsibility to create and return an instance of a game character for the given input argument (`unit_type`). The following is the `Kingdom` class after this refactoring:

```
class Kingdom:
    def __init__(self, factory):
        self.factory = factory

    def recruit(self, unit_type):
        unit = self.factory.create_unit(unit_type)
        self.pay_gold(unit)
        self.update_records(unit)
        return unit

    def pay_gold(self, something):
        print("GOLD PAID")

    def update_records(self, something):
        print("Some logic (not shown) to update database of units")
```

The `self.factory` instance represents `UnitFactory`. In the `recruit` method, the responsibility for creating game characters is delegated to this factory object. The `pay_gold` and `update_records` methods are just shown for completeness. Let's not worry about the logic inside these two methods. They remain unchanged. Finally, the following is one way to use the factory. The code is self-explanatory:

```
if __name__ == "__main__":
    factory = UnitFactory()
    k = Kingdom(factory)
    elf_unit = k.recruit("ElfRider")
    print(elf_unit)
```

What we have not shown in this example is the actual implementation of the concrete product classes that our factory uses to create products, such as `ElfRider`, `Knight`, and so on. These classes are going to be similar to the ones we have discussed so far. For example, all these concrete classes can be subclasses of `AbstractGameUnit`. These details were not shown in the example we just covered. However, this is not the only way to implement a simple factory. In Python, we can deal with this problem in other ways as well. One such approach will be discussed next.

Simple factory solution 2 – Pythonic approach

There is one problem with the solution presented in the previous section. You still need to maintain the `if..else` block in `create_unit`. Another thing to ask is, do we really need to instantiate `UnitFactory`? Depending on your application, the answer could be yes or no. In this example, the `create_unit` code would be identical for each instance of the factory you create. So, we do not really need an instance of `UnitFactory`. Let's discuss how to implement a simple factory without actually instantiating it.

What is illustrated here is not the only way to implement a simple factory. The source code is available in the supporting material as `simplefactory_pythonic.py`. Depending on the type of problem you are dealing with, you can tweak this approach further, and come up with a different solution. For example, you can choose a factory instance, and access its methods as normal instance methods. This approach is illustrated in the `simplefactory_pythonic_alternatesolution.py` file.

Here is the reworked `UnitFactory` class from the file `simplefactory_pythonic.py`:

```python
class UnitFactory:
    units_dict = {
        'elfrider': ElfRider,
        'knight': Knight,
        'dwarffighter': DwarfFighter,
        'orcrider': OrcRider,
        'fairy': Fairy,
        'wizard': Wizard,
        'elflord': ElfLord,
        'orcfighter': OrcFighter
    }

    @classmethod
    def create_unit(cls, unit_type):
        key = unit_type.lower()
        return cls.units_dict.get(key)()
```

A Python dictionary created as a 'class variable'

Defined as a class method (@classmethod). See the calling code

Earlier in the chapter, we reviewed some Python language features that come in handy for design patterns. Let's see how first-class classes and class methods can be used in a simple factory:

- `units_dict` is a Python dictionary object declared as a class variable (for the class `UnitFactory`).

- Python classes are first-class objects. So we can simply put them as values of the dictionary, `units_dict`. The dictionary keys can be unique strings of your choice. Just make sure that the calling code knows which key corresponds to which class.

- The method `create_unit` is defined as a class method using the decorator `@classmethod`. What this means is that the first argument passed to this method is the class itself (denoted by `cls`) instead of being self (an instance of the class).

- Now look at the `return` statement of the `create_unit` method:

  ```
  return cls.units_dict.get(key)()
  ```

  Here, we access `units_dict`, a class variable, as `cls.units_dict`, and get the value for a particular key given as an input argument. This can be better explained with an example. Assume that the given key is `elfrider`. The corresponding value in the dictionary is the `ElfRider` class. So, the `create_unit` method will return `ElfRider()`, which is an instance of the `ElfRider` class.

Compare this code with the one we saw in the previous heading, *Simple factory solution 1 – Traditional approach*. As can be noticed, the number of lines of code has not been reduced significantly. But the code clarity is much better here. You still need to maintain the dictionary object (`units_dict`) for all future requirements, which is relatively easy compared to maintaining the `if..else` clause.

Now observe the `Kingdom` class. It has just a few changes:

```
class Kingdom:                      factory is declared as a
    factory = UnitFactory           class variable

    def recruit(self, unit_type):
        unit = type(self).factory.create_unit(unit_type)
        self.pay_gold(unit)
        self.update_records(unit)        type(self).factory is
        return unit                      equivalent to
                                         Kingdom.factory
    def pay_gold(self, something):
        print("GOLD PAID")

    def update_records(self, something):
        print("Some logic (not shown) to update database of units")
```

Let's review the preceding code snippet

- First, we assign the `UnitFactory` class to a class variable, `factory`. Again, we can do this because Python classes are first-class objects.

- The `recruit` method is just a normal instance method of `Kingdom`. The class variable `factory` is accessed as `type(self).factory`.

- In this example, `type(self).factory.create_unit` is equivalent to `UnitFactory.create_unit`. We could have directly written it that way, but if a subclass of `Kingdom` defines its `factory` as a different class, say `DwarfUnitFactory`, then it will require you to write some extra code, such as overriding the `recruit` method.

Finally, here is the calling code. Notice that we are not creating any `factory` instances:

```
if __name__ == "__main__":
    k = Kingdom()
    elf_unit = k.recruit("ElfRider")
    print(elf_unit)
```

The discussion on the simple factory has set the stage for the formal design pattern called the abstract factory pattern. Let's review that next.

Abstract factory pattern

We have just learned how to create and use a simple factory in a program. Let's go a little further and study a formal pattern known as the abstract factory pattern.

Imagine we have a master factory and some follower factories. Further assume that each follower factory is responsible for producing its own trademark products (objects). The follower factories are related in some sense. They create products that share a common theme. For example, each follower factory produces its own version of tomato ketchup. The factories have their own ordering form for their product.

The customers have a hard time in keeping up with so many forms for ordering a tomato ketchup. For example, one factory says you should call it MyRedTomatoKetchup, otherwise it won't understand. So, the master factory says:

> *We make products that are like a part of an extended family. Our customers would benefit if we can simplify and standardize the procedure to order these products from our group of factories. From now on, every follower factory is required to implement a common ordering form.*

The customers benefit, as they just need to know the high-level name tomato ketchup and the factory that can supply this product. Let's put this into programming terminology:

- The master factory is an abstract factory, and the follower factories are concrete factories.

- The tomato ketchup is an abstract class. Every concrete factory creates its custom version of tomato ketchup; we will call this a concrete object (an instance of a concrete class).

- The standardization procedure referenced earlier is called an interface. The abstract factory declares such an interface (or in Python terms, a set of abstract methods) that is required to be implemented by the concrete factories for creating families of concrete objects.

- The customer is the client code. It doesn't need to know the details of the concrete object received from a concrete factory. It just needs to have knowledge of the abstract class.

> The Java programming language has a provision to create an abstract type called interface. If a class implements an interface, it must implement all the methods described by that interface. For more information on interface in the Java language, visit the wiki page: `https://en.wikipedia.org/wiki/Interface_(Java)`. In Python, there is no such formal provision to create and implement an interface. Instead, we can use inheritance, where concrete factories inherit from the abstract factory. Instead, we can use the first-class features offered by Python, as discussed earlier. Let's see these next.

Quite a mouthful? Let's dig deeper into the abstract factory pattern with a game scenario.

Abstract factory scenario – An accessory store

Imagine you have implemented a new feature that enables buying accessories for your army. At the moment, you can buy an armored jacket or a gold locket, as shown in the following code fragment:

```python
class Kingdom:
    def buy_accessories(self):
        armor = Jacket()
        locket = GoldLocket()
        accesories = [armor, locket]
        self.pay_gold(accesories)
        self.update_records(accesories)
    def pay_gold(self):
        print("GOLD PAID")
    def update_records(self, accesories):
        print("Some logic (not shown) to update database of accesories")
```

More choices for armor and lockets were added as follows:

```python
class Kingdom:
    def buy_accessories(self, armor_type, locket_type):
        if armor_type == 'ironjacket':
            armor = IronJacket()
        elif armor_type == "powersuit":
            armor = PowerSuit()
        elif (type == 'mithril'):
            armor = MithrilArmor()

        if locket_type == "goldlocket":
            locket = GoldLocket()
        elif locket_type == "superlocket":
            locket = SuperLocket()
        elif locket_type == "magiclocket":
            locket = MagicLocket()

        accesories = [armor, locket]
        self.pay_gold(accesories)
        self.update_records(accesories)
```

You reworked the preceding piece of code, and implemented a simple factory instead. This factory would produce all the accessories for the game characters. In this example, it would return armor and locket objects.

The reworked code, which implements a simple factory, is shown next:

```
class AccessoryFactory:
    armor_dict = {
        'ironjacket': IronJacket,
        'powersuit': PowerSuit,
        'mithril': MithrilArmor
    }
    locket_dict = {
        'goldlocket': GoldLocket,
        'superlocket': SuperLocket,
        'magiclocket': MagicLocket
    }

    @classmethod
    def create_armor(cls, armor_type):
        return cls.armor_dict.get(armor_type)()

    @classmethod
    def create_locket(cls, locket_type):
        return cls.locket_dict.get(locket_type)()
```

The Kingdom class and the main execution code is shown next. The Kingdom class has an instance variable, self.factory, which represents our simple factory:

```
class Kingdom:
    def __init__(self, factory):
        self.factory = factory

    def buy_accessories(self, armor_type, locket_type):
        armor = self.factory.create_armor(armor_type)
        locket =  self.factory.create_locket(locket_type)
        print("Kingdom armor:", armor)
        accesories = [armor, locket]
        self.pay_gold(accesories)
        self.update_records(accesories)

    def pay_gold(self, accessories):
        print("GOLD PAID")
    def update_records(self, accesories):
        print("Some logic (not shown) to update database of accesories")

if __name__ == '__main__':
    factory = AccessoryFactory()
    k = Kingdom(factory)
    k.buy_accessories("mithril", "magiclocket")
```

The `self.factory` variable is used to create `armor` and `locket` instances, as indicated in the `buy_accessories` method.

 As illustrated in the section on simple factories, the factory can also be specified as a class attribute accessed as `Kingdom.factory`, instead of creating an instance, `self.factory`.

The changes you made simplified the implementation. Looks like Sir Foo is quite happy with his new Iron jacket, however, that doesn't seem to be the case with others! There is a new problem...

Abstract factory – The problem

One size doesn't fit all! The DwarfKingdom is now using this AccessoryFactory, and has reported problems with the products:

The new accessory store is no good. The IronJacket is oversized. The GoldLocket does not have 'Great Dwarf' imprinted on it. I would just close it down.

The Great Dwarf has reason to be annoyed. The factory does not support customization for the products it creates. How do we address this?

This is one scenario where we can use the abstract factory pattern.

Abstract factory – Rethinking the design

Observe the following class diagram. It represents a typical abstract factory pattern, our approach to solve the problem:

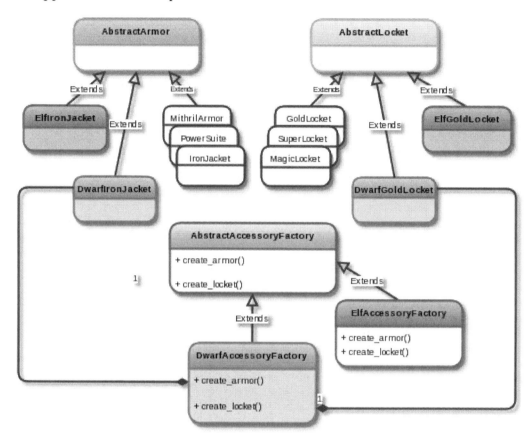

Let's review the components of the UML-like diagram presented here, and correlate them with the terms used in the earlier definition of an abstract factory:

- `DwarfAccessoryFactory`, `ElfAccessoryFactory`: The follower or concrete factories. Recall that each concrete factory creates products that share a common theme. Here, they create accessories for the game characters. As mentioned earlier, they are required to implement standard procedures set by the master factory.

- `AbstractAccessoryFactory`: This is the abstract factory class, or what we referred to as a master factory earlier. It defines an interface (a set of abstract methods) that must be implemented by the concrete factories. In this case, each of the concrete factories is required to implement methods to create armors and lockets.

- In this example, each concrete factory implements the `create_armor` and `create_locket` methods. These methods return instances of concrete product classes. Thus, each factory creates its own flavor of the products. For instance, `create_locket` of `DwarfAccessoryFactory` returns an instance of `DwarfGoldLocket`, whereas the same method in `ElfAccessoryFactory` returns an instance of `ElfGoldLocket`.

- `AbstractArmor`, `AbstractLocket`: These are abstract product classes. There could be several concrete product types that inherit from these abstract classes. For example, the concrete product classes `DwarfGoldLocket` and `SuperLocket` inherit from `AbstractLocket`, and so on.

- **The client code**: This is not shown in the class diagram. The client code doesn't need to know which concrete product class gives it the desired product. It just knows the high-level name of the product (for example, `create_locket`). Essentially, it chooses the factory, and invokes the standard API methods, such as `create_locket`, to get the required objects. See the next solution section for an example.

Simplifying the design further

The preceding class diagram shows a classic way of implementing the abstract factory pattern. For ease of understanding, let's simplify the problem further. We will assume that all the concrete factories define the required methods without the abstract factory enforcing the rule (interface) to do so.

With this assumption, we could even remove the `AbstractAccessoryFactory` class from the design, and just have the concrete factories. Recall that we discussed duck typing at the beginning of this chapter. So as long as the concrete factories implement the required methods, the client code (see `Knight.buy_accessories` in the next example) won't complain.

For conceptual understanding, we will retain the inheritance hierarchy in the upcoming discussion. We will call this class simply `AccessoryFactory`, and won't define `create_armor` and `create_locket` as abstract methods. Enforcing an interface will require some minor adjustments in the code. We will briefly discuss this as an optional or advanced topic at the end of the next section, where we look at the actual implementation.

Abstract factory solution – Pythonic approach

In the previous section, we saw a representative class diagram that shows the implementation details for the abstract factory pattern. We will discuss only a Pythonic solution for implementing this pattern. Since we have already covered the simple factory in depth, the abstract factory pattern is just a few steps away. We will limit our discussion to some of the important classes. Look at the `abstractfactory_pythonic.py` file in the supporting code for the complete source.

The `Kingdom` and `DwarfKingdom` classes are shown next. The code is self explanatory, and was pretty much discussed earlier:

```python
class Kingdom:
    factory = AccessoryFactory

    def buy_accessories(self, armor_type, locket_type):
        armor = type(self).factory.create_armor(armor_type)
        locket = type(self).factory.create_locket(locket_type)
        accessories = [armor, locket]
        self.pay_gold(accessories)
        self.update_records(accessories)
        self.print_info(armor, locket)

    def pay_gold(self, accessories):
        print("GOLD PAID")
    def update_records(self, accessories):
        print("Updated database of accessories")
    def print_info(self, armor, locket):
        print("Done with shopping in        :", type(self).__name__)
        print("   concrete class for armor  :", type(armor).__name__)
        print("   concrete class for locket :", type(locket).__name__)


class DwarfKingdom(Kingdom):
    factory = DwarfAccessoryFactory
```

Let's look at the `AccessoryFactory` class (see a note on design simplification under the previous heading, *Simplifying the design further*):

```
class AccessoryFactory:
    armor_dict = {
        'ironjacket': IronJacket,
        'powersuit': PowerSuit,
        'mithril': MithrilArmor
    }
    locket_dict = {
        'goldlocket': GoldLocket,
        'superlocket': SuperLocket,
        'magiclocket': MagicLocket
    }

    @classmethod
    def create_armor(cls, armor_type):
        return cls.armor_dict.get(armor_type)()

    @classmethod
    def create_locket(cls, locket_type):
        return cls.locket_dict.get(locket_type)()
```

This is very similar to the `UnitFactory` class we reviewed in the section on simple factory implementation. The only difference is that the factory produces two separate products, `armor` and `locket`. So, we have two different class methods (factory methods) for creating each of the concrete products. The `armor_dict` dictionary holds armor-related concrete classes as its values, and `locket_dict` is used for the locket-related classes. Both of these are defined as class variables.

The following code snippet is for `DwarfAccessoryFactory`, one of the concrete factories. Here, we have only redefined the `armor_dict` and `locket_dict` dictionaries. Nothing else changes. Likewise, you can define other concrete factories such as `ElfAccesoryFactory`. If you want a strict abstract factory pattern implementation, you should also enforce an interface in the concrete factory. This is briefly discussed at the end of this section:

```
class DwarfAccessoryFactory(AccessoryFactory):
    armor_dict = {
        'ironjacket': DwarfIronJacket,
        'powersuit': DwarfPowerSuit,
        'mithril': DwarfMithrilArmor
    }
    locket_dict = {
        'goldlocket': DwarfGoldLocket,
        'superlocket': DwarfSuperLocket,
        'magiclocket': DwarfMagicLocket
    }
```

The last piece of the puzzle is the main execution code. It creates two kingdoms, the first is a default Kingdom, and the second is a kingdom of *The Great Dwarfs* — DwarfKingdom. This is done as follows:

```
if __name__ == '__main__':
    print("Buying accesories in default Kingdom...")
    k = Kingdom()
    k.buy_accessories("ironjacket", "goldlocket")
    print("-"*56)
    print("Buying accesories in DwarfKingdom...")
    dwarf_kingdom = DwarfKingdom()
    dwarf_kingdom.buy_accessories("ironjacket", "goldlocket")
```

Observe that buy_accessories is invoked for both the kingdoms with the same arguments, ironjacket and goldlocket. But what each kingdom gets as the concrete product depends on the factory chosen. For example, as the DwarfKingdom has selected DwarfAccessoryFactory as its factory, for the abstract product named ironjacket it would get an instance of DwarfIronJacket. The following is a sample output of the code in the abstractfactory_pythonic.py file:

```
[user@hostname ch6]$ python abstractfactory_pythonic.py
Buying accesories in default Kingdom...
GOLD PAID
Updated database of accessories
Done with shopping in        : Kingdom
  concrete class for armor   : IronJacket
  concrete class for locket  : GoldLocket
--------------------------------------------------------
Buying accesories in DwarfKingdom...
GOLD PAID
Updated database of accessories
Done with shopping in        : DwarfKingdom
  concrete class for armor   : DwarfIronJacket
  concrete class for locket  : DwarfGoldLocket
```

Advanced topic – enforcing an interface

This section illustrates one way of enforcing an interface in Python. If this does not mean anything to you right now, just ignore this and move on to the next topic.

Recall that for ease of illustrating a Pythonic solution, we had simplified the problem. `AccessoryFactory` does not enforce any rule that requires the subclasses to implement the `create_armor` and `create_locket` methods. Actually, it is easy to do so. If you are using Python 3.3 or higher, you can simply define these methods as abstract methods in addition to being class methods, using the two decorators, `@classmethod` and `@abstractmethod`, like so:

```
@classmethod
@abstractmethod
def create_armor(cls, armor_type):
    return cls.armor_dict.get(armor_type)()
```

In subclasses such as `DwarfAccessoryFactory`, you just need to implement these class methods. For completeness, make `AccessoryFactory` abstract by inheriting from `ABCMeta`. Technically, that would confirm the formal design of an abstract factory. But if you look at the code inside this method (`create_armor`), it hasn't changed a bit. Thus, in this example, declaring an abstract method would help only to enforce the rule that subclasses must implement certain methods.

Adapter pattern

The adapter design pattern enables a handshake between two incompatible interfaces. Here, the incompatible interface of a class or a library is transformed into the one expected by your client code. This transformation is accomplished by an adapter class. The other class with a different interface than what the client expects is often referred to as an adaptee.

There are two broad categories of adapter pattern, namely a class adapter pattern and an object adapter pattern. In the former, the adapter inherits from the adaptee. It is possible to implement a class adapter in Python, as the language supports multiple inheritance. However, it is better to choose object composition (has a relationship) over inheritance. In the object adapter pattern, the adapter object has an adaptee object instead of inheriting from the adaptee class. The object adapter pattern helps maintain a loose coupling between the adaptee and the client code, wherein the client does not need to have any knowledge of the adaptee interface. This offers more flexibility when compared to the class adapter pattern.

In the upcoming discussion, we will only talk about the object adapter pattern.

Adapter scenario – Elf's distant cousin

Let's fast-forward to an imaginary future one more time. A group of developers has approached you. They have been working on a similar fantasy game application. Given the popularity of your game, they would like to collaborate. It's a win-win situation for both parties. You happily accept this proposal, as it will give you access to several game characters in their collection.

Adapter – The problem

You begin the integration work, and notice a problem. Let's hear it from our friend, the Elf:

The code that follows highlights this problem further. What is shown here is a simplified version of the new WoodElf class that only shows the leap() method. Assume that all its other methods match our existing interface.

There is no correlation between the jump method (rather, the jump strategies) discussed in the section on *Strategy pattern* with the one illustrated here. For easier understanding of the pattern, only the bare minimum code is shown. For example, the AbstractGameUnit class is not used here. As an exercise, try to use the code from the strategy pattern here, and implement an adapter so that we can talk to WoodElf (the solution is not provided)!

```python
class WoodElf:
    """WoodElf class from third party developers"""
    def leap(self):
        print("Inside WoodElf.leap")

class ElfRider:
    def jump(self):
        print("Inside ElfRider.jump")

class Knight:
    def jump(self):
        print("Inside Knight.jump")

if __name__ == '__main__':
    # With our existing API, client code can call jump() method
    # for characters like ElfRider, Knight and so on.
    elf = ElfRider()
    knight =Knight()
    elf.jump()
    knight.jump()

    # But the new WoodElf class doesn't support jump() as an API method.
    # The client is forced to call leap() instead.
    wood_elf = WoodElf()
    #wood_elf.jump() # <-- Will throw an AttributeError
    wood_elf.leap()
```

Adapter – Attempted solution

The new class doesn't have a `leap()` *method. How can we solve this problem? Any thoughts, Fairy?*

> Simple! You just open up the class WoodElf and add a new method jump() that delegates this to leap()

```
class WoodElf:
    def jump(self):
        self.leap()

    def leap(self):
        print("Inside WoodElf.leap")
```

We could have possibly done that, but this code is owned by a third party. If they have shared the source, then you can update it. But that is going to be a maintenance overhead for you. If you don't have the source code, then you have to depend on them to get this method supported. For all these reasons, the solution suggested by the Fairy may not be the best way to go forward. That said, the Fairy is on the right track! She has a `jump()` method that delegates this to the `leap()` method. Let's see how the adapter pattern can help here.

How about adding a new class that enables a handshake between these two interfaces? Look at the following code fragment:

```python
class WoodElfAdapter:
    def __init__(self, wood_elf):
        self.wood_elf = wood_elf
    def jump(self):
        self.wood_elf.leap()

class WoodElf:
    """WoodElf class from third party developers"""
    def leap(self):
        print("Inside WoodElf.leap")

if __name__ == '__main__':
    elf = ElfRider()
    elf.jump()

    wood_elf = WoodElf()
    wood_elf_adapter = WoodElfAdapter(wood_elf)
    wood_elf_adapter.jump()
```

This last code fragment seems to address one issue. We do not need to make any changes to the third-party class WoodElf. We feed an instance of WoodElf to the adapter, WoodElfAdapter. This adapter class has a jump method, which calls the leap method of WoodElf. The client code simply needs to use this adapter instance instead of the WoodElf instance. However, there are two main problems with this solution:

- The adapter class seems to be tied to the WoodElf class. What if we have a new class, MountainElf, which implements the spring method as an equivalent of the jump method?

- Imagine that the WoodElf class has other methods such as attack, info, climb, and so on. Some might already be compatible with the existing interface, while for others, there is no equivalent. All such methods can be directly called without any special processing like what was done for leap(). If we follow the approach discussed in the preceding code fragment, you will have to define each of these methods in the adapter class WoodElfAdapter. Without implementing them, you won't be able to use the adapter class seamlessly in your client code. That's quite a bit of work.

It is very easy to address both these problems. Let's write a generalized solution next.

Adapter solution – Pythonic approach

To summarize the problem, a new class, WoodElf, provided by third-party developers, has a leap() method instead of jump(). Put another way, it has an incompatible interface. We are seeking a solution that doesn't require us to touch the WoodElf class. We created an adapter, WoodElfAdapter, but it had its own shortcomings, as discussed in the previous section, *Adapter – Attempted Solution*.

Let's generalize the adapter class further to address these issues. See the supplementary adapterpattern.py file for the source code. This will be illustrated next. First look at the following code fragment, and then we will talk through it:

```python
class ElfRider:
    def jump(self):
        print("Inside ElfRider.jump")

class WoodElf:
    def leap(self):
        print("Inside WoodElf.leap")
    def climb(self):
        print("Inside WoodElf.climb")

class MountainElf:
    def spring(self):
        print("Inside MountainElf.spring")
```

```
class ForeignUnitAdapter:
    def __init__(self, adaptee, adaptee_method):
        self.foreign_unit = adaptee
        self.jump = adaptee_method          We can assign a Python
                                            function to a variable.

    def __getattr__(self, item):
        return getattr(self.foreign_unit, item)

if __name__ == '__main__':
    elf = ElfRider()               calls __getattr__, as
    elf.jump()                     climb() is not defined
                                   in the adapter class.
    wood_elf = WoodElf()
    wood_elf_adapter = ForeignUnitAdapter(wood_elf, wood_elf.leap)
    wood_elf_adapter.jump()
    wood_elf_adapter.climb()

    mountain_elf = MountainElf()
    mountain_elf_adapter = ForeignUnitAdapter(mountain_elf,
                                              mountain_elf.spring)
    mountain_elf_adapter.jump()
```

The following things are to be noted in the preceding code screenshots:

- The adapter class is renamed as `ForeignUnitAdapter`.

- The first input argument, `adaptee`, represents the instance of the class for which we need an adapter. The second argument, `adaptee_method`, is the instance method that needs to be adapted (for example, `wood_elf.leap` needs to be interpreted as a `jump` method).

- Next, we take advantage of the Python first-class functions to assign `adaptee_method` to `self.jump`. For example, calling `self.jump()` is now equivalent to calling `wood_elf.leap()`. This eliminates the need to create a separate `jump` method inside the adapter class.

- Earlier in the chapter, we learned about the `__getattr__` method. Here, we have implemented it in the adapter class `ForeignUnitAdapter`. The client code assumes that the adapter object (which represents a third-party game character), has defined methods such as `info()`, `attack()`, and `climb()`. The client calls these methods using the adapter object. In reality, the adapter class has not defined any of them. It relies on `self.foreign_unit` to provide these methods.

- This handling code is written in the `__getattr__` method. Here, `getattr(self.foreign_unit, item)` would simply return `self.foreign_unit.item`.

- You can create multiple adapter objects by passing in different instances of the game units, and the method that needs to be the adapter. One such example is shown in the preceding code fragment.

Adapter – Multiple adapter methods

In the earlier illustration, we assumed that `self.jump` would be the handling adapter method. What if we have multiple methods that need to be an adapter to conform to our existing API? You can generalize this implementation further. Here is one way to handle multiple methods. This source can be found in the supporting code bundle. Look for the `adapterpattern_multiple_methods.py` file:

```python
class FooElf:
    def leap(self):
        print("FooElf.leap")
    def hit(self):
        print("FooElf.hit")

class ForeignUnitAdapter:
    def __init__(self, adaptee):
        self.foreign_unit = adaptee

    def __getattr__(self, item):
        return getattr(self.foreign_unit, item)

    def set_adapter(self, name, adaptee_method):
        setattr(self, name, adaptee_method)
```

The following is the main execution code:

```python
if __name__ == '__main__':
    foo_elf = FooElf()
    foo_elf_adapter = ForeignUnitAdapter(foo_elf)

    foo_elf_adapter.set_adapter('jump', foo_elf.leap )
    foo_elf_adapter.set_adapter('attack', foo_elf.hit)

    # Optionally, assign the adapter methods directly:
    # foo_elf_adapter.jump = foo_elf.leap
    # foo_elf_adapter.attack = foo_elf.hit

    foo_elf_adapter.attack()
    foo_elf_adapter.jump()
```

Again, we take advantage of the Python first-class functions. The `set_adapter` method uses a built-in method, `setattr()`, to set new attributes for the `ForeignUnitAdapter` class. These act as the adapter methods. Alternatively, you can also set the attributes as follows:

```
foo_elf_adapter.jump = foo_elf.leap
foo_elf_adapter.attack = foo_elf.hit
```

Summary

This chapter provided an introduction to design patterns in Python, an important aspect of application development. We started this chapter with an introduction and saw how design patterns are classified. Next we reviewed some key features offered by the Python language that help simplify several design patterns. With practical illustrations, you learned how design patterns can be implemented to provide a solution to recurring problems in application development. More specifically, you learned about strategy, abstract factory, and adapter patterns. For each of these patterns, we first used an interesting game scenario to describe the problem. We then discussed how the design pattern can tackle this problem, and further implemented the design pattern using a Pythonic approach. For some patterns, we also reviewed a traditional approach to implementing the design pattern. Last but not the least, we met some of Sir Foo's new friends.

So far, we have discussed several important aspects of application development. This discussion helped us write better code, make the application more robust, and increase the application's life expectancy. In the next three chapters, we will learn various ways to improve the performance of the application.

7

Performance – Identifying Bottlenecks

So far, you have learned various ways to make the application robust and accommodating for new features. Now, let's discuss techniques to improve the application performance. This broad topic is split into a series of three chapters—this is the first one in this series. It will cover the following topics:

- Basic ways to clock the application runtime
- How to identify the runtime performance bottlenecks by profiling the code
- Basic memory profiling with the `memory_profiler` package
- **Big O** notation for the computational complexity

To understand these concepts better, we will develop an interesting game scenario called *Gold Hunt*. You will soon realize that the application runs very slow when you increase the input data size. This chapter will elaborate on techniques to pinpoint such problems.

Overview of three performance chapters

Before we dive into the main discussion, let's first understand how the chapters on performance improvement are organized. As mentioned earlier, this discussion is split into a series of three interlinked chapters.

More focus on the runtime performance

The term performance improvement can mean several things. One can be talking about improving the runtime (CPU usage), making the application memory efficient, reducing the network consumption, or a combination of these. In this book, we will primarily focus on the runtime performance improvement. We will also discuss the memory consumption aspect, but the discussion will be limited to the **memory profiling** technique and the use of generator expressions.

The first performance chapter

You are reading the first chapter in this series. It does some preparatory work to improve the application performance. This preparation involves measuring the runtime, identifying pieces of the code that cause the performance bottlenecks, understanding the big O notation, and so on.

*Of course! We will develop the earlier mentioned **Gold Hunt scenario**, and then identify the performance bottlenecks in the code. The next two chapters will use this groundwork to gradually improve the application performance.*

The second performance chapter

The next chapter is all about learning various performance improvement techniques. The first half aims at improving the application runtime for the *Gold Hunt* application. The second half teaches several tricks to optimize the code. The chapter covers some built-in modules designed for high performance and memory efficiency. It also talks about list comprehension, generator expressions, choice of data structures, algorithmic changes, and so on.

The third performance chapter

The last chapter in this series will briefly talk about the **NumPy** package and **parallelization** using the `multiprocessing` module in Python. We will use these techniques to drastically improve the runtime performance of the application.

Sneak peek at the upcoming application speedup

Here is a preview of how the *Gold Hunt* program will evolve from a turtle to a rabbit. The following figure shows   the approximate runtime after each major step of performance improvement. By the time we complete *Chapter 9, Improving Performance – Part two, NumPy and Parallelization*, the application runtime will be brought down to approximately 14 seconds from an initial value of nearly 106 seconds.

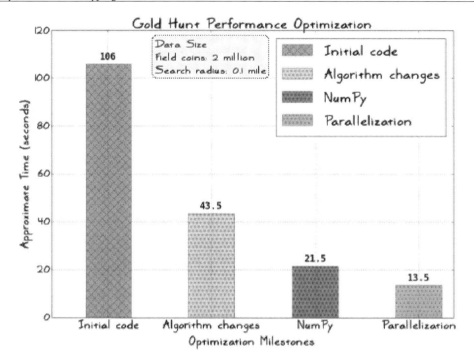

No need to spend any time trying to understand the elements presented in this chart; things will become clear once you read all three chapters on performance. For now, all you need to know is that we will learn some techniques to drastically improve the application runtime in the upcoming chapters.

Caution

The chapters on performance will show some examples of inefficient code. Running these examples can consume a lot of compute resources. Instead of using the problem size illustrated in these chapters, you should choose an appropriate data size depending on what your machine can handle.

Scenario – The Gold Hunt

You recently introduced a new scenario in the game – to meet the expenses of his army, Sir Foo is out on a mission to collect gold from a recently acquired territory. The scenario starts with Sir Foo arriving at a place full of gold coins, jewelry, and so on. There are a couple of problems though. Firstly, the gold is scattered all over the field. Secondly, Sir Foo doesn't have time to collect all the gold on the field.

*What you see behind Sir Foo is an imaginary **gold field**. Sir Foo will enter from the left side and travel across the field. He will only collect the coins lying along his path and **ignore all the remaining gold** scattered across the field.*

Let's represent this gold field as a circle with a radius of nearly 10 miles (diameter of 20 miles), and center located at coordinates $x = 0$ and $y = 0$, as shown in the following screenshot:

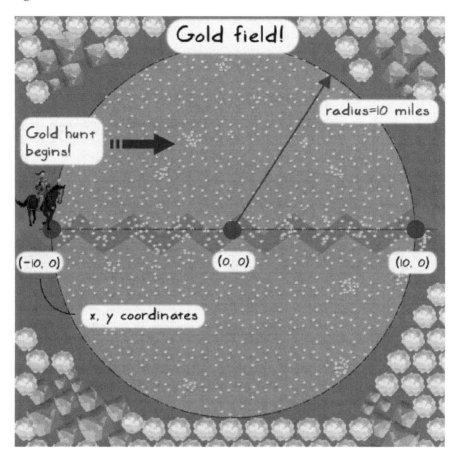

Observe the following screenshot. The *dotted line* (the diameter of the field) shows the path that Sir Foo traverses on his way out. During this 20 mile journey, he stops at 10 *equally spaced points*. In other words, these points are 2 miles apart, represented by the centers of the small "search circles". For each stop, he collects the gold within a search circle. The total collected gold is the sum of the coins inside each of those 10 tiny circles. Let's not worry about the gold lying outside of these search circles.

Assume that the remaining gold on the field is irrelevant for the problem we are solving.

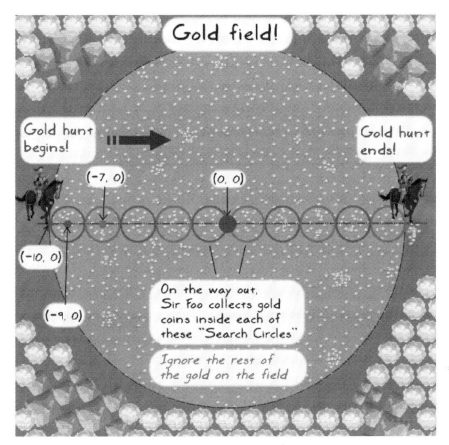

High-level algorithm

With the preceding screenshot as a reference, let's write the high-level algorithm. We will keep it simple. The task is to collect the gold coins found inside each of the small circles in this image (recall that these circles are referred to as *search circles*). We will call the radius of each of these circles a *search radius*. In the present scenario, the search radius is 1 mile, or let's simply call it 1 unit:

1. Randomly create points representing the gold coins inside a gold field. The gold field is represented by a large circle with a radius of 10 units and center at *(x = 0, y = 0)*. Each gold coin is represented with a *(x,y)* location.

2. Start with the leftmost search circle, the center of which represents Sir Foo's current location. The coin hunt is constrained within this search circle.

3. For each search circle:

  ° Get Sir Foo's current location coordinates.

  ° Find the distance between each gold coin on the field and Sir Foo's location, the center of a search circle.

  ° Collect all the coins with distance less than the *search radius*. These are the coins lying inside the perimeter of the current search circle.

  ° Advance Sir Foo to the center of the next search circle.

  ° Repeat the preceding steps until you reach the rightmost circle.

4. Report the total number of collected gold coins.

Reviewing the initial code

Let's review the code next (it can also be found in the supporting code bundle, just look for the goldhunt_inefficient.py file). Here is a new GoldHunt class:

```
class GoldHunt:
    """Class to play a scenario 'Great Gold Hunt'"""
    def __init__(self, field_coins=5000, field_radius=10.0,
                 search_radius=1.0):
        self.field_coins = field_coins
        self.field_radius = field_radius
        self.search_radius = search_radius

        # Game unit's initial coordinates e.g. (-9.0, 0)
        self.x_ref = - (self.field_radius - self.search_radius)
        self.y_ref = 0.0

        # Distance by which the game unit advances
        # for the next gold search.
        self.move_distance = 2*self.search_radius
```

move distance

The `play` method of this class contains the main logic, as shown in the following screenshot:

```python
def play(self):
    """Logic to play the scenario Great Gold Hunt"""
    total_collected_coins = []

    x_list, y_list = generate_random_points(self.field_radius,
                                            self.field_coins)

    # Loop to collect the gold coins in all the 'search circles'
    while self.x_ref <= 9.0:
        # Find all the coins within a circle defined by 'search_radius'
        coins = self.find_coins(x_list, y_list)

        # Update the list that keeps record of all the collected coins.
        total_collected_coins.extend(coins)

        # Move to the next position along positive X axis
        self.x_ref += self.move_distance

    print("Total collected coins: ", len(total_collected_coins))
```

Let's review the code in the preceding screenshots:

- The input arguments for the `play` method, `field_coins` and `field_radius`, set the number of coins and the radius of the circular gold field, respectively. These are optional arguments with default values, as shown in the `__init__` method. The third optional argument, `search_radius`, helps define the radius of the smaller search circles.

- The `x_ref` and `y_ref` variables represent the *center* of the current search circle. We simplified the problem by assuming a constant `y_ref` of `0.0`.

- The `play` method starts by generating random points representing the scattered gold coins. The `generate_random_points` function returns two Python lists containing the `x` and `y` coordinates of all the coins on the field.

- In a `while` loop, the `total_collected_coins` list stores the coordinates of coins inside the *search circles*, starting with the leftmost one.

- The actual search operation is performed by the `find_coins` method.

Next, let's review the `GoldHunt.find_coins` method:

```python
def find_coins(self, x_list, y_list):
    """Return list of coins that lie within a given distance."""
    collected_coins = []
    for x, y in zip(x_list, y_list):
        # Find distance between the current point and the center
        # of the search circle.
        delta_x = self.x_ref - x
        delta_y = self.y_ref - y
        dist = math.sqrt(delta_x*delta_x + delta_y*delta_y)

        # Check if the point is inside the search circle
        if dist <= self.search_radius:
            collected_coins.append((x, y))

    return collected_coins
```

This method loops over all the points (gold coins) on the field and for each point, it computes its distance from the center of the search circle. With this distance, we can determine whether or not the given gold coin lies inside the perimeter of the search circle. This is shown schematically in the following diagram. The (x_ref, y_ref) coordinates represent the center of the search circle. The (x, y) parameters are the coordinates of any gold coin on the field.

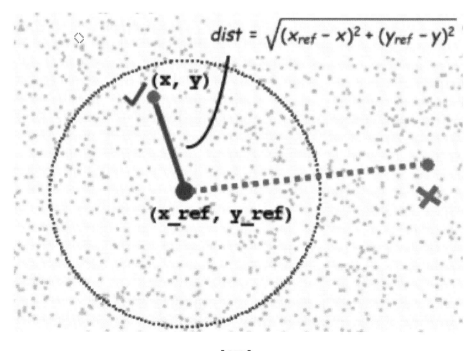

In this diagram, the distance between a point and the center is represented by **dist**. It shows two representative points (or coins). The first one with a *check mark* next to it lies inside the circle, whereas the other one with a *cross mark* is outside. Only the point lying inside the circle is collected. The method returns a `collected_coins` list that contains the location tuples `(x, y)` of all such points.

Let's review the function that creates random points on the field:

```python
def generate_random_points(ref_radius, total_points):
    """Return x.y coords representing random points inside a circle"""
    x = []
    y = []
    for i in range(total_points):
        theta = random.uniform(0.0, 2*math.pi)
        r = ref_radius*math.sqrt(random.uniform(0.0, 1.0))
        x.append(r*math.cos(theta))
        y.append(r*math.sin(theta))

    return x, y
```

You should be able to understand this code fragment fairly easily if you have a basic math background. Here is how it works:

- Consider a point with radius `r` and an angle `theta`.

- The Cartesian coordinates of this point are $x = r*cos(theta)$ and $y = r*sin(theta)$.

- The built-in function, `random.uniform`, is used to randomly vary `r` between `0.0` (the field center) and `ref_radius` (the field radius). Note that the `import` statements are not shown. For that, refer to `goldhunt_inefficient.py`.

- Similarly, the `theta` angle is randomly varied between `0.0` and `2*math.pi` (360 degrees).

Plotting the points

You can visualize the generated random distribution of gold coins using **matplotlib**, a Python plotting library. We won't discuss the plotting techniques here. Check out their website (`http://matplotlib.org`) that hosts a number of tutorials and installation instructions. Python distributions, such as Anaconda, come preinstalled with matplotlib. You can also use the plotting function, `plot_points`, provided in the `goldhunt_inefficient.py` file.

Running the code

The main execution code is as follows:

```
if __name__ == '__main__':
    game = GoldHunt()
    game.play()
```

This code uses the default arguments to instantiate `GoldHunt`. With the default arguments, the code should run smoothly and finish within a few seconds. The actual time will vary depending on your machine configuration, available RAM, and so on. You can add some informative `print` statements to see how the game is progressing. Here is a sample output using the default arguments:

```
[user@hostname ch7]$ python goldhunt_inefficient.py
Circle# 1, center:(-9.0, 0.0), coins: 55
Circle# 2, center:(-7.0, 0.0), coins: 37
Circle# 3, center:(-5.0, 0.0), coins: 54
Circle# 4, center:(-3.0, 0.0), coins: 47
Circle# 5, center:(-1.0, 0.0), coins: 53
Circle# 6, center:(1.0, 0.0), coins: 60
Circle# 7, center:(3.0, 0.0), coins: 44
Circle# 8, center:(5.0, 0.0), coins: 50
Circle# 9, center:(7.0, 0.0), coins: 51
Circle# 10, center:(9.0, 0.0), coins: 51
Total_collected_coins = 502
```

The problem

*In the game scenario, you allowed the users to tweak certain parameters. For example, the users can control the **total number of coins** on the field or modify the **radius of the search circle**. Unknowingly, you opened a new can of worms. For a large input size, the program runs very slow. For example, one variant of the game, **The Great Dwarf of the Foo mountain**, is performing the gold hunt. Let's hear what he has to say:*

If you change `field_coins` from `5000` to `1000000` and set `search_radius` to `0.1`, the application will take quite a bit of time to finish. Here is the updated main execution code with these new parameters:

```
if __name__ == '__main__':
    game = GoldHunt(field_coins=1000000, search_radius=0.1)
    game.play()
```

If you increase the coins further or make the search radius even smaller, it will severely affect the application runtime.

Warning!

If you run the following code, depending on your machine configuration, it can slow down your machine, take longer time to finish, and in some cases (a machine with an average configuration) the computer can stop responding. If you are unsure, it is better not to run it! It is presented here just as an example. If you really want to, then do it at your own risk!

For example, it can take several seconds or minutes to complete this operation. What can we do here to improve the performance? Before jumping to that, let's first review some techniques to identify the bottlenecks.

Identifying the bottlenecks

In the previous section, we saw how a different choice of input parameters degrades the application runtime. Now, we need some way to accurately measure the execution time and find out the performance bottlenecks or the time consuming blocks of the code.

Measuring the execution time

Let's start by monitoring the time taken by the application. To do this, we will use Python's built-in `time` module. The `time.perf_counter` function is a performance counter that returns a clock with the highest available resolution. This function can be used to determine the time interval or the system-wide time difference between the two consecutive calls to the function.

> The `time.perf_counter` function is available in Python versions 3.3 onwards. If you have an older version of Python (for example, version 2.7), use `time.clock()` instead. On Unix, `time.clock()` returns a floating point number within seconds that represents the processor time. On Windows, it returns the elapsed wall-clock time within seconds after the first call to the function.

The original file, `goldhunt_inefficient.py`, already has the following code:

```
import time

if __name__ == '__main__':
    start = time.perf_counter()
    game = GoldHunt()
    game.play()
    end = time.perf_counter()
    print("Total time interval:", end - start)
```

At the beginning of the file, we import the `time` module. The `start` variable marks the beginning of the performance counter, and the `end` variable represents its second consecutive call. In between, we will run the main execution code. The difference between the two values of the counter can be used as an indicator for the runtime of the application. Similarly, you can insert these calls elsewhere in the code to monitor individual code fragments.

Measuring the runtime of small code snippets

The built-in `timeit` module is a useful tool for quickly checking the execution time of a small code fragment. It can be used from the command line or imported and called inside the code. Here is one way to use this functionality using the command-line interface:

```
$ python -m timeit "x = 100*100"
100000000 loops, best of 3: 0.0155 usec per loop
```

The `-m` option allows running the `timeit` module from the command line. In the preceding example, it measures the execution time for the `x = 100*100` statement.

Let's review the output of this execution. The `100000000 loops` in the output indicates how many times the code is executed by `timeit`. It reports the best of three timings. In this example, the best time taken is `0.0155` microseconds for a single execution. You can also tweak the number of times the code is run by using the `--number` argument, as shown in the following code snippet. Here, the code is run only `10` times:

```
$ python -m timeit --number=10  "x = 100*100"
10 loops, best of 3: 0.0838 usec per loop
```

Internally, `timeit` uses `time.perf_counter` to measure the time taken. This is the default implementation since Python version 3.3. For further details, check out the documentation (`https://docs.python.org/3/library/timeit.html`).

Code profiling

The performance measurement techniques that we have seen so far work quite well, especially when you want to run benchmarks for the application. However, it is often cumbersome to implement these timers throughout your project to get a full execution profile. This is where the code profiling helps. It is a technique that analyzes a program while it is running and gathers some important statistics. For example, it reports the duration and frequency of various function calls within that program. This information can be used to identify the performance bottlenecks in the code.

The cProfile module

Let's see how to use `cProfile`, Python's built-in module for code profiling. For illustration purposes, we will use the `profile_ex.py` file from the supporting code bundle. It has three simple functions that do some trivial tasks, as shown in the following screenshot:

```python
def test_1():
    return 100*100

def test_2():
    x = []
    for i in range(10000):
        temp = i/1000.0
        x.append(temp*temp)
    return x

def test_3(condition=False):
    """Trivial recursion example"""
    if condition:
        test_3()

if __name__ == "__main__":
    a = test_1()
    b = test_2()
    c = test_3(True)
```

The cProfile command can either be run from the command prompt or by importing it inside the module to be tested. Here is the output when run from the Command Prompt:

```
File  Edit  View  Search  Terminal  Help
[user@hostname ch]$ python -m cProfile profile_ex.py
        10007 function calls (10006 primitive calls) in 0.008 seconds

   Ordered by: standard name

   ncalls  tottime  percall  cumtime  percall filename:lineno(function
      2/1    0.000    0.000    0.000    0.000 profile_ex.py:12(test_3)
        1    0.000    0.000    0.008    0.008 profile_ex.py:2(<module>
        1    0.000    0.000    0.000    0.000 profile_ex.py:2(test_1)
        1    0.007    0.007    0.008    0.008 profile_ex.py:5(test_2)
        1    0.000    0.000    0.008    0.008 {built-in method exec}
    10000    0.001    0.000    0.001    0.000 {method 'append' of 'lis
        1    0.000    0.000    0.000    0.000 {method 'disable' of '_l

[user@hostname ch]$ █
```

The **IPython** interactive shell also provides a convenient magic command called %prun. With this, you can quickly profile a Python statement. For more information, check out https://ipython.org/ipython-doc/3/interactive/magics.html.

Let's understand the output of this run:

- The first line of the output shows the total number of function calls monitored. A majority of these are due to for loop inside test_2. For each iteration, it calls the append function of the Python list datatype.

- On the same output line, it also reports the number of primitive calls. These are the function calls that do not involve **recursion**. The test_3 function shows an example of recursion. To understand this better, run the code by printing the value of the input argument condition. In this case, there is only one recursive function call.

- The ncalls column indicates the number of function calls. If you add them up, the total number of calls becomes 10007, same as the ones reported on the first line of the output. Notice that for test_3, it reports the function calls as 2/1. It means that the function was called twice but one of the calls was recursive.

- The tottime column indicates the total time spent in a given function.

- The percall column records the quotient of the totcall/ncalls division.

- The time spent inside a particular function, including its sub-functions, is reported by cumtime (the cumulative time).

- The percall column reports the cumtime/primitive calls quotient.

- The last column is, essentially, the data related to the functions. It includes the built-in function calls, such as the append method of the Python list, and so on.

By default, the output is sorted by standard name. To understand the bottlenecks, this sorting order is not quite useful. Instead, you can sort by cumulative time, number of function calls, and so on. This is accomplished using the command-line option, -s. For a complete list of available sorting options, refer to https://docs.python.org/3/library/profile.html.

The following screenshot shows the output sorted by `tottime`. Observe that it spends the most time in the `test_2` function.

```
e  Edit  View  Search  Terminal  Help   ■■■■■■■■■■■■■
er@hostname ch]$ python -m cProfile -s tottime profile_ex.py
       10007 function calls (10006 primitive calls) in 0.008 seconds

Ordered by: internal time

ncalls  tottime  percall  cumtime  percall filename:lineno(function
     1    0.007    0.007    0.008    0.008 profile_ex.py:5(test_2)
 10000    0.001    0.000    0.001    0.000 {method 'append' of 'lis
     1    0.000    0.000    0.008    0.008 profile_ex.py:2(<module>
     1    0.000    0.000    0.008    0.008 {built-in method exec}
   2/1    0.000    0.000    0.000    0.000 profile_ex.py:12(test_3)
     1    0.000    0.000    0.000    0.000 profile_ex.py:2(test_1)
     1    0.000    0.000    0.000    0.000 {method 'disable' of '_l
```

Now that we know how to use `cProfile`, let's use it to analyze the *Gold Hunt* problem. Run the original `goldhunt_inefficient.py` file with all the default options, as follows:

```
$ python -m cProfile goldhunt_inefficient.py
```

It prints a lot of information in the terminal window as there are several of the internal function calls involved. Optionally, you can redirect `stdout` to a text file. To effectively analyze this data, Python provides a built-in module called `pstats`. Let's see how to use it in the following section.

The pstats module

The `pstats` module can be used to further process the profiling data generated by `cProfile`. It gives you greater control over creating your reports as compared to the limited options provided by `cProfile`. The analysis of the data generated by `cProfile` is done using the `pstats.Stats` class. To make the `cProfile` output usable by `pstats`, we will need to write it to a file using the command-line option, `-o`, as follows:

```
$ python -m cProfile -o profile_output goldhunt_inefficient.py
```

The `profile_output` file, thus generated, is not human readable. While we can go on and feed this file to `pstats.Stats`, it is better to automate the whole process by stitching together these two utilities. Here is a simplified code that does this:

```python
import cProfile
import pstats
from goldhunt_inefficient import GoldHunt

def view_stats(fil, text_restriction):
    """View the pstats for the given file"""

    stats = pstats.Stats(fil)
    # Remove the long directory paths
    stats.strip_dirs()
    # Sort the stats by the total time (internal time)
    sorted_stats = stats.sort_stats('tottime')
    # Only show stats that have "goldhunt" in their 'name column'
    sorted_stats.print_stats("goldhunt")

def play_game():
    """Control function to execute the GoldHunt game"""
    game = GoldHunt()
    game.play()

if __name__ == '__main__':
    filname = 'profile_output_new'
    cProfile.run('play_game()', filname)
    # View the pstats
    view_stats(filname, "goldhunt")
```

Warning

This is a simplified example without any error checks! For example, the code does not check if the output file already exists. To make the code robust, add such checks and the try...except clauses wherever appropriate.

This code is also available as `profiling_goldhunt.py` in the supporting code bundle for this chapter. Let's quickly review what this code does:

- The main execution code shows a way to run `cProfile` using its `run` method. The first argument to `run` is the function (or statement) to be monitored, whereas the second argument is the filename where the profiling output is stored.

- The `view_stats` function is where we use the functionality from `pstats`. This function takes the generated profiling output (`filname`) as the first argument. It is used while creating an instance of `pstats.Stats`.

- The `strip_dirs` method of the `Stats` class is used to remove all leading path information strings from filenames. This reduces the clutter in the final output by just displaying the name of the file.

- Using the `print_stats` method, we can impose some restrictions in the final output. In this example, it looks for the `goldhunt` string in the rightmost columns and displays the matching row, ignoring all others. Put in another way, it limits the information related to the function calls inside `goldhunt_inefficient.py`.

> The `pstats.Stats` class provides several other useful features. For example, the `print_callees` method prints a list of all the functions that were called by the function being monitored. For further details, check out the Python documentation (`https://docs.python.org/3/library/profile.html#pstats.Stats`).

This code can be run from the command prompt, as follows (it has a dependency on `goldhunt_inefficient.py` so put it in the same directory as this file):

```
$ python profiling_goldhunt.py
```

Here is the sample output of this run (only the output pertaining to the statistics is shown):

```
     95556 function calls in 0.042 seconds

Ordered by: internal time
List reduced from 19 to 5 due to restriction <'goldhunt'>

ncalls  tottime  percall  cumtime  percall filename:lineno(function)
    10    0.023    0.002    0.027    0.003 goldhunt_inefficient.py:101(find_coins)
     1    0.008    0.008    0.015    0.015 goldhunt_inefficient.py:32(generate_random_points)
     1    0.000    0.000    0.042    0.042 profiling_goldhunt.py:30(play_game)
     1    0.000    0.000    0.042    0.042 goldhunt_inefficient.py:119(play)
     1    0.000    0.000    0.000    0.000 goldhunt_inefficient.py:85(__init__)
```

This is significantly less output and is restricted to the function calls from the program we wish to monitor. As indicated in the output, only 5 out of 19 function calls are listed. The list is sorted by the total internal time taken to execute the functions. The two functions, `find_coins` and `generate_random_points`, top the chart! Their order may vary depending on the values we choose for the `field_coins` and `search_radius` variables. But essentially, the code profiling has helped us identify the most time consuming code in our application.

Good question! It will certainly help if we can peep inside the function and see the line-by-line profiling output. Luckily, there is a tool that enables exactly this. Let's review it next.

The line_profiler package

The `line_profiler` package is a third-party Python package that can be installed using `pip`:

```
$ pip install line_profiler
```

This package can be used to monitor the performance of a function, line by line. When you install the package, it also creates an executable `kernprof`.

On Linux, this executable is created at the same location as your Python executable. For example, on Linux, if Python is available as `/usr/bin/python`, this executable is created as `/usr/bin/kernprof` (or look for the `kernprof.py` script). On Windows OS, it should be created at the same location as `pip.exe`. Refer to *Chapter 1, Developing Simple Applications* for the `pip.exe` path.

 On Windows OS, if you encounter any error, such as **error: Unable to find vcvarsall.bat**, you will probably need to use Visual C++ Express. Check out https://www.visualstudio.com/en-US/products/visual-studio-express-vs for more information.

Using this tool requires trivial changes to the code. All you need to do is add a @profile decorator above the function or method name, as shown in the following screenshot:

```
@profile
def find_coins(self, x_list, y_list):
    """Return list of coins that lie within a given distance...."""
    collected_coins = []
    # Rest if the code follows (not shown)...
```

Then, run the tool using the kernprof command as follows:

```
$ kernprof -v -l goldhunt_inefficient.py
```

The -v or --view option displays the results of the profile output in the terminal window. The profiler also creates an output file, goldhunt_inefficient.py.lprof. The -l or --line-by-line option uses the line-by-line profiler from the line_profiler module.

> Be sure to remove the decorator @profile when you are not profiling the application using the line_profiler. In other words, remove it while running the application, as:
>
> ```
> $ python goldhunt_inefficient.py
> ```
>
> Otherwise, it will raise a NameError exception.

The line_profiler output for the find_coins method is shown below.

As you can see, quite a bit of time is spent computing the distance between the points (gold coins) and the center of the search circle.

```
Total time: 0.147367 s
File: goldhunt_inefficient.py
Function: find_coins at line 100
```

Line #	Hits	Time	Per Hit	% Time	Line Contents
100					@profile
101					def find_coins(self, x_list, y_list):
102					"""Return list of coins that lie within a given distanc
103					
104					:param x_list: List of x coordinates of all the coins (
105					:param y_list: List of y coordinates of all the coins (
106					:return: A list containing (x,y) coordinates of all the
107					"""
108	10	11	1.1	0.0	collected_coins = []
109					# Rest if the code follows (not shown)...
110	50010	26679	0.5	18.1	for x, y in zip(x_list, y_list):
111	50000	28873	0.6	19.6	delta_x = self.x_ref - x
112	50000	26053	0.5	17.7	delta_y = self.y_ref - y
113	50000	36244	0.7	24.6	dist = math.sqrt(delta_x*delta_x + delta_y*delta_y)
114					
115	50000	29127	0.6	19.8	if dist <= self.search_radius:
116	467	373	0.8	0.3	collected_coins.append((x, y))

Similarly, if you see the output for the `generate_random_point` function, the majority of the time is spent while creating a random combination of the `theta` angle and the `r` radius, which is used to define a point (a gold coin).

Memory profiling

The profiling techniques we have covered so far aim at finding the runtime bottlenecks. Let's briefly discuss memory profiling, another important aspect of profiling.

The memory_profiler package

For memory profiling, we will use a popular Python package called `memory_profiler`. It can be installed using `pip`. Here is how to install it on Linux from the command line:

```
$ pip install memory_profiler
```

The documentation highly recommends installing the `psutils` module. It also suggests that, in order for `memory_profiler` to work on Windows OS, you will need the `psutil` module. The `psutil` module can be installed using `pip`, as follows:

```
$ pip install psutil
```

 For more information on `memory_profiler`, check out the following page: `https://pypi.python.org/pypi/memory_profiler`.

Just like `line_profiler`, the `memory_profiler` package uses the `@profile` decorator above the function name. Let's add the decorator `@profile` just above the `generate_random_points` function, and then run the memory profiler on the `goldhunt_inefficient.py` file. The command to run this is as follows:

```
$ python -m memory_profiler goldhunt_inefficient.py
```

Here is the output of the memory profiler. It reports the line-by-line memory consumption. Note that the profiler prints the whole function, including the docstrings. For ease of illustration, part of the docstring is not shown.

```
Line #    Mem usage    Increment   Line Contents
================================================
    30    52.188 MiB   0.000 MiB   @profile
    31                             def generate_random_points(ref_radius, total_points):
    32                                 """Return x, y coordinate lists representing random points
    33    52.188 MiB   0.000 MiB       x = []
    34    52.188 MiB   0.000 MiB       y = []
    35    52.188 MiB   0.000 MiB       show_plot = False
    36
    37    52.574 MiB   0.387 MiB       for i in range(total_points):
    38    52.574 MiB   0.000 MiB           theta = random.uniform(0.0, 2*math.pi)
    39    52.574 MiB   0.000 MiB           r = ref_radius*math.sqrt(random.uniform(0.0, 1.0))
    40    52.574 MiB   0.000 MiB           x.append(r*math.cos(theta))
    41    52.574 MiB   0.000 MiB           y.append(r*math.sin(theta))
    42
    43    52.574 MiB   0.000 MiB       if show_plot:
    44                                     plot_points(ref_radius, x, y)
    45
    46    52.574 MiB   0.000 MiB       return x, y
```

The line number in the code is shown in the first column. The second column, Mem Usage, tells us how much memory the Python interpreter consumes after executing that line number. The unit of the memory is **mebibyte (MiB)**.The third column, Increment, gives the memory difference between the current line and the previous line. If the memory is released by the current line of code, then the Increment column shows a negative number. The last column shows the actual line of code. As can be seen from the Increment column, the memory is mainly consumed in the for loop. We will use the memory profiler in the next chapter to compare the memory efficiency of a **generator expression** and a **list comprehension**.

Algorithm efficiency and complexity

An algorithm is a set of instructions to solve a particular problem. In this context, an algorithm can be a function or even a simple operation that adds two numbers. Let's understand two related terms: algorithm efficiency and algorithm complexity.

Algorithm efficiency

Algorithm efficiency indicates the computation resources consumed by an algorithm. Typically, the lower the resource consumption, the better the efficiency. The computational resources can mean several things. One can be talking about the runtime (CPU usage), the memory consumption (RAM or hard disk) or the network consumption, or a combination of these.

The application requirement determines which resource takes precedence over the others. For example, in a web application, the network usage can be more important than the disk space. For a scientific application, you might have all the memory you need but the runtime can be a pain in the neck, and so on. In this book, we will limit our discussion to the runtime efficiency only.

Algorithm complexity

Suppose you have a program (an algorithm) that processes some data in five minutes. If you increase the size of the data, how much time will the program need? The answer lies in the algorithm complexity. It tells us how well the algorithm will scale if you increase the size of the problem. In other words, the computational complexity influences the performance of the algorithm. In the next section, you will learn how to represent the computational complexity.

Big O notation

In simple terms, the big O or big Oh notation is a way to represent the computational complexity of an algorithm. Here, the O is the letter *O*, as in *order*, and not the number zero. The big O indicates an upper bound or the worst-case scenario of the complexity of an algorithm (details to follow in the next section). This concept can be better explained with an example. Let's take a look at the following code:

```
num = 100
x = []
for i in range(num):
    x.append(i)
```

Let's call this trivial code fragment an algorithm. It is a simple operation that appends a number to the `list` inside a `for` loop. Here, `num` represents the size of the input used by the algorithm. If you increase `num`, the algorithm will have to do more work inside the `for` loop. Increase it further, and the poor algorithm will have to do even more work. Thus, the time taken by the algorithm depends on the value of `num` and can be expressed as a growth function, *f(n)*. Here, *n* represents the size of the input that corresponds to `num` in this example.

 Making sense so far? You can also test this by measuring the execution time. To see a real difference, choose a larger value of num.

In this algorithm, the most time consuming piece is the `for` loop, and it will determine the overall runtime of the algorithm. Inside the `for` loop, each call to `x.append(i)` takes constant time, *t*, to finish. For a large value of `num`, the total time taken by the loop will be approximately *num*(t)*. Thus, the runtime efficiency of the whole algorithm relative to `num` is linear. In terms of the big O notation, this particular algorithm is said to have *O(n)* complexity.

Big O complexity classes

Let's review some big O complexity classes. The following chart annotates various complexity classes and shows how *f(n)* influences the running time of algorithms:

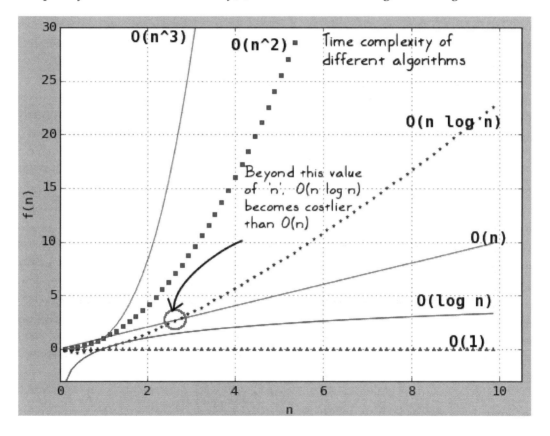

On the *y* axis, we have the *f(n)* function, and the *x* axis represents the input size, *n* (the `num` variable in the previous discussion). The plot compares some common functions that represent the time complexity of algorithms.

It should be noted that the big O representation does not include the constants. So, even if two algorithms share the same big O complexity, they can clock a very different runtime performance. The circle marker in the plot shows a typical crossover point between two complexity functions. In this example, this is between *O(n)* and *O(n log n)*. As noted earlier, the individual algorithms representing these complexity functions will have different constant multipliers (not reflected in the big O notation). Tweaking those multipliers can change where this crossover happens.

Let's briefly review these notations now.

O(1) – constant time

Regardless of the value of the input size, the time taken by the algorithm remains constant. Getting the length of a Python list (`len(x)`, where x is the list) or the `append` list operation we saw earlier, are a few examples of *O(1)* complexity.

O(log n) – logarithmic

The time required by the algorithm is proportional to the logarithm of the input size. One of the examples of logarithmic complexity is a **binary search algorithm**. It starts with inspecting the middle element of a sorted array. If the value being searched is lower than the middle element, the entire upper half, including this middle element, is eliminated from the search. We can do this because it is a **sorted array**. This process is repeated for the remaining half and it continues until we find the desired value.

Confused? Let's see what Fairy is up to these days…

Fairy has lost her enchanted locket in a room full of treasure chests. These boxes are numbered 1 to 100 and are arranged in increasing order. In other words, the boxes are sorted and the locket is placed in one of them. She is trying to find it with the help of her magical wand. The wand knows that the locket is in, for instance, box number 82, but it won't give a straight answer! It expects her to ask the right questions.

She is standing exactly in the middle of the room and in front of box 50. Towards her left, she sees numbers 1 to 49; and towards the right, numbers 51 to 100, in that order.

She asks her wand, is the locket in box 50? The wand says "no". She further asks, is the number greater than 50 or less than 50? The wand answers "greater than 50".

With this answer, she ignores the boxes on the left side (1-49), including box 50, and stands in the middle of the group, to her right (51-100). Now, she has box 75 in front of her. She repeats the questions with box 75 as the reference. Each time, half of the remaining chests are eliminated. The search operation goes on until she finds her locket in box 82.

This is the binary search in a nutshell. You can find more information on Wikipedia (`https://en.wikipedia.org/wiki/Binary_search_algorithm`). In the worst case scenario, the time complexity of this search is *O(log n)*. Another way to look at the logarithmic complexity is as follows. For an exponential increase in the size of the problem *n*, the time taken by the algorithm increases linearly. As can be seen in the earlier chart, the *O(log n)* time complexity is better compared to the *O(n)* (linear-time) complexity, but not as good as *O(1)*.

O(n) – Linear time

We already saw an example where a `for` loop makes the algorithm of the *O(n)* complexity. Finding a min or max element in a Python list and copying a list or a dictionary are some other examples of this complexity.

O(n log n) – Log linear

An example of a log linear time complexity is a **quicksort algorithm**. Let's call Fairy one more time to get a better idea of the working of this algorithm.

Fairy enters another treasure room and finds it extremely disorganized. The treasure chests are randomly scattered everywhere in the room. Not liking this, she decides to sort the chests in an increasing order of their value (or price). Initially, the chests are randomly placed, like this:

[5 3 2 4 9 7 8 8]

Here, the number represents the value of each chest. Fairy starts picking a pivot chest, say with a value tag of 5. She then rearranges the chests into three sections: (i) The ones with a value lower than 5 are on the left side of the pivot, (ii) the pivotal chest 5, (iii) and the values greater than 5 are on the right side. This is shown below:

[3 2 4 5 9 7 8 8]

Next, with 5 fixed to its position, she repeats the preceding procedure to the items on the left and right sides of 5. For example, consider only the left side of 5:

[3 2 4]

The fairy chooses number 3 as a new pivot and arranges the values to the left and right of 3, as shown earlier. This rearrangement results in:

[2 3 4]

The process goes on until all the chests are sorted in the increasing order of the valuables, as shown below:

[2 3 4 5 7 8 8 9]

This is the basic quicksort operation and has the complexity of *O(n log n)*. As shown in the earlier chart, for a higher value of *n*, the *O(n log n)* complexity is expensive compared to *O(n)*, but it is much better than the quadratic complexity.

It should be noted that *O(n log n)* is the **average-case** complexity of the quicksort algorithm. Refer to the section, *Upper bound (worst-case) of the complexity*, of this chapter to learn about average-case and worst-case complexities.

O(n²) – Quadratic

This represents the quadratic runtime complexity. The time required to run the program grows as square of the size of the input to the algorithm. Let's extend the previous example to understand this further:

```
num = 100
x = []
for i in range(num):
    for j in range(num):
        x.append(i)
```

It is a nested `for` loop. Let *t* be the time it takes to append an element to the list. As mentioned earlier, a single append operation is of *O(1)* complexity. The inner `for` loop will take approximately *n*t* (or *num*t*) to execute. Since we have an outer `for` loop, the total time complexity becomes *n*(n*t)*. A classic example of this complexity is a **bubble sort algorithm** (https://en.wikipedia.org/wiki/Bubble_sort). This algorithm sorts a list in an iterative manner, and it repeatedly swaps the adjacent elements of the list if these elements are placed in a wrong order.

O(n³) – cubic

This is a cubic complexity, which is worse than the quadratic complexity. A small increase in the problem size will result in a big increase in the runtime. Adding another outer `for` loop in the illustration on quadratic complexity will make it *O(n³)*.

This is only a partial list of complexity classes. There are many more. For further information, check out https://en.wikipedia.org/wiki/Big_O_notation.

Upper bound of the complexity

Let's revisit the statement we made earlier: "Big O notation indicates an upper bound or the worst-case scenario of the complexity of an algorithm". Quite a mouthful? An explanation is in order. We will reuse the illustration used in the discussion on the $O(n^2)$ complexity:

```
num = 100
x = []
for i in range(num):
    for j in range(num):
        x.append(i)
```

We already saw that a single `x.append(i)` operation is $O(1)$, the inner loop is $O(N)$, and the full nested `for` loop has the time complexity of $O(n^2)$. Then why do we say that the complexity of the algorithm as a whole is $O(n^2)$?

If you look at the earlier chart that compared various complexities, $O(n^2)$ is the costliest among these three complexities and thus the most significant part of it. In other words, the algorithm complexity cannot get worse than $O(n^2)$. Now, read the earlier statement on upper bounds one more time. The big O notation represents the worst-case scenario of the complexity of the algorithm. This is the reason why the big O complexity class for this algorithm is represented as $O(n^2)$.

Average-case time complexity:

Most of the time, an algorithm is analyzed by measuring its worst-case complexity. However, there are some problems where it makes practical sense to measure the **average-case time complexity**. Here, the amount of time taken to run the algorithm is averaged over all possible inputs. The quicksort algorithm we saw earlier is a classic example where average-case complexity is useful. It determines the real (or practical) efficiency of the algorithm. The average-case time complexity of this algorithm is $O(n \log n)$, whereas the worst-case complexity is $O(n^2)$. For more information, check out `https://en.wikipedia.org/wiki/Average-case_complexity`.

Complexity for common data structures and algorithms

The following table summarizes the time complexity of a few frequently performed operations on some Python data structures. This is not an exhaustive list, for that, see the Python wiki (`https://wiki.python.org/moin/TimeComplexity`). It documents the time complexity of several other operations on these data structures.

Data structure	Operation	Time complexity	Example
list	search (check for membership)	O(n)	`x in lst`
	index (accessing a value)	O(1)	`x[i]`
	append	O(1)	`x.append(10)`
	delete	O(n)	`del lst[i]`
	iteration	O(n)	`for i in lst`
dict	search (check for membership)	O(1) (average-case)	`x in d`
	index (accessing a value)	O(1) (average-case)	`d[key]`
	delete	O(1) (average-case)	`del d[key]`
	iteration	O(n)	`for key in d`
set	search (check for membership)	O(1) (average-case)	`x in s`
	index (accessing a value)	O(1) (average-case)	`d[x]`
	delete	O(1) (average-case)	`del s[e]`
	iteration	O(n)	`for i in s`

The following table summarizes the time complexity of some common algorithms along with the Python functions that implement them. Note that the functions listed are from the NumPy library. Although the next chapter will introduce you to NumPy, we won't specifically talk about these functions in this book.

Algorithm	Time complexity		Python functions (standard functions in numpy library)	Notes
	Average-case	Worst-case		
Binary search	O(log n)	O(log n)	`numpy.searchsorted`	Also called half-interval search algorithm
Quicksort	O(n log n)	O(n²)	`numpy.sort`	Use optional argument kind='quicksort'
Mergesort	O(n log n)	O(n log n)	`numpy.sort`	Use optional argument kind='mergesort'
Heapsort	O(n log n)	O(n log n)	`numpy.sort`	Use optional argument kind='heapsort'
Bubblesort	O(n²)	O(n²)	---	No standard Python function available

The first algorithm listed in the preceding table is a binary search algorithm. This was already illustrated when we talked about the *O(log n)* or logarithmic complexity. The `numpy.searchsorted` function uses binary search to find array indices where the elements need to be inserted to maintain order. The remaining algorithms in this table are a few common sorting algorithms that put elements in a list in a specific order. We already talked about quicksort. To learn more about the other algorithms, refer to `https://en.wikipedia.org/wiki/Sorting_algorithm`.

Wrapping up the big O discussion

Let's summarize what you learned about the big O notation so far:

- Big O enables us to compare different algorithms in terms of their time (or space) complexity. This helps us choose the right algorithm (if possible) or determine the strategy to implement changes that speed things up.

- It gives us the growth rate of an algorithm, but it will not give us the absolute value of the runtime. For example, some algorithm A takes 10 minutes to execute. On the same machine, algorithm B takes 200 minutes to execute, and guess what—both algorithms have the same complexity, say *O(n)*. Although they have different execution times, they have one thing in common, the time taken linearly increases with their problem size.

> *Glad you brought that up! The big O notation indicates the worst-case scenario of an algorithm, and it rules other (less costly) complexity classes present in that algorithm. In other words, the worst-case complexity drives the performance of that algorithm.*

It is good to be aware of the complexity, especially when the problem size is large. For a very small problem, it may or may not make a huge difference. A good practice is to analyze the existing algorithm for the performance bottlenecks, and then see if it is worth revamping the algorithm for speedup. Weigh in the factors, such as the time you spend on changing the algorithm and its impact on the quality (bugs and testing) versus the long term benefit of the speedup accomplished. In a nutshell, choose the strategy that best fits your needs.

It is also worth noting that sometimes you have to live with an algorithm with a certain complexity class. But that is not the end of the road. You can still implement techniques to speedup the code without changing its order of complexity. The performance improvement obtained will depend on the problem in hand. For example, you can parallelize the code or compute some parameters in advance to achieve speedup. Later in this book, we will cover basics of parallelization in Python.

Summary

This chapter was the first one in the series of three chapters based on performance. It laid the ground work to improve application performance. We learned how to record the runtime using the `time` module. We also saw how the `timeit` module can be used to measure the performance of small pieces of code. We took a practical problem where an application ran fine when working with a small input, but, as the input grew larger, it slowed down considerably. With this example, we learned how to identify the bottlenecks using `cProfile` and display the results using `pstats`.

We saw how the `line_profiler` module can help locate the time consuming statements inside a function. While most of the discussion was focused on the runtime performance, we briefly covered the `memory_profiler` module. This module enabled line-by-line analysis of memory consumption for the given functions. Finally, we learned about the big O notation that represents the computational complexity of an algorithm.

Now that we have identified the performance bottlenecks, let's move on to the next chapter to improve the application performance.

8
Improving Performance – Part One

Let's recap what you learned in the previous chapter. We started with a program that appeared harmless until some parameters were tweaked. This change revealed performance issues. Hence, we performed a *search operation* (profiling) to catch the *culprits* (the bottlenecks). Now, let's see what we can do to speed up the application code. To be specific, we will cover the following topics:

- Cutting down the runtime of the *Gold Hunt* application

- Learning to improve the application performance using the following ways:

    ° Making changes to the algorithm

    ° Avoiding the function re-evaluation

    ° Using the list and dictionary comprehensions

    ° Using generator expressions

    ° Using tricks to improve the performance of code involving loops

    ° Choosing the right data structures

    ° Discussing the `collections` and `itertools` modules briefly

In summary, this chapter will cover several (but not all) techniques to speed up the application. Some of these can be directly applied to alleviate the performance problems of the *Gold Hunt* scenario from the previous chapter. For the rest, we will use generic examples to illustrate the efficacy of those techniques.

Prerequisite for the chapter

Have you already read *Chapter 7, Performance – Identifying Bottlenecks*? It teaches you how to identify the performance bottlenecks. A part of this chapter uses the same problem that was discussed in the previous chapter and gradually improves its performance. Also, in this chapter, it is assumed that you already know how to profile the code.

This is how the chapter is organized

We will start with first part of the performance improvements for the *Gold Hunt* scenario. The aim is to provide you with a practical example of how to approach the problem and gradually cut down the runtime. The following chart shows a preview of what will be accomplished by the end of this chapter—this is the same chart shown in the previous chapter. The application runtime is about to be cut down by more than 50%!

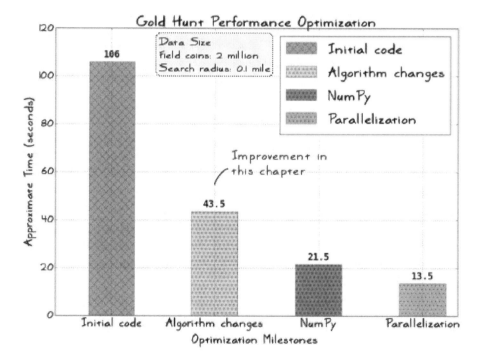

The second half of this book will show you many ways to improve the application speed. For this discussion, we will use generic examples, as not all techniques can be applied directly to the *Gold Hunt* scenario. The second half will serve as a handy reference for performance improvements.

The Python wiki has documented several performance improvement tips. Some of these will be covered here. Refer to `https://wiki.python.org/moin/PythonSpeed/PerformanceTips` for further details.

Revisiting the Gold Hunt scenario

At this point, you should go back to *Chapter 7, Performance – Identifying Bottlenecks*, and refresh your memory on the *Gold Hunt* scenario. To summarize the problem, a circular field has gold coins scattered all over and you need to pick as many coins as you can while traveling across the field. However, you can only pick the coins lying inside the small search circles. We wrote an application code and discussed how tweaking the `search_radius` and `field_coins` (total scattered coins) parameters impact the performance. In the upcoming discussion, we will gradually improve the performance of this code.

Selecting a problem size

*In order to see a real difference in the timing after optimizing the code, let's increase the problem size further. In the previous chapter, **The Great Dwarf** wanted us to put one million coins on the field. **Let's double the deal**. Now, there are **two million** gold coins up for grabs! In short,* `search_radius` *and* `field_coins` *will be set to* `0.1` *and* `2000000`, *respectively.*

Caution! Read this before running any example

Running the examples in this chapter can consume a lot of computational resources (the sample output will be shown in this chapter so you don't have to run these). The `goldhunt_0.py` file, for instance, takes nearly two minutes to complete on a 64 bit Linux machine with an 8 GB RAM and a good processor with only a few running tasks. It also consumes quite a bit of memory during the execution. The performance is not that bad for this system configuration. In general, it will depend on the specifications of your machine. So, be careful! One strategy is to set `field_coins=5000` and `search_radius=1` and see how well the application runs. Then, progressively tweak these parameters to an acceptable configuration.

Profiling the initial code

We will start with the source `goldhunt_0.py` file (see the supporting code for the chapter). This is same as `goldhunt_inefficient.py` except for the following:

- It profiles the game execution using `cProfile` and prints the statistics. Thus, it also includes the functions from the `profiling_goldhunt.py` module. Although combining these two modules is not the best practice, it will help simplify the upcoming illustrations.

- The updated `play_game()` function is shown next. It uses the new parameter values, as shown:

```python
def play_game():
    """Control function to execute the GoldHunt game"""
    game = GoldHunt(field_coins=2000000, search_radius=0.1)
    game.play()


if __name__ == '__main__':
    filname = 'profile_output_new'
    cProfile.run('play_game()',filname)
    # View the pstats
    view_stats(filname, "goldhunt")
```

The code can be run as follows—if necessary, tweak the input arguments to `GoldHunt()`:

```
$ python goldhunt_0.py
```

The following screenshot shows the profiling statistics for this run:

```
     208019639 function calls in 106.265 seconds

Ordered by: internal time
List reduced from 21 to 5 due to restriction <'goldhunt'>

ncalls  tottime  percall  cumtime  percall filename:lineno(function)
    95   87.911    0.925  100.041    1.053 goldhunt_0.py:105(find_coins)
     1    3.469    3.469    6.172    6.172 goldhunt_0.py:35(generate_random_points)
     1    0.045    0.045  106.265  106.265 goldhunt_0.py:163(play_game)
     1    0.002    0.002  106.220  106.220 goldhunt_0.py:124(play)
     1    0.000    0.000    0.000    0.000 goldhunt_0.py:88(__init__)
```

Notice that `find_coins` eats up a significant amount of time. The next on the list is `generate_random_points`. Let's see what we can do to improve the performance.

Optimizing Gold Hunt – Part one

It is time for some action. This section is organized in the following manner—you will learn some techniques to optimize the code and speedup the application. These techniques will be directly applied to improve the performance of the *Gold Hunt* game.

This is the first part of the optimization task. Here, the performance will be improved in three steps. We will call these *optimization pass one*, *pass two*, and *pass three*. After implementing each of these strategies, the code will be re-profiled to get an understanding of the speedup accomplished. Let's get started with *optimization pass one*.

Tweaking the algorithm – The square root

The profiling output (refer to the *Profiling the initial code* section) shows the `find_distance` method as the bottleneck. As a starter, let's make some changes to this algorithm so that it runs faster. Here is the original method that was presented in the *Reviewing the initial code* section in *Chapter 7, Performance – Identifying Bottlenecks*:

```python
def find_coins(self, x_list, y_list):
    """Return list of coins that lie within a given distance."""
    collected_coins = []
    for x, y in zip(x_list, y_list):
        # Find distance between the current point and the center
        # of the search circle.
        delta_x = self.x_ref - x
        delta_y = self.y_ref - y
        dist = math.sqrt(delta_x*delta_x + delta_y*delta_y)

        # Check if the point is inside the search circle
        if dist <= self.search_radius:
            collected_coins.append((x, y))

    return collected_coins
```

The method computes the distance to each gold coin from the center of the search circle and determines whether or not the given gold coin lies inside the search circle. The computed distance, denoted by `dist`, is a square root.

Do we really need to compute a square root? The square root computation is time consuming and in this case unnecessary. All we are doing is just comparing two numbers. Can we avoid that by comparing the square of two numbers instead? Confused? Have a look at the following comparison:

$$a = 4, \quad b = 9 \implies a < b$$

$$\sqrt{a} = 2, \quad \sqrt{b} = 3 \implies \sqrt{a} < \sqrt{b}$$

We have two positive numbers, *a*=4 and *b*=9. Obviously, *a* is smaller than *b*. So, the comparison *a* < *b* will always return `true`. This is applicable even for the comparison of their square roots. The same logic can be applied to our problem. The `dist` and `self.search_radius` variables can be considered as square roots of two numbers. We have got the following code:

```
dist = math.sqrt(delta_x*delta_x + delta_y*delta_y)
```

Or, we can say `dist` is the square root of some number, `dist_square`, given as follows:

```
dist_square = delta_x*delta_x + delta_y*delta_y
```

Next, we already know the value of `self.search_radius`. Now, imagine it as a square root of another number, `search_radius_square`. This number is not already available, and it needs to be computed as follows:

```
search_radius_square = self.search_radius*self.search_radius
```

As the last step, we will need to compare these two numbers instead of their square roots:

```
if dist_square <= search_radius_square:
    # more code follows...
```

> OK, we are not finding the 'square root', but now it requires us to do a new computation... the 'square' of the search radius! How is that going to help??

That's a good observation! It requires us to do an extra computation to find out the square of self.search_radius. *But, we do not need to compute that for every iteration inside the* for *loop. The* self.search_radius *does not change inside the loop. So, this computation can be done just once before the* for *loop.*

Gold Hunt optimization – Pass one

Putting it all together, the updated `find_coins` method is shown next:

```python
def find_coins(self, x_list, y_list):
    """Return list of coins that lie within a given distance...."""
    collected_coins = []
    # Compute the square
    search_radius_square = self.search_radius*self.search_radius

    for x, y in zip(x_list, y_list):
        delta_x = self.x_ref - x
        delta_y = self.y_ref - y
        # No need to compute the actual distance which is
        # square-root of the following number.
        dist_square = delta_x*delta_x + delta_y*delta_y

        # Just compare the squares of the distances!
        if dist_square <= search_radius_square:
            collected_coins.append((x, y))

    return collected_coins
```

It is now time to profile this code again and see if we get any improvement in the performance. The supporting source file, `goldhunt_pass1.py`, has these changes incorporated. It can be run as follows:

`$ python goldhunt_pass1.py`

The following screenshot shows the profiling statistics for this run:

```
        18019402 function calls in 55.740 seconds

Ordered by: internal time
List reduced from 21 to 5 due to restriction <'goldhunt'>

ncalls  tottime  percall  cumtime  percall filename:lineno(function)
    95   49.703    0.523   49.708    0.523 goldhunt_pass1.py:107(find_coins)
     1    3.260    3.260    5.981    5.981 goldhunt_pass1.py:38(generate_random_points)
     1    0.043    0.043   55.740   55.740 goldhunt_pass1.py:169(play_game)
     1    0.002    0.002   55.697   55.697 goldhunt_pass1.py:127(play)
     1    0.000    0.000    0.000    0.000 goldhunt_pass1.py:91(__init__)
```

Compare the timings with that of the original code. There is a significant improvement in the application's runtime. Earlier, the total runtime was more than 100 seconds, but this optimization has brought it down to less than 60 seconds! You can also compare the first row in the output (find_coins) against the original timings. The timings noted by the profiler will depend on the machine specifications and the input values chosen.

> The timings will vary slightly even if you run the same program again. There are two reasons behind this; first, we are distributing the gold coins randomly on the field. As a result, for each run, there will be a variation in the total number of coins appended to the list. The second factor that influences this is the other running processes on your system. Ideally, you should run it under the same environment to reduce these variations (or *noise*). For example, close other running applications so that they don't interfere with the timing. During the performance benchmarking process, quite often, the same application is run multiple times and an average time is noted to reduce the effect of these variations.

Skipping the dots

The **dot** notation in Python enables access to the attributes of the given object. Take a look at the following code from the previous example. This is taken from the for loop of the find_coins method:

```
for x, y in zip(x_list, y_list):
    # Some code follows...
    # ...
    if dist_square <= search radius square:
        collected_coins.append((x, y))
```

In this loop, for every iteration, the collected_coins.append function is re-evaluated. Recall that in *Chapter 6, Design Patterns*, you learned about the first-class functions. Let's represent collected_coins.append with a local function. This avoids the function re-evaluation (skips the dots) and will help speed up the loop.

Gold Hunt optimization – Pass two

In pass two, we will improve the code from the earlier pass (*optimization pass one*). The `goldhunt_pass2.py` file in the supporting code bundle incorporates all the changes to be discussed next. Here is the modified `find_coins` method:

```python
def find_coins(self, x_list, y_list):
    """Return list of coins that lie within a given distance...."""
    collected_coins = []
    search_radius_square = self.search_radius*self.search_radius

    # Assign collected_coins.append to a local function
    append_coins_function = collected_coins.append
    # Create local variables to represent the instance vars
    local_xref = self.x_ref
    local_yref = self.y_ref

    for x, y in zip(x_list, y_list):
        delta_x = local_xref - x
        delta_y = local_yref - y
        dist_square = delta_x*delta_x + delta_y*delta_y

        if dist_square <= search_radius_square:
            # See the definition of append_coins_function
            # before the for loop. It is used in place of
            # collected_coins.append for speedup
            append_coins_function((x, y))

    return collected_coins
```

Here, a local function called `append_coins_function` is assigned to the built-in `append` function of a Python `list`. This avoids the re-evaluation of the `append` function. Similarly, `self.xref` and `self.yref` are represented with local variables. Let's profile this new code and see if we get any improvements. The command is as follows:

```
$ python goldhunt_pass2.py
```

```
     18019513 function calls in 44.545 seconds

Ordered by: internal time
List reduced from 21 to 5 due to restriction <'goldhunt'>

ncalls  tottime  percall  cumtime  percall  filename:lineno(function)
    95   38.553    0.406   38.559    0.406  goldhunt_pass2.py:107(find_coins)
     1    3.247    3.247    5.935    5.935  goldhunt_pass2.py:38(generate_random_points)
     1    0.044    0.044   44.545   44.545  goldhunt_pass2.py:172(play_game)
     1    0.002    0.002   44.501   44.501  goldhunt_pass2.py:130(play)
     1    0.000    0.000    0.000    0.000  goldhunt_pass2.py:91(__init__)
```

There is an improvement in the performance, but the results are not as impressive as the first pass of the optimization. It is still a reasonable improvement of about 10 seconds or more than 15%.

You can make similar changes elsewhere in the code, but before you jump the gun, Sir Foo has an important message for you.

That is an excellent point! Care should be taken while adopting such techniques. You should document the code or define a project-specific coding convention so that the local functions clearly stand out. This will help other developers understand the purpose of such assignments. More generally, do not overdo it and see if there is a real benefit.

Using local scope

While looking for a variable or a function definition, Python first searches the following **namespaces** in that order: **local**, **global**, and **built-in**. In simpler terms, it first looks for local variables or functions, then performs the search at the module level, and if nothing can be found, it looks for a built-in function or variable name. So, the look up for local variables or functions is the fastest. Using a local function in place of a global or built-in function may help improve the performance. The amount of speedup you get will depend on the problem.

Let's review the `generate_random_points` function. The original code is shown next. Refer to the *Reviewing the initial code* section in *Chapter 7, Performance – Identifying Bottlenecks*, where it was explained.

```python
def generate_random_points(ref_radius, total_points):
    """Return x,y coords representing random points inside a circle"""
    x = []
    y = []
    for i in range(total_points):
        theta = random.uniform(0.0, 2*math.pi)
        r = ref_radius*math.sqrt(random.uniform(0.0, 1.0))
        x.append(r*math.cos(theta))
        y.append(r*math.sin(theta))

    return x, y
```

In the original function, we are calling various functions of the built-in modules, `random` and `math`. Let's update `generate_random_points` in the next optimization pass.

Gold Hunt optimization – Pass three

Let's go further into the optimization process. We will replace the built-in function calls in the `generate_random_points` function with local ones. The reworked code is shown next. Here, the `l_uniform` variable represents the `random.uniform` function. Likewise, you can see the other assignments in this code snippet.

```python
def generate_random_points(ref_radius, total_points):
    """Return x, y coordinate lists representing random points inside a cir
    x = []
    y = []
    # Combination of avoiding the dots (function reevaluations)
    # and using local variable
    l_uniform = random.uniform
    l_sqrt = math.sqrt
    l_pi = math.pi
    l_cos = math.cos
    l_sin = math.sin

    for i in range(total_points):
        theta = l_uniform(0.0, 2*l_pi)
        r = ref_radius*l_sqrt(l_uniform(0.0, 1.0))
        x.append(r*l_cos(theta))
        y.append(r*l_sin(theta))

    return x, y
```

The optimization accomplished after this step is a combination of using local scope and skipping the dots. As an exercise, you can try to separate these components. For example, to avoid using dots, at the top of the module, import pi, cos and other symbols, and directly use them in the function. Then compare the performance with and without the use of local functions.

Also, before implementing such a code, ask yourself a few questions: By using local scope, is the code quality getting compromised (is it harder to read and maintain)? Does the final performance improvement outweigh all other factors?

You can also find this code in goldhunt_pass3.py. The following is the cProfile output for this file. There is only a minor improvement in the overall timing. The real difference will be noticeable if you compare the second row of the list (generate_random_points) with the corresponding output of *optimization pass two*:

```
         18019605 function calls in 43.564 seconds

   Ordered by: internal time
   List reduced from 21 to 5 due to restriction <'goldhunt'>

   ncalls  tottime  percall  cumtime  percall filename:lineno(function)
       95   38.267    0.403   38.272    0.403 goldhunt_pass3.py:114(find_coins)
        1    2.618    2.618    5.240    5.240 goldhunt_pass3.py:38(generate_random_points)
        1    0.044    0.044   43.564   43.564 goldhunt_pass3.py:179(play_game)
        1    0.002    0.002   43.520   43.520 goldhunt_pass3.py:137(play)
        1    0.000    0.000    0.000    0.000 goldhunt_pass3.py:98(__init__)
```

The total runtime has been reduced to ~2.6 seconds from an initial ~ 3.2 seconds. Increasing the problem size (number of coins) could make this difference further noticeable.

But it looks like someone is not quite impressed with the speedup...

*Absolutely! The task to improve the **Gold Hunt** game performance is far from over! Before we do that, let's discuss some other techniques that help speed up the application. We will use generic examples as many of these techniques are not relevant in the context of the previously mentioned game scenario.*

*In the next chapter, we will revisit the **Gold Hunt** problem and speed up the application further using NumPy and parallelization. It will be a drastic improvement in the performance. If you do not want to break the continuity, read the next chapter first and then come back here for the rest of the discussion.*

Performance improvement goodies

Let's spend some time discussing miscellaneous tips and tricks that help improve the runtime performance of the code. You can still apply a few of these techniques to the *Gold Hunt* problem, but let's just use generic examples to explain these concepts.

All the illustrations in this section can be found in the supporting file, `misc_performance.py`. To compare the performance, we will use the `timeit` module that was discussed in *Chapter 7, Performance – Identifying Bottlenecks* (refer to the *Measuring runtime of small code snippets* section). See also the `timeit` documentation, `https://docs.python.org/3/library/timeit.html`.

List comprehension

List comprehension is a compact way of creating a Python `list`. It is often used to replace the nested `for` loops or the `map` and `filter` functionality. Besides being compact, it is also efficient compared to, for instance, an equivalent `for` loop. The basic syntax is as follows:

```
a = [i*i for i in range(5)]
```

This creates a list with elements: `[0, 1, 4, 9, 16]`

The preceding syntax is equivalent to the following:

```
mylist = []
for i in range(5):
    mylist.append(i*i)
```

Let's wrap these code blocks in two functions. We will measure the performance of each function using the `timeit` module. The previously mentioned file, `misc_performance.py`, also has these functions. To get a better idea of the performance gain, we will select a larger problem size. As noted a few times earlier in this book, select a problem size depending on what your machine can comfortably handle.

The following code fragment shows these functions:

```python
import timeit

sample_size_1 = 1000000

def list_comprehension_ex1():
    mylist = [i*i for i in range(sample_size_1)]

def no_list_comprehension_ex1():
    mylist = []
    for i in range(sample_size_1):
        mylist.append(i*i)

if __name__ == '__main__':
    t1 = timeit.timeit(
        "no_list_comprehension_ex1()",
        setup="from __main__ import no_list_comprehension_ex1")

    t2 = timeit.timeit(
        "list_comprehension_ex1()",
        setup="from __main__ import list_comprehension_ex1")

    print("Without list comprehension :", t1)
    print("With list comprehension    :", t2)
```

The `sample_size_1` variable is chosen sufficiently large to see a difference. The runtime is captured using the `timeit.timeit` method, whose first argument is a string representing the function name. The second argument is a `setup` parameter that tells us where to look for this function. The runtime performance can be compared by executing the script, as:

```
$ python misc_preformance.py
```

As can be seen from the following output, the list comprehension is faster compared to an equivalent `for` loop:

```
Without list comprehension : 1.218718248004734
With list comprehension    : 0.8486306999984663
```

As an exercise, try comparing the timings of a nested `for` loop and an equivalent list comprehension syntax. Refer to the `list_comprehension_ex2` function in the `misc_performance.py` file.

In the *Gold Hunt* problem, it is also possible to use list comprehension in the generate_random_points function. For example, you can optionally write theta as follows:

```
theta = [random.uniform(0.0, 2*math.pi)
        for i in range(total_points)]
```

But before making such changes, read the next chapter, which shows how the NumPy package drastically improves the performance of this function.

Recording execution time

In the previous section, we used the timeit.timeit function to record and compare the performance of list comprehension against a classical for loop. Let's wrap the timeit code into a utility function so that we can reuse it for the rest of the discussion. The run_timeit function is shown next:

```
def run_timeit(func_1, func_2, num=1):
    """Run timeit.timeit for the given function names (input args)"""

    t1 = timeit.timeit("%s()"%func_1,
                        setup="from __main__ import %s"%func_1, number=num)
    t2 = timeit.timeit("%s()"%func_2,
                        setup="from __main__ import %s"%func_2, number=num)

    print("Function: {func}, time: {t}".format(func=func_1, t=t1))
    print("Function: {func}, time: {t}".format(func=func_2, t=t2))
```

Here, func_1 and func_2 are the function names (strings) whose execution time needs to be recorded. The number argument in the timeit.timeit function indicates the number of times the given function is executed. The callers of run_timeit can tune this number by using the optional num argument. See the documentation for further details.

 This function does not do any error checking. As an exercise, you can add that capability. For example, add the try...except clause to catch errors if the function is not found.

In the upcoming discussion, we will use run_timeit to compare the performance of two functionally equivalent code blocks.

Dictionary comprehension

Just like the list comprehension, a **dictionary comprehension** is the syntactic construct to create a Python dictionary object. The following functions show two ways to create a dictionary. The first one (`no_dict_comprehension`) uses a `for` loop to create a dictionary, whereas the second function shows the dictionary comprehension syntax.

```python
def no_dict_comprehension():
    d = {}
    for i in range(sample_size_1):
        d[i] = i*i

def dict_comprehension():
    d = {i: i*i for i in range(sample_size_1)}

if __name__ == '__main__':
    run_timeit("dict_comprehension", "no_dict_comprehension")
```

As noted in the previous section, from now onwards, we will use the `run_timeit` utility function to record timings. The `timeit` output after executing this code is shown next:

```
Function: no_dict_comprehension, time: 0.14393422298599035
Function: dict_comprehension, time: 0.13295511799515225
```

Swapping conditional block and for loops

Consider the following trivial code. There is a top-level `for` loop with an `if...else` condition block. Depending on the value of the `num` variable (assume it changes), either `if` or `else` condition is executed. As before, an appropriate integer for the `sample_size_1` variable should be chosen:

```python
def no_if_condition_loop_opt():
    num = 1000
    val = 0
    for i in range(sample_size_1):
        if num < 100:
            val += i*i
        else:
            val += i*i*i
    return val
```

We can write the same code by swapping the `for` loop and the `if...else` block. The new function has a top-level `if...else` block. Inside each condition statement, we have the same `for` loop. The following `if_condition_loop_opt` function shows this (its output remains the same):

```python
def if_condition_loop_opt():
    num = 1000
    val = 0
    if num < 100:
        for i in range(sample_size_1):
            val += i*i
    else:
        for i in range(sample_size_1):
            val += i*i*i
    return val

if __name__ == '__main__':
    run_timeit("no_if_condition_loop_opt", "if_condition_loop_opt")
```

Let's find out the winner between these two functions:

```
Function: no_if_condition_loop_opt, time: 0.1894498920009937
Function: if_condition_loop_opt, time   : 0.15955313100130297
```

To summarize, the function with a top-level `if...else` block runs faster compared to the function with a top-level `for` loop.

> This was a simple example where the swapping of the `for` loop and condition blocks was easy. However, in the real world, weigh in the advantages of making such modifications over the risk of introducing bugs. Does the profiling really show this code block as a major bottleneck? If you finally decide to go ahead with it, add enough automated tests to make sure that the function output remains the same! See *Chapter 5, Unit Testing and Refactoring*, to learn how to write unit tests.

'try' it out in a loop

Remember the **Easier to ask for forgiveness than permission (EAFP)** principle that encourages using the `try...except` clause? It was discussed briefly in *Chapter 2, Dealing with Exceptions*. Let's see how a `try...except` clause can save some execution time. Consider the following function, which populates a list in a `for` loop based on the value of `i`. Only for the first iteration of the `for` loop (i=0), the `if` statement is executed. For all other values of i, it executes the `else` block, `val /=i`.

```python
def not_using_try():
    mylist = []
    val = 1
    for i in range(sample_size_1):
        if (i == 0):
            val /= 10
        else:
            val /= i
        mylist.append(val)
```

Let's replace the `if...else` block with a `try...except` clause. The `try` clause will always try to execute the `val /= i` statement. When we have i=0, it raises the `ZeroDivisionError` exception, which is handled in the `except` clause.

```python
def using_try():
    mylist = []
    val = 1
    for i in range(sample_size_1):
        try:
            val /= i
        except ZeroDivisionError:
            val /= 10
    mylist.append(val)

if __name__ == '__main__':
    run_timeit("not_using_try", "using_try")
```

Here, we need to catch the error only for the initial value, i=0. For the rest of the loop, the code should run smoothly. The `try...except` clause effectively gets rid of the extra checks imposed by the `if...else` condition block. In other words, we will no longer need to check if i==0 for each value of i. As a result, the code runs faster. The execution time for these functions is shown next—clearly, the `using_try` function performs better:

```
Function: not_using_try, time: 0.1821241550205741
Function: using_try, time   : 0.09502803898067214
```

Choosing the right data structures

This is fairly a broad topic. The choice of data structure largely depends on the problem you are trying to solve. In this section, we will limit our discussion to just one example that shows how the right choice of data structure improves the runtime performance. Observe the `data_struct_choice_list` function; it first creates a list object, `mylist`. Next, inside a `for` loop, the code checks if `j` is one of the elements of `mylist` and updates the `val` parameter accordingly.

```python
def data_struct_choice_list():
    mylist = [i*i for i in range(1000)]
    val = 0
    for j in range(100000):
        if (j in mylist):
            val += j
        else:
            val += j*2

    return val
```

Now look at the following `data_struct_choice_set` function. Instead of a `list` object, it creates a `set` object denoted by the `myset` variable. The syntax is similar to the `list` or dictionary comprehension syntax we saw earlier (the rest of the code remains the same and both the functions return the same value).

```python
def data_struct_choice_set():
    # Python 'set' comprehension just like a dict or list
    myset = {i*i for i in range(1000)}
    val = 0
    for j in range(100000):
        if (j in myset):
            val += j
        else:
            val += j*2

    return val

if __name__ == '__main__':
    run_timeit("data_struct_choice_list", "data_struct_choice_set")
```

When it comes to checking the membership of an element, the Python `set` is faster compared to a `list`. In other words, the `"if (j in myset)"` operation is faster compared to `"if (j in mylist)"`. As summarized in a table in *Chapter 7, Performance – Identifying Bottlenecks*, the average-case time complexity of this operation is $O(1)$ for set and $O(n)$ for list.

The `timeit` output for these two functions is shown next. Clearly, the function that implements `set` is much faster compared to the one that implements `list`:

```
Function: data_struct_choice_list, time: 1.7527358299994376
Function: data_struct_choice_set, time: 0.015494994004257023
```

 Have you noticed a problem in this example? The runtime reported by `timeit` includes the time required to create the `list` and `set` objects. For an accurate comparison, you should only compare the `for` loops in these functions. In other words, move the `list` and `set` creation part out of the function definition and then do the timing comparison.

Let's continue the discussion on the data structures and review Python's `collections` module next.

The collections module

The `collections` module offers a number of special purpose container data types. Let's review a few of the common ones. If you want to know about the other data structures in this module, see the Python documentation (https://docs.python.org/3/library/collections.html).

The deque class

The `deque` class enables appending or deleting elements from either side of the `deque` data structure. The `append` and `pop` operations in `deque` class are memory efficient and thread-safe with a complexity of *O(1)*. The following code shows a simple way to create `deque` and then remove the rightmost element:

```
>>> dq = deque(range(10))
>>> dq
deque([0, 1, 2, 3, 4, 5, 6, 7, 8, 9])
>>> dq.pop()
9
>>> dq
deque([0, 1, 2, 3, 4, 5, 6, 7, 8])
```

Let's compare the performance of `deque` with an equivalent `list`. Observe the following two functions, where we call the `pop()` method of the `list` and `deque` classes—note that we are creating the `list` and `deque` objects outside of these functions to make sure that the reported timing is not influenced by the object creation:

```
from collections import deque

# Create the list and deque objects
lst = list(range(sample_size_1))
dq = deque(range(sample_size_1))

def list_example():
    for i in range(sample_size_1):
        lst.pop()

def deque_example():
    for i in range(sample_size_1):
        dq.pop()

if __name__ == '__main__':
    run_timeit("list_example", "deque_example")
```

The following `timeit` output shows that the `pop()` operation on `deque` is faster compared to that of `list`:

```
Function: list_example, time: 0.1243858500092756
Function: deque_example, time: 0.0937135319982189
```

So, when should we use `deque`? In general, if your code involves a lot of operations where the data needs to be appended or popped from one of the ends, `deque` is preferred over a `list`. But, if the code needs fast random access to the elements, `list` is a better choice of data structure.

The defaultdict class

The `defaultdict` class is derived from the built-in `dict` class. If you try to access a key that doesn't exist, a simple Python dictionary throws a `KeyError` exception. But, a `defaultdict` class creates a new key instead. This can be better explained with the following example:

```
>>> d1 = {}
>>> d1['a']
Traceback (most recent call last):
  File "<stdin>", line 1, in <module>
KeyError: 'a'
```

The standard dictionary object, d1, doesn't have an 'a' key, so it throws an error. If you try to access this key with a defaultdict class, it simply creates it, as shown in the following example:

```
>>> from collections import defaultdict
>>> d2 = defaultdict(int)
>>> d2['a']
0
>>> d32
defaultdict(<class 'int'>, {'a': 0})
```

The built-in setdefault() method of the standard dictionary does a similar job. If the key you are trying to access does not exist, it inserts a new key in the dictionary, assigns a default value to it, and returns this default. However, using defaultdict is faster compared to the setdefault method. Refer to the documentation (https://docs.python.org/3/library/stdtypes.html#dict) for more information.

This is just one of the features offered by defaultdict. It also provides an efficient means to count the number of times an element occurs in a container. Let's see this with an example. The following dict_counter function defines a list called game_characters. There are many repeating elements in this list. The function uses a standard dictionary to count how many times each element occurs, and then returns this dictionary.

```
def dict_counter():
    unit_headcount = {}
    game_characters = ['elf', 'knight', 'orc',
                       'orc', 'knight', 'knight']*sample_size_1
    # Loop over the list
    for unit in game_characters:
        # Count the occurance of each character and store
        # the result in the dictionary object unit_headcount
        if unit in unit_headcount:
            unit_headcount[unit] += 1
        else:
            unit_headcount[unit] = 1

    return unit_headcount
```

For example, the output of this function will be a dictionary:

```
{'orc': 2000000, 'knight': 3000000, 'elf': 1000000}
```

The `sample_size_1` is just a multiplication factor to make this list big enough to see the difference in the execution time. In this example, it is chosen as `100000`. Now, let's write a function that uses a `defaultdict` class to do the same job. Take a look at how compact the resulting code is:

```
from collections import defaultdict

def defaultdict_counter():
    unit_headcount = defaultdict(int)
    game_characters = ['elf', 'knight', 'orc',
                       'orc', 'knight', 'knight']*sample_size_1

    for unit in game_characters:
        unit_headcount[unit] += 1

    return unit_headcount

if __name__ == '__main__':
    run_timeit("dict_counter", "defaultdict_counter")
```

Let's compare the performance of these two functions. The following `timeit` output confirms that the function implementing `defaultdict` runs faster:

```
Function: dict_counter, time: 0.6270602609729394
Function: defaultdict_counter, time: 0.4926446119789034
```

The counting operation can also be performed using the `collections.Counter` class. The syntax is simple and efficient compared to a `defaultdict` class (we will not discuss the `Counter` class in this book). As an exercise, read the documentation and write a function that uses the `Counter` class for the earlier example.

Generators and generator expressions

A **generator** is basically an iterator. It is a powerful tool to handle a very large, or an infinite data set. A generator function is written just like a regular function, but is characterized by the use of the `yield` statement. It is similar to a `return` statement, in the sense that it returns a value. However, a generator function "freezes" the current environment after it yields. So, the next time you want a value, the generator function continues from where it left off and yields the next value.

In other words, a generator returns values (say from a list) one at a time, keeps track of the current state of the iteration (remembers all the values it has returned in the previous calls), and when called again, it picks up from the position where it left off. When you add a `yield` statement to a function, it automatically becomes a generator function. Let's write a trivial example to understand this concept better:

```
>>> def get_data():
...     for i in range(3):
...         yield i*i
...
>>> g = get_data()
>>> g
<generator object get_data at 0x7f704c55fb40>
```

The `get_data()` function returns a generator object, g. The `next()` function is just one way of getting the values from the generator:

```
>>> next(g)
0
```

For the first iteration in the `get_data()` function, we have `i=0`. So, the value returned by the generator is `i*i=0`. Now comes the interesting part. Let's call the `next()` function again:

```
>>> next(g)
1
```

It returned the value as `1`. This corresponds to the next value of the iterator in the `get_data()` function, `i=1`, which makes `i*i=1`. If we call `next()` one more time, it will return the result for `i=2`, as follows:

```
>>> next(g)
4
```

This will continue until the generator is exhausted with all the values. If we call `next()` again, it raises a `StopIteration` exception, as shown next:

```
>>> next(g)
Traceback (most recent call last):
  File "<stdin>", line 1, in <module>
StopIteration
```

Using the `yield` statement is one way of creating a generator function, and hence a generator object. Let's learn about the generator expression, which provides another way to create a generator object.

Generator expressions

The generator expression is proposed as *PEP 289* and is summarized as a high performance memory efficient generalization of list comprehension and generators.

 Refer to `https://www.python.org/dev/peps/` `pep-0289` for further details on *PEP 289*.

The basic syntax for a generator expression is similar to that of a list comprehension. Instead of square brackets `[]`, it uses the round brackets `()` to create a generator object:

```
>>> g = (i*i for i in range(3))
>>> g
<generator object <genexpr> at 0x7f0b71b0c8b8>
```

We already saw how to use the `next()` function to get values out of a generator object. You can also get the data from a generator using a `for` loop, as follows:

```
>>> g = (i*i for i in range(3))
>>> for data in g:
...     print(data)
...
0
1
4
```

Let's see a simple example where a generator expression can be used. The built-in `sum` function accepts an iterable as an input. It sums all the elements of that iterable and returns the total sum as a single value:

```
>>> g = (i*i for i in range(3))
>>> sum(g)
5
```

Note that you can even pass a `list` to the `sum()` method to get the same result. Next, we will compare the memory efficiency of a generator expression with that of a list comprehension.

Comparing the memory efficiency

For a moderately-sized problem, the runtime performance of a list comprehension is typically better compared to an equivalent generator expression. We won't make that comparison here. Instead, we will see how the generator expression and the list comprehension compare when it comes to memory consumption.

In the previous chapter, we saw how to use the memory_profiler package. Let's use it here to profile the memory usage. Create a compare_memory.py file or download it from the supporting code bundle for this chapter. The code is shown next:

```
@profile
def list_comp_memory():
    sample_size = 10000
    my_data = [i for i in range(sample_size)]

@profile
def generator_expr_memory():
    sample_size = 10000
    my_data = (i for i in range(sample_size))

if __name__ == '__main__':
    list_comp_memory()
    generator_expr_memory()
```

The list_comp_memory function creates a list using the list comprehension syntax. The generator_expr_memory function creates a generator object using the generator expression syntax. The @profile decorator marks the function for profiling by the memory profiler. Let's run the memory_profiler function on this file:

```
$ python -m memory_profiler compare_memory.py
```

Here is the output of this run:

```
Filename: compare_memory.py

Line #    Mem usage    Increment   Line Contents
================================================
    14   19.625 MiB    0.000 MiB   @profile
    15                             def list_comp_memory():
    16   19.629 MiB    0.004 MiB       sample_size = 10000
    17   20.008 MiB    0.379 MiB       my_data = [i for i in range(sample_size)]


Filename: compare_memory.py

Line #    Mem usage    Increment   Line Contents
================================================
    19   19.840 MiB    0.000 MiB   @profile
    20                             def generator_expr_memory():
    21   19.840 MiB    0.000 MiB       sample_size = 10000
    22   19.840 MiB    0.000 MiB       my_data = (i for i in range(sample_size))
```

Let's review the output achieved from the profiling done on the `compare_memory.py` file:

- The `Increment` column indicates that the list comprehension creates a `list` and puts it in the memory. In the present example, it consumes about 0.37 MiB.

- The memory profiler reports the usage in MiB. For the generator expression, it reports 0.0 MiB or interprets it as only a few bytes in this example.

- If you increase the `sample_size` variable further, the memory consumed by the list comprehension will increase accordingly.

- For a very large `sample_size`, your computer may even choke while creating the `list` with the list comprehension.

- With the generator expression, the memory consumed will remain constant, no matter how large the data size gets. This is an extremely useful feature when operating on a very large or an infinite data set.

Generator expressions or list comprehensions?

Good question. How to decide between generator expressions and list comprehensions? The choice depends on the type of problem you are dealing with. The following points should help you make that decision:

- Use generator expressions when you are working with a very large (or infinite) data set, iterated over only once. The list comprehension puts the whole list in the memory, which works fine on small or mid-sized data sets. However, as the data size grows bigger, you will notice problems. The generator expression, on the other hand, uses constant memory. It returns data on the fly. Once the data is generated, the memory is freed.

- This is really another way to put the first point. Do not use generator expressions if you want to loop over the whole data set several times. In such cases, use the list comprehension.

- Generator expressions do not support list operations such as **slicing**. So, if you want to perform such operations, use the list comprehension.

The itertools module

Now that we know how the generator expressions work, let's briefly review `itertools`, another important built-in module in Python. It provides functionality to create iterators for efficient looping. The `itertools` module offers several building blocks for iterators. Some of the frequently used iterators include `count()`, `repeat()`, `chain()`, `groupBy()`, `tee()`, `product()`, `permutation()`, `combination()`, and so on. This is just a partial list of the supported functionality. In this chapter, we will only review the `chain()` iterator.

 Refer to `https://docs.python.org/3/library/itertools.html` for information on other iterators offered by the `itertools` module.

The itertools.chain iterator

This iterator is used to chain multiple iterators together. It can take lists, tuples, generators, or even a combination of these iterators as an input. Let's review a simple example that shows how to create a `chain` object:

```
>>> from itertools import chain
>>> mylist_1 = [1, 2, 3]
>>> mytuple = ('x', 'y')
>>> mylist_2 = [10, 20]
>>> mychain = chain(mylist_1, mytuple, mylist_2)
>>> mychain
<itertools.chain object at 0x7fc6fcc1c2e8>
```

The simplest way to view the contents of this `chain` object is to print it as a new `list` object:

```
>>> print(list(mychain))
[1, 2, 3, 'x', 'y', 10, 20]
```

As can be seen, the `chain` iterator combined the two input lists and a tuple (or the iterators). Sometimes, you want to perform identical operations on more than one list or any other iterable data structures. The `chain` iterator enables this by combining or chaining these data structures. More importantly, it does not consume any significant amount of memory. Just like a generator, the memory consumed by a `chain` object remains constant even when the size of the data grows bigger. It is also important to note that, just like a generator, a `chain` object can be used to iterate over a given data set only once. This is illustrated by the following code:

```
>>> mychain = chain(mylist_1, mytuple, mylist_2)
>>> for item in mychain:
...         print(item)
...
1
2
3
x
y
10
20
>>> next(chain)
Traceback (most recent call last):
  File "<stdin>", line 1, in <module>
TypeError: 'type' object is not an iterator
```

You can compare the memory efficiency of a `chain` object with an equivalent code that combines the input lists. The code is shown next. The `for` loop in these functions is just to illustrate how the `chain` object can be used in a loop.

```python
from itertools import chain

# Create some lists. these will be 'chained' together
data_1 = ['x']*10000
data_2 = ['y']*10000
data_3 = ['z']*10000

@profile
def chain_memory():
    mychain = chain(data_1, data_2, data_3)
    for i in mychain:
        pass

@profile
def list_memory():
    mylist = data_1 + data_2 + data_3
    for i in mylist:
        pass

if __name__ == '__main__':
    chain_memory()
    list_memory()
```

You can also find this code in `compare_memory.py`. In this file, just add the `@profile` decorator. With this change, run the memory profiler as an exercise. The following can be observed from the memory profiler output (not shown here):

- The `chain` object consumes about 0.004 MiB memory and the consumption remains constant even after you increase the size of the input lists, `data_1`, `data_2` and `data_3`.

- The `list_memory` function consumes nearly 0.383 MiB of memory to create the `mylist` object. The memory consumed by this function increases with the input data size.

Exercises

A few exercises were already suggested. Let's list a few of these. (Note that the solution are not provided for these exercises.):

- Write a list comprehension syntax for a nested `for` loop. Compare the timings of a nested `for` loop and the list comprehension. Here is an example:

  ```
  x = [ i*j for i in range(4) for j in range(4)]
  ```

- Write a generator expression for the preceding list comprehension. You just need to change the outer square brackets `[]` to the round brackets `()`.

Summary

In this chapter, you learned many techniques that help cut down the application's runtime. We started by improving the speed of the *Gold Hunt* application. The total time taken to run this application was improved by more than 50%—we accomplished this by changing the algorithm so that it does not need to compute the square root for distance comparison. Two more changes knocked off a few more seconds from the total execution time. We avoided the function re-evaluation (skipped the "dots") and preferred local scope for the variables over global scope. This was the end of *part one* of the performance improvement for the *Gold Hunt* program.

Moving on, the chapter taught you a number of ways that help speed up the code. It illustrated how a list comprehension does a better job compared to an equivalent `for` loop. We also saw how the choice of data structure affects the performance. The chapter further introduced us to the generator expressions that offer memory advantage over the list comprehensions. Additionally, we also briefly reviewed the functionality offered by the `itertools` and `collections` modules.

We promised *The Great Dwarf* further improvements to the application. In the next chapter, let's learn the things that will help us keep our promise!

9
Improving Performance – Part Two, NumPy and Parallelization

This is the final chapter in the series of the three chapters on performance improvement. It will introduce you to two important libraries, **NumPy**, a third-party package, and the built-in **multiprocessing** module. In this chapter, we will cover the following topics:

- A brief introduction to the NumPy package
- Using NumPy to speed up the *Gold Hunt* application
- An introduction to parallel processing using the `multiprocessing` module
- Using the `multiprocessing` module to further improve the application runtime

Prerequisites for this chapter

You should read the last two chapters, *Chapter 7*, *Performance – Identifying Bottlenecks*, and *Chapter 8*, *Improving Performance – Part one*, on performance that teaches you how to identify the performance bottlenecks and improve the runtime using built-in functionality. This chapter takes the application to the next level by drastically improving performance.

This is how the chapter is organized

This chapter will be the *Part two* of performance improvement. Just like the previous chapter, the performance of the *Gold Hunt* program will be improved in steps. We will start with a quick introduction to NumPy, just enough to use its functionality for *optimization passes four* and *five*, which follow next. Moving ahead, there will be a superficial introduction to the `multiprocessing` module. In *optimization pass six*, we will use this module to parallelize a portion of the application code. Let's pull up the same bar chart from the previous chapter. The last two bars indicate the speedup accomplished by the end of this chapter.

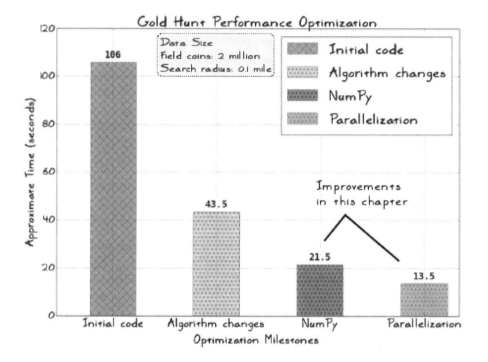

But the chart does not tell the full story. The *optimization pass four*, will significantly speedup the `generate_random_points` function of the *Gold Hunt* program. This speedup is not reflected in the chart as the function does not significantly contribute to the runtime in this scenario. Towards the end, the chapter will provide preliminary information on **PyPy** for further reading. PyPy is a Python interpreter that provides a **Just In Time (JIT)** compiler.

Running Gold Hunt optimization examples

If you look closely at the profiling output shown in the upcoming discussion, you will notice a filename, `goldhunt_run_master.py`. Using this file is optional but it provides a convenient way to run any of the optimization passes. You can find this file in this chapter's supporting code bundle.

Introduction to NumPy

NumPy is a powerful Python package for scientific computing. It provides a multidimensional `array` object that enables efficient implementation of numerical computations in Python. It also has a relatively smaller memory footprint when compared to a list. An `array` object is just one of the many important features of NumPy. Among other things, it offers linear algebra and random number generation capabilities. It also provides tools to access codes written in other languages, such as C/C++ and Fortran. Let's start with a short introduction that gives a flavor of its capabilities. What we will discuss in this book is more like scratching the surface of NumPy! This chapter covers some features to be used later to speed up the *Gold Hunt* application.

Review the official NumPy documentation (`http://docs.scipy.org`) to learn about several other features that are not covered here.

If you are already familiar with NumPy, you can optionally skip this introduction and directly move on to the *Optimizing Gold Hunt – Part two* section.

Installing NumPy

Some Python distributions, such as Anaconda (`https://www.continuum.io/downloads`), provide NumPy by default. If unavailable, use `pip` to install it. Here is how to do it on Linux, assuming `pip` is available as a command in the terminal:

```
$ pip install numpy
```

This should install NumPy. If you encounter problems, refer to the platform specific installation instructions at `http://www.scipy.org/install.html`. Alternatively, you can use the earlier mentioned Anaconda Python distribution.

Once installed, open the Python interpreter and type the following command:

```
>>> import numpy as np
```

Assuming the installation is successful, it should import NumPy. For the rest of the discussion, we will use the notation np as the alias for numpy. Keep the interpreter window open. For the rest of the introduction, we will run some simple NumPy operations.

Creating array objects

As noted before, a multidimensional (**N-dimensional**) array object is one of the core NumPy capabilities. This array is provided by a built-in class, numpy.ndarray. It represents a collection of elements of the same type. In other words, it is a homogeneous array. There are several ways to create a Numpy array. Type the following code in your Python interpreter:

```
>>> import numpy as np
>>> x = np.array([2, 4])
>>> x
array([2, 4])
```

This creates an array instance denoted by the x variable with two elements. This is of the numpy.ndarray type. It is a single dimensional array. You can access any element or change its value, just like a Python list:

```
>>> x[0]
2
>>> x[0]=8
>>> x
array([8, 4])
```

In this simple example, the size of the array is 2. This is also called the *shape* of an array. NumPy represents the array shape as a tuple of integers. It gives the size of the array along each dimension. This is shown in the following line of code:

```
>>> x.shape
(2,)
```

Continuing further, here is another example that creates a two-dimensional array:

```
>>> p = np.array([[4, 8], [10, 20]])
>>> p
```

```
array([[ 4,   8],
       [10, 20]])
>>> p.ndim
2
>>> p.shape
(2, 2)
```

Here, `ndim` represents the number of dimensions of an array. The array shape indicates the size of two in each dimension.

Let's review the `numpy.arange` function. This is similar to the Python `range` function. But, `arange` returns an `array` object instead of a `list`. The following is another way to create an array using `numpy.arange`:

```
>>> a = np.arange(10)
>>> a
array([0, 1, 2, 3, 4, 5, 6, 7, 8, 9])
```

There are many other ways to create arrays in NumPy. Refer to the documentation, (`http://docs.scipy.org/doc/numpy/reference/`) for more details. Specifically, look for array creation routines.

Simple array operations

We will review some basic mathematical operations that can be performed on NumPy arrays. Let's create two arrays, `x` and `y` (these are one-dimensional arrays or vectors):

```
>>> import numpy as np
>>> x = np.array([2, 4])
>>> y = np.array([2, 4])
```

Using these arrays, you can perform mathematical operations, such as addition, subtraction, multiplication, and so on. NumPy performs all these operations element by element:

```
>>> x - y
array([0, 0])
>>> x + y
array([4, 8])
>>> x*y
array([ 4, 16])
```

It is important to note here that x*y is not the inner product. It is just a multiplication of the corresponding elements in the x and y arrays. The inner product of these vectors can be accomplished using the dot function, as follows:

```
>>> x.dot(y)
20
```

The following code illustrates the concept using a two-dimensional array. Here, x2.dot(y2) is a matrix multiplication operation:

```
>>> x2 = np.array([[2, 4], [6, 8]])
>>> y2 = np.array([[2, 4], [1, 2]])
>>> x2*y2
array([[ 4, 16],
       [ 6, 16]])
>>> x2.dot(y2)
array([[ 8, 16],
       [20, 40]])
```

Array slicing and indexing

For single dimensional arrays, the **indexing** and **slicing** operations are similar to a Python list. If you are unfamiliar with the list slicing operation, refer to https://docs.python.org/3/tutorial/introduction.html#lists. This is an important concept. In this chapter, we will only need to perform a few basic indexing operations.

Indexing

Array indexing is essentially an operation that enables us to access a particular element in an array. Here is a simple one-dimensional array with a size of five:

```
>>> b = np.arange(5)
>>> b
array([0, 1, 2, 3, 4])
```

The simplest indexing operation is shown below, which accesses an element of this array. This operation is similar to how it is done for a Python list:

```
>>> b[2]
2
```

Here is how you can retrieve elements from a two-dimensional array:

```
>>> p = np.array([[2,2], [4,4]])
>>> p
array([[2, 2],
       [4, 4]])
>>> p[0]
array([2, 2])
```

Once complete, it returns an array with only the first row.

 It is important to note that the basic array indexing does not return a copy of the original array. It just points to the same memory location as the original array. Refer to the following link where the basic and advanced indexing has been comprehensively documented: http://docs.scipy.org/doc/numpy/reference/arrays.indexing.html

The following code will retrieve a single value from a two-dimensional array:

```
>>> p[0][1]
2
```

With this basic introduction to array indexing, let's learn about some common slicing operations.

Slicing

Suppose you want to get an array with only the first two elements. Just like a `list`, you will need to specify a start and an end. For example, `b[start:stop]` means the resulting (sliced) array will begin at the `start` index and end at the `stop-1` index:

```
>>> b[0:2]
array([0, 1])
```

Similarly, to get any array with only the elements at the positions 1 and 2, you can do as follows:

```
>>> b[1:3]
array([1, 2])
```

For the N-dimensional arrays, you have to give the slicing instructions in each direction. Consider the following array with four rows and columns:

```
>>> z2 = np.array([[2, 4, 6, 8], [1, 5, 7, 9], [3, 3, 3, 3], [4, 4, 9, 4]])
>>> z2
array([[2, 4, 6, 8],
       [1, 5, 7, 9],
       [3, 3, 3, 3],
       [4, 4, 9, 4]])
>>> z2.shape
(4, 4)
```

Let's slice this array so that it returns only the first row. Here is the syntax to do that:

```
>>> z2[0:1, :]
array([[2, 4, 6, 8]])
```

If you want to get only the first column of z2 instead, then specify the slicing as follows:

```
>>> z2[:, 0:1]
array([[2],
       [1],
       [3],
       [4]])
```

The following slicing operation will create a new array using elements of the first two rows and columns:

```
>>> z2[0:2, 0:2]
array([[2, 4],
       [1, 5]])
```

To gain a better understanding of array slicing operations, try more examples in a Python interpreter. See the documentation for details (search the Web for NumPy array slicing).

Broadcasting

Broadcasting is another important NumPy feature. Let's understand this concept with a simple example. We have two arrays, p0 and p1, as shown in the following example:

```
>>> p0 = np.array([10])
>>> p1 = np.array([[1, 2], [3,4]])
```

The shapes of these arrays are as follows:

```
>>> p0.shape
(1,)
>>> p1.shape
(2,2)
```

Although the arrays have different shapes, NumPy can perform arithmetic operations on these arrays. A basic multiplication operation is shown next:

```
>>> p0*p1
array([[10, 20],
       [30, 40]])
```

This is referred to as broadcasting. The p0 array has a smaller shape relative to p1. The broadcasting enables this array to work with p1. In this example, it enables the multiplication operation. Of course, the two arrays need to meet certain requirements to take advantage of this feature. Refer to the NumPy documentation to learn more about broadcasting.

Miscellaneous functions

Let's look at some advanced mathematical operations that you can perform using the NumPy arrays.

 Most of the operations illustrated here will be used in the upcoming discussion on performance improvement using NumPy. So, pay close attention to this section.

numpy.ndarray.tolist

This is a handy function that returns the NumPy array as a Python `list` object. Depending on the array dimension, it can be a nested list. Here is an example that shows this function in action:

```
>>> x = np.array([2, 4])
>>> x_list = x.tolist()
>>> x_list
[2, 4]
```

numpy.reshape

As the name suggests, it changes the shape of an array without actually changing its data. Look at the following code; the x array is one dimensional and has a size (shape) of 9:

```
>>> x = np.arange(9)
>>> x
array([0, 1, 2, 3, 4, 5, 6, 7, 8])
>>> x.shape
(9,)
```

Let's see how to reshape this into a matrix that has three rows and columns. In other words, the following code returns an array with a new shape of (3,3):

```
>>> np.reshape(x, (3,3))
array([[0, 1, 2],
       [3, 4, 5],
       [6, 7, 8]])
```

The new shape selected should be compatible with the original shape of the array; otherwise, it will throw an error. For the preceding example, if you reshape it as `np.reshape(x, (3,2))`, it will throw a value error complaining about changed size.

numpy.random

This module provides several functions for random sampling. For a detailed list, refer to http://docs.scipy.org/doc/numpy/reference/routines.random.html.

Let's review `np.random.uniform` that draws samples from a uniform distribution:

```
>>> np.random.uniform(0.0, 2.0, size=3)
array([ 0.24061728,  0.66123504,  1.86137435])
```

```
>>> np.random.uniform(0.0, 2.0, size=4)
array([ 1.81382452,  1.20355728,  1.07085075,  0.9653697 ])
```

The first two arguments of this function represent the lower (0.0) and upper (2.0) boundaries of the output interval. You can specify any float value as the limit. All the random values or samples generated by the function lie within these two limits. The default lower and upper limits are 0.0 and 1.0, respectively. The size argument represents the shape of the output array. In the preceding example, it is specified as a single integer value. If you do not specify the size argument, it defaults to None. In that case, the function will simply return a single floating point number. The following is a slightly complicated example of when the size (or shape) argument is a tuple (2,2):

```
>>> np.random.uniform(0.0, 2.0, size=(2,2))
array([[  1.02970767e+00,   4.48798719e-02],
       [  5.20609066e-04,   6.10167655e-01]])
```

Have you already noticed a difference between Python's built-in random.uniform function and NumPy equivalent's np.random.uniform? The Numpy np.random. uniform function, can optionally give us an array object with samples drawn from uniform distribution, whereas the built-in random.uniform can only give us a single number. We will use this NumPy function in *optimization pass four*.

numpy.dstack

This provides a simple way to stack or concatenate a sequence of arrays along a third axis. Consider two NumPy arrays, x and y, representing the x and y coordinates of some points in space. These arrays are shown below:

```
>>> x = np.array((1, 2, 3, 4))
>>> y = np.array((10, 20, 30, 40))
```

Thus, x[0]=1 and y[0]=10 represent a point (1, 10). Likewise, we can represent other points for the remaining elements. Sometimes, it is convenient to use a single array to express the coordinates of several such points, as follows:

```
    points = [ [1,10], [2,20], [3, 30], [4, 40]]
```

How do we create such an array using the x and y arrays shown earlier? There are multiple ways to do this. One option is to use numpy.dstack. This function enables stacking arrays along a third axis to create a single array. The following code shows how to create a points array discussed earlier using the input x and y arrays:

```
>>> points = np.dstack((x,y))
>>> points
```

```
array([[[ 1, 10],
        [ 2, 20],
        [ 3, 30],
        [ 4, 40]]])
```

Notice that the resultant array is three-dimensional:

```
>>> points.ndim
3
```

The size of the array along each axis (or dimension) is given by its shape:

```
>>> points.shape
(1, 4, 2)
```

We will use this function in *optimization pass five*. Similarly, there are other ways of stacking arrays, for example, `numpy.hstack` or `numpy.vstack`. These are not discussed in this book. Refer to the NumPy documentation for further details.

numpy.einsum

This function provides a way to compute the **Einstein notation** (or **Einstein summation convention**) on the input arrays for the operations (called **operands**). In terms of performance, this function offers great efficiency. Later in the chapter, we will exploit it to find the square of the distance between two points.

> Understanding the mathematical concept behind `einsum` can be a bit challenging, especially if you do not have a math background. In that case, just remember one key thing about `numpy.einsum`—It is a function that allows you to perform some highly efficient operations involving arrays. For example, a matrix multiplication operation between two NumPy arrays or a dot product can be done more efficiently using `numpy.einsum`.
>
> Refer to the NumPy documentation for more information on this function. Also, see `https://en.wikipedia.org/wiki/Einstein_notation` for information on Einstein notation.

This can be better explained with an example. Consider the following equations that represent two vectors, A and B:

$$\vec{A} = A_x\hat{x} + A_y\hat{y} + A_z\hat{z}$$

$$\vec{B} = B_x\hat{x} + B_y\hat{y} + B_z\hat{z}$$

These are two points in space with some x, y, and z coordinates. The dot product of these vectors is represented as follows:

$$\vec{A} \cdot \vec{B} = A_x B_x + A_y B_y + A_z B_z$$

 To learn more about a dot product, see
https://en.wikipedia.org/wiki/Dot_product.

It is a scalar product and can be represented as a summation, as shown in the following equation:

$$\mathbf{A} \cdot \mathbf{B} = \sum_{i=1}^{3} A_i B_i$$

The Einstein summation convention for the preceding equation is written as follows:

$$\vec{A} \cdot \vec{B} = A_i B_i$$

Here, it is implied that A_iB_i is a summation over i with a lower bound of 1 and upper bound of 3. This is the Einstein summation convention in a nutshell.

`numpy.einsum` evaluates the Einstein summation convention on the given input arrays. The basic syntax is shown below—there are other optional arguments as well, but those are not shown here:

```
numpy.einsum(subscripts, *operands)
```

The first argument, subscripts, is a string that represents a list of subscript labels. These are separated by a comma and each label represents a dimension of a particular operand. In the example we just saw, there was only one subscript label, *i*. The second argument, operands, represents the input arrays (*A* and *B* in the example).

Suppose the *A* and *B* vectors are one dimensional. Their inner product can be represented with the subscript string 'i,i'. This can be better explained with the following example:

```
>>> import numpy as np
>>> a = np.array([2, 2])
>>> b = np.array([4, 4])
>>> np.einsum('i,i', a, b)
16
```

The arrays a and b are one dimensional. You can also cross-check the answer using the numpy.inner function, which returns the same answer:

```
>>> np.inner(a,b)
16
```

The numpy.einsum function is faster and also memory efficient. Now, take a look at the following code—it represents a dot product (or matrix multiplication) of two vectors, a2 and b2:

```
>>> a2 = np.array([[1,1], [2, 2]])
>>> b2 = np.array([[4,4], [6, 6]])
>>> np.einsum('ij,jk', a2, b2)
array([[10, 10],
       [20, 20]])
```

The subscript string for numpy.einsum is 'ij,jk', where ij is the subscript for two dimensions of array a2, and jk is the one for array b2. The dot product can also be obtained by following this example:

```
>>> np.dot(a2, b2)
array([[10, 10],
       [20, 20]])
```

Computing distance square with einsum

The examples shown so far should just give you a flavor of the `einsum` function. Let's only discuss how to use this function to calculate the square of the distance between two points. Again, for a comprehensive reference, refer to the NumPy documentation.

Consider any point `p1` with coordinates (0, 2). Furthermore, assume that the center is located at (0, 0). As the x coordinate of the `p1` point is 0, you can easily determine the distance between `p1` and center as 2 units. The square of the distance can be found using the `einsum` function, as follows:

```
>>> p1 = np.array([0,2])
>>> center = np.array([0, 0])
>>> d = p1 - center
>>> d
array([0, 2])
>>> np.einsum('i,i', d, d)
4
```

Now, imagine that there are multiple such points and you want to find the square of the distance of each point from the center. Here is one way to compute this using `einsum`:

```
>>> points = np.array([[0,2], [0,4], [2, 2], [4, 4]])
>>> center = np.array([0,0])
```

The `points` array represents a list of points. For each of these points, we will find a vector, with center as its starting point and the given point (from the `points` array) as its end. Let's represent the array of such vectors as `diff`, as shown in the following example:

```
>>> diffs = points - center
>>> diffs.shape
(4, 2)
>>> diffs
array([[0, 2],
       [0, 4],
       [2, 2],
       [4, 4]])
```

As the center is $(0, 0)$, the `diff` array is essentially the same as the `points` array. The following line of code shows the `einsum` syntax—it uses the ellipsis notation (...), to the left of each term in the subscripts argument:

```
>>> np.einsum('...i,...i', diffs, diffs)
array([ 4, 16,  8, 32])
```

It returns an array that contains a square of the distances for each point in the `points` array. That's all we need!

What does this ellipsis notation do? Why didn't we use the earlier syntax?

```
>>>  np.einsum('i,i', d, d)
```

The earlier syntax involved single dimensional arrays (d) that had only one subscript label. We cannot use it here as the operand (or the `diffs` array) for the Einstein sum is a two-dimensional array. To understand this, let's look at the `diffs` array one more time:

```
>>> diffs
array([[0, 2],
       [0, 4],
       [2, 2],
       [4, 4]])
```

Consider any row of this array. It is essentially a vector between a point and the center. For example, `[0, 2]` represents a vector between a center `[0,0]` and a point `[0,2]`. The other dimension of the array is to hold many such vectors. The ellipsis symbol, "...", is a convenient way to broadcast the second dimension. The alternative syntax to get the same result is as follows:

```
>>> np.einsum('ij,ij->i', diffs, diffs)
array([ 4, 16,  8, 32])
```

However, if the array shapes change further, you will need to work on constructing a proper subscript string for the `einsum` function again. The NumPy documentation has several examples that show how to use `einsum`. Here is a NumPy version 1.10 documentation: http://docs.scipy.org/doc/numpy-1.10.0/reference/generated/numpy.einsum.html.

Where to get more information on NumPy?

In the NumPy introduction, you were presented with several links to the documentation. Just for the completeness, let's summarize where to find more information on NumPy. You can start by visiting their website (`http://www.numpy.org/`) or just do a web search on NumPy to get to its homepage.

SciPy is another project worth mentioning. It is a library that integrates several open source tools for mathematics, science, and engineering disciplines. NumPy, matplotlib, and pandas are some of its core packages. See the project website (`https://www.scipy.org/`) for more information.

In an earlier discussion, several links were provided to the NumPy documentation. Looking at those links, you must have already noticed that they all point to the SciPy website. The documentation for both NumPy and SciPy is located at `http://docs.scipy.org/doc/`.

The open source pandas library is used for data analysis using Python. It provides high performance data structures and tools to analyze data. Refer to `http://pandas.pydata.org/` for more information.

Optimizing Gold Hunt – Part two

The previous section served as a short introduction to NumPy. Recall that, in earlier chapters, we gradually improved the runtime performance of the game. The last recorded timing was the one obtained with *optimization pass three*. We successfully reduced the total runtime down to nearly 44 seconds from the original time of about 106 seconds. NumPy supports vectorized calculation routines such as element-wise multiplication. It internally uses efficient C loops that help run such operations faster. Let's leverage NumPy capabilities to speed up the *Gold Hunt* game even further.

Gold Hunt optimization – pass four

It is now time to resume the optimization operation for the *Gold Hunt* problem. Let's start with *optimization pass four*. We will focus our attention once again on the function, generate_random_numbers. As a refresher, the cProfiler output of the last optimization run reported the total time as ~ 2.6 seconds and a cumulative time, which includes the time spent by sub-functions, was ~ 5.2 seconds.

You are right. For this example, it is not worth optimizing this piece of code. The 5.2 seconds time doesn't look that bad. At this time, the function is called only once, as indicated by the ncalls column of the cProfile output. But any future requirements can potentially make this function a new bottleneck. As an example, imagine a new game scenario where there are hundreds of such gold fields or places full of abandoned weapons. We might need to call such a function many times. This will increase the total time spent in generating points. Keeping this in mind, let's work on improving its performance.

We will revamp the code from the previous optimization run (goldhunt_pass3.py). The supporting source code is in the goldhunt_pass4.py file. The first thing we will add is the NumPy import statement at the beginning of the file:

```
import numpy as np
```

The reworked `generate_random_points` function is illustrated in the following code snippet:

```python
def generate_random_points(ref_radius, total_points):
    """Return x, y coordinate lists representing random points inside a cir
    l_uniform = np.random.uniform
    l_sqrt = np.sqrt
    l_pi = np.pi
    l_cos = np.cos
    l_sin = np.sin

    theta = l_uniform(0.0, 2.0*l_pi, total_points)
    radius = ref_radius*l_sqrt(l_uniform(0.0, 1.0, total_points))
    x = radius*l_cos(theta)
    y = radius*l_sin(theta)

    # x and y thus obtained are NumPy arrays. Return these as lists
    return x.tolist(), y.tolist()
```

It is optional to use local variables such as `l_uniform`. Those are used here to skip the function reevaluation. This was already discussed in the *Skipping the dots* section from the previous chapter. Let's review this function next:

- Compare the new function with the previous implementation. The key thing to note here is the use of the NumPy functions, such as `np.random.uniform`, `np.sqrt`, and others in place of the built-in functions.

- Another major difference is that we no longer need a `for` loop. The `np.random.uniform` function returns a NumPy array. The last argument specifies its size. Refer to the earlier introductory section on NumPy for more information on the `random.uniform` functionality.

- The x and y coordinates are computed using the `radius` and `theta` arrays. Note that the variables, x and y, are created as NumPy arrays. For efficiency reasons, we will return these as Python lists. This is accomplished by using `numpy.ndarray.tolist()`, a method accessible to NumPy `array` objects.

Let's profile this code and compare the performance with the previous optimization pass. Here is the command to execute this code:

```
$ python goldhunt_pass4.py
```

The profiler output is shown next:

```
     19434 function calls in 38.391 seconds

Ordered by: internal time
List reduced from 18 to 5 due to restriction <'goldhunt'>

ncalls  tottime  percall  cumtime  percall filename:lineno(function)
    95   37.993    0.400   37.999    0.400 goldhunt_pass4.py:107(find_coins)
     1    0.164    0.164    0.346    0.346 goldhunt_pass4.py:40(generate_random_points)
     1    0.038    0.038   38.391   38.391 goldhunt_pass4.py:173(play_game)
     1    0.002    0.002   38.353   38.353 goldhunt_pass4.py:131(play)
     1    0.000    0.000    0.000    0.000 goldhunt_pass4.py:91(__init__)
```

Observe the cumulative time column for the `generate_random_points` function. The cumulative time for the original function was ~ 5.2 seconds, that is now reduced to `0.346` seconds. This is already a significant improvement.

It is possible to further improve the performance of the `generate_random_points` function. For example, at the beginning of the function, you can compute the product `2*1_pi`, for example:

```
two_pi = 2*np.pi
```

Then use this variable in the computation of `theta`. However, this will only result in a marginal improvement in the runtime.

Gold Hunt optimization – pass five

In this optimization pass, we will further improve the runtime performance of the `GoldHunt.find_coins` method. The original method is shown in the following code snippet for convenience. You can also find it in an earlier `goldhunt_pass4.py` file. For more details, see the previous chapter's, *Gold Hunt Optimization – Pass two* section.

```
def find_coins(self, x_list, y_list):
    """Return list of coins that lie within a given distance...."""
    collected_coins = []
    search_radius_square = self.search_radius*self.search_radius

    # Assign collected_coins.append to a local function
    append_coins_function = collected_coins.append
    # Create locak variables to represent the instance vars
    local_xref = self.x_ref
    local_yref = self.y_ref
                                          Optimization pass-4
    for x, y in zip(x_list, y_list):
        delta_x = local_xref - x
        delta_y = local_yref - y
        dist_square = delta_x*delta_x + delta_y*delta_y

        if dist_square <= search_radius_square:
            # See the definition of append_coins_function
            # before the for loop. It is used in place of
            # collected_coins.append for speedup
            append_coins_function((x, y))

    return collected_coins
```

Recall that the last recorded runtime for this method was about 38 seconds. Our task is to improve it further. We will start the optimization work by making a small change to the generate_random_points function. Recall that this function returns the x and y coordinates of the *gold coins* on the field as Python lists. Instead, let's return these as NumPy arrays.

If you have skipped reading the earlier introductory section on NumPy, now would be the time to go back and read it! The *optimization pass five* uses the NumPy functions discussed in that section. More specifically, the code presented next uses the einsum and dpstack functions. You may find the einsum syntax confusing. Therefore, it is recommended that you read the introduction first before diving into the code.

In the `find_coins` method, we will use the NumPy functions that work efficiently with these NumPy arrays. The following code fragment shows the updated function:

```python
def generate_random_points(ref_radius, total_points):
    """Return x, y coordinate lists representing random points inside a cir
    # Combination of avoiding the dots (function reevaluations)
    # and using local variable. This is similar to the
    # optimization pass-3 but here we use equivalent NumPy functions.
    l_uniform = np.random.uniform
    l_sqrt = np.sqrt
    l_pi = np.pi
    l_cos = np.cos
    l_sin = np.sin

    # Note that the variables theta and radius are now NumPy arrays.
    theta = l_uniform(0.0, 2.0*l_pi, total_points)
    radius = ref_radius*l_sqrt(l_uniform(0.0, 1.0, total_points))
    x = radius*l_cos(theta)
    y = radius*l_sin(theta)

    # Unlike optimization pass-4 (which returns x and y as Python lists,
    # here it returns the NumPy arrays directly to be consumed by
    # the GoldHunt.find_coins method
    return x, y
```

With this change, let's quickly review the reworked `find_coins` method next:

```python
def find_coins(self, x_list, y_list):
    """Return list of coins that lie within a given distance...."""
    collected_coins = []
    # Compute the square of the search radius needed later
    search_radius_square = self.search_radius*self.search_radius
    # Assign collected_coins.append to a local function
    append_coins_function = collected_coins.append

    # Create a single 'points' array from          Optimization pass-5
    # (x_list, y_list) representing x, y coordinates.
    points = np.dstack((x_list, y_list))
    # Array representing the center of search circle
    center = np.array([self.x_ref, self.y_ref])
    diff = points - center

    # Use einsum to get array representing distance squares
    distance_squares = np.einsum('...i,...i', diff, diff)
    # Convert it to Python list
    dist_sq_list = distance_squares[0].tolist()

    for i, d in enumerate(dist_sq_list):
        # i is the index. d is the value of the list item
        if d <= search_radius_square:
            append_coins_function((x_list[i], y_list[i]))

    return collected_coins
```

Let's review the preceding code snippet:

- Recall that our task is to find the square of the distance between any gold coin on the field and the center of the search circle, and then use this value to check if the gold coin lies inside the search circle.

- The input argument, `x_list` and `y_list`, are the NumPy arrays representing the x and y positions of the gold coins on the field.

- Using these coordinates, we will create a single `points` array that contains (x, y) coordinate pairs as its elements. This is accomplished using `numpy.dstack`. See the earlier introductory section on NumPy for an example usage.

- Next, we will find the vector between each point in the `points` array and the `center` array for the search circle. These vectors are stored as the elements of the `diff` array.

- Using this `diff` array, we will find the square of the distances between all the gold coins from the center using `einsum`. See an earlier, *Computing distance square with einsum* section, where this was discussed in detail.

- Finally, we will check if the gold coin lies inside the circle by comparing the distance squares. The `enumerate()` function is a built-in function that presents a cleaner way to get the current index (i) of the loop and the corresponding value (d).

The code is ready. Now, it is time to profile it:

```
$ python goldhunt_pass5.py
```

The profiler output is shown below:

```
        21345 function calls in 21.487 seconds

Ordered by: internal time
List reduced from 25 to 5 due to restriction <'goldhunt'>

ncalls  tottime  percall  cumtime  percall filename:lineno(function)
    95   14.843    0.156   19.504    0.205 goldhunt_pass5.py:148(find_coins)
     1    1.754    1.754   21.483   21.483 goldhunt_pass5.py:192(play)
     1    0.161    0.161    0.219    0.219 goldhunt_pass5.py:40(generate_random_points)
     1    0.003    0.003   21.486   21.486 goldhunt_run_master.py:37(play_game)
     1    0.000    0.000    0.000    0.000 goldhunt_pass5.py:132(__init__)
```

Observe that the cumulative time taken by the `find_coins` function has gone down to ~19.5 seconds from the earlier ~ 38 seconds. It is nearly a 50% improvement for this function alone. Also, the total runtime is now ~ 21.5 seconds compared to the previous timing of ~38 seconds.

It is possible to improve the performance of `find_coins` by using list comprehension instead of the `for` loop. However, the improvement will be marginal. You can try it as an exercise (no solution is provided). Here is a sample code that uses list comprehension:

```
collected_coins = [(x_list[i], y_list[i])
                    for i, d in enumerate(dist_sq_list)
                    if d <= search_radius_square]
```

Parallelization with the multiprocessing module

Before jumping onto the discussion of the `multiprocessing` module, let's first understand what we mean by parallelization. This will be a very short introduction to parallelization, just enough to understand how to use some features of the `multiprocessing` module.

Introduction to parallelization

Imagine you are standing in a long queue at a checkout counter in a grocery store, waiting for your turn. Now, three more counters are opened to serve the customers and the existing queue is split. As a result, you can pay and get out of the store quickly.

Parallelization, in some sense, accomplishes similar results. In this example, each counter can be imagined as a separate process, carrying out independent tasks of accepting payments. The initial queue of the customers can be imagined as your program. This long queue is then divided into independent queues (or tasks), processing them parallely on separate counters (processes).

The *Gold Hunt* program we have written so far runs serially. The program executes a set of tasks one after another on a single processor. This is analogous to the single counter in the previously mentioned grocery store example. Many times, it is possible to split the program into smaller tasks and run them independently using multiple processes or threads.

Let's quickly review two broad programming models that handle parallel process communications. These are **shared memory** and **distributed memory** parallelization.

Shared memory parallelization

In the shared memory programming model, the parallel processes access the same memory segment. Thus, the exchange of data and the communication between processes happens through this common memory. This programming model is often referred to as *threaded programming*. The disadvantage of the shared memory model is something known as a **race condition**. Here, multiple threads compete to access or modify, for instance, data at a memory location. The race condition can be avoided by controlling access to that critical information using *locks*. However, this adds to the programming overhead. Refer to `https://en.wikipedia.org/wiki/Shared_ memory` for further information.

Distributed memory parallelization

Here, each process gets its own memory space. The processes do not share any memory resources, and they run independent of each other. The communication between the processes happens over inter-process communication channels. This is referred to as **message passing**. To learn more about message passing, see `https://en.wikipedia.org/wiki/Message_passing`. Since the processes do not share the same memory space, there is an additional communication overhead associated with the distributed memory mechanism.

Global interpreter lock

In Python, the `threading` module provides a high-level interface for thread based parallelization. To avoid the race condition discussed earlier, Python employs a mechanism called **global interpreter lock** (GIL). When a thread is executing a block of code, a global lock is acquired. This lock makes sure that only one thread is executed at a time in the Python interpreter environment. The disadvantage of GIL is that you cannot take full advantage of a multiprocessor machine.

The multiprocessing module

The `multiprocessing` module addresses the GIL problem and provides a simple way to parallelize Python programs. Instead of using threads, it uses sub-processes and avoids GIL. In this module, the exchange of data between processes is supported using two communication channels, a `Queue` class and a `Pipe` function. This module also provides several other useful features, such as *managers* and *proxy objects*. The `Manager` object is created using `multiprocessing.Manager()`. It controls a server process that manages the Python objects. The manager also enables other processes to manipulate these Python objects using proxies. Discussing these features is beyond the scope of this book. Python documentation has great examples of how these features work. Refer to `https://docs.python.org/3/library/multiprocessing.html` for more information.

In this chapter, we will cover only a few features of the `Pool` class.

The Pool class

The `multiprocessing.Pool` class provides a simple approach to parallelize the program. It is used to manage a pool of worker processes and defines methods that enable various ways to run the given tasks parallely.

> The other basic approach is to use the `Process` class, which is not
> discussed in this book. See the previous documentation link for details.

The `Pool.map` and `Pool.apply` methods are among the ones frequently used. These
are the parallel equivalents of the Python built-in `map` and `apply` functions. Both
these methods block the main program until a worker process is finished and the
results are ready. The blocking nature is useful if you are interested in getting a
sequential output from the parallel processes. They also have their asynchronous
variants, namely `map_async` and `apply_async`. The asynchronous variants are better
suited to run parallel jobs where you don't care about the order in which results are
returned by the processes.

> The `apply` function is no longer a built-in function in Python 3.
> However, it was supported in Python 2.7. You can refer to Python 2
> documentation to learn what this function does.

Let's work on a simple example that shows how to use the `Pool` class and its
methods, `map` and `apply`. Observe the following code:

```python
import multiprocessing


def get_result(num):
    """Trivial function used in multiprocessing example"""
    process_name = multiprocessing.current_process().name
    print("Current process:", process_name, ", Input Number:", num)
    return 10*num


if __name__ == '__main__':
    numbers = [2, 4, 6, 8]
    # Create two worker processes.
    pool = multiprocessing.Pool(2)
    # Use Pool.map method to run the task using the pool of processes.
    mylist = pool.map(func=get_result, iterable=numbers)
    # Stop the worker processes
    pool.close()
    # Join the processes
    pool.join()
    print("Output:", mylist)
```

Let's review the preceding code snippet:

- We start by importing the `multiprocessing` module.

- The `pool` instance is created with two worker processes. You can specify the number of worker processes as an optional input argument.

- After creating a pool of workers, the `pool.map` method is called. As previously stated, this is a parallel equivalent of the built-in `map` function. The first argument is a trivial function called `get_result`. This function is applied to the `iterable` specified as the second argument.

- In this case, the `get_result` function is applied on each element of the `numbers` list. Inside this function, we also print the name of the current worker process doing the job.

- The `pool.close()` method stops the worker processes after execution, whereas the `pool.join()` method blocks until the worker process terminates. This mimics the API provided by the `threading` module.

The preceding code can also be found in `pool_example.py`. In this file, you just need to enable the relevant code and disable the other function calls. The file can be run from the Command Prompt, as follows:

```
$ python pool_example.py
```

Here is a sample command-line output after this execution:

```
Current process: ForkPoolWorker-1 , Input Number: 2
Current process: ForkPoolWorker-2 , Input Number: 4
Current process: ForkPoolWorker-2 , Input Number: 6
Current process: ForkPoolWorker-1 , Input Number: 8
Output: [20, 40, 60, 80]
```

Notice that the elements of the output list (`mylist`) are arranged in the same order as the input list (`numbers`). In other words, we have the input as `[2, 4, 6, 8]` and the output is 10 times each element, given as `[20, 40, 60, 80]`. This may or may not be the case for asynchronous variants. It will depend on which order the processes finish and return the results for.

With just a single line change, we can run the same example using `Pool.apply`. The following code snippet shows how to do this. The `get_result` function is not shown as it remains the same as before, as follows:

```
if __name__ == '__main__':
    numbers = [2, 4, 6, 8]
    # Create two worker processes.
    pool = multiprocessing.Pool(2)
    # Use Pool.apply method to run the task using pool of processes
    mylist = [pool.apply(get_result, args=(num,)) for num in numbers]
    # Stop the worker processes
    pool.close()
    # Join the processes
    pool.join()
    print("Output:", mylist)
```

Here, we created `mylist` using list comprehension. For each element of the `numbers` list, it calls the `Pool.apply` method. The first argument to the method is the name of the function whereas the second argument, `args`,is used to specify the other arguments to this function. This method offers convenient syntax to specify any number of arguments to the function being sent to the worker processes. The rest of the code and programming output remains the same, as shown in the `Pool.map` method example. Let's review one of the asynchronous variants, `Pool.apply_async`. The code is shown as follows:

```
if __name__ == '__main__':
    numbers = [2, 4, 6, 8, 10]
    # Create two worker processes.
    pool - multiprocessing.Pool(2)

    # Use Pool.apply_async method to run the tasks
    results = [pool.apply_async(get_result, args=(num,))
                    for num in numbers]

    # The elements of results list are instances of Pool.ApplyResult.
    # Use the object's get() method to get the final values.
    mylist = [p.get() for p in results]

    # Stop the worker processes
    pool.close()
    # Join the processes
    pool.join()
    print("Output:", mylist)
```

Let's talk through this code:

- This involves two changes. The first one is a trivial one. The `apply` method is simply replaced with `apply_async` (shown highlighted). There is no change in the method syntax.

- However, the output of the `apply_async` call does not directly give us the final values we need. Instead, it returns the object of a `Pool.ApplyResult` class.

- In this example, `apply_async` is used inside a list comprehension. So, the elements of the `results` list are objects of the `ApplyResult` class.

- The final value can be obtained using the `ApplyResult.get()` method. We do this using a list comprehension, as shown in the preceding image. Alternatively, you can also use the generator expression syntax discussed in the previous chapter.

With this short introduction on parallelization, let's see how to parallelize some functionality from the *Gold Hunt* application.

Parallelizing the Gold Hunt program

Looking at the previous profiler output, the `find_coins` function is still the main bottleneck with ~19.5 seconds of cumulative time. Let's see how parallelization can help speed it up further.

Revisiting the gold field

Here is the *gold field* image from *Chapter 7, Performance – Identifying Bottlenecks*:

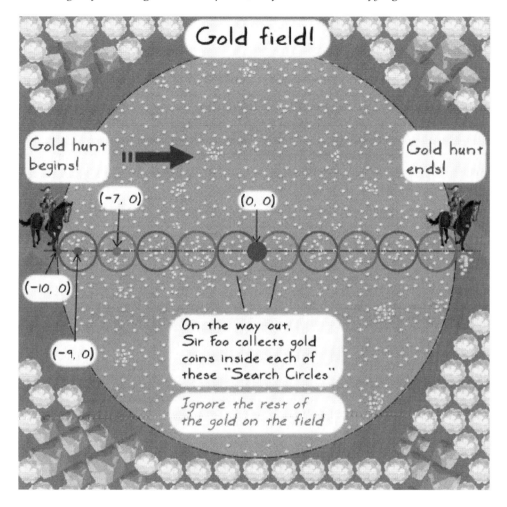

Let's quickly summarize what we already saw in *Chapter 7, Performance – Identifying Bottlenecks*:

- The `find_coins` method is called for each of the small search circles shown in the figure. So, if there are 10 search circles, `find_coins` will be called 10 times, one after the other.

- The `find_coins` method returns the coordinates of the gold coins lying inside the given search circle.

- The information about all such collected coins is maintained in a list object.

There is one important thing to note here. It is a serial execution. You start with the first circle, collect the coins and move on to the next one, and repeat the procedure until you hit the other end of the field.

So how can we further enhance the search operation? Any thoughts, Mr. Great Dwarf?

Perfect! The search operation inside each circle is independent of the others. Therefore, the find_coins *function can be independently executed for each search circle. This is an ideal candidate for parallelization.*

That is even better!

Since the order in which the results are returned (by the worker processes) is not important, we can use Pool.apply_async *to parallelize this task.*

Gold Hunt optimization – Pass six, parallelization

As a first step, you should skim through the play method of the last *optimization pass five*. Most of the changes we are about to make will be in this method. Additionally, we will pass some more arguments to the find_coins method.

So, we decided to use a pool of worker processes represented by a `Pool` object. The *work queue* of this `Pool` object consists of all the search circles inside the gold field shown earlier. Each worker process will parallely run the search operation (`find_coins`), and it doesn't depend on other search circles. Generally, the worker processes within a `Pool` object are not terminated until the complete work queue is processed. When a worker process is done finding the coins in a particular search circle, it may get assigned to perform this operation for another search circle.

So what changes are required to be done to the `play` *method? The code will be very similar to the basic example of* `apply_async`, *as seen earlier. Does anything else need to be changed in the existing method? Our friend Elf has a question...*

```python
def play(self):
    """Top level logic to play the g⟨ From Optimization pass-5
    total_collected_coins = []
    x_list, y_list = generate_random_points(self.field_radius,
                                            self.field_coins)
    count = 0
    while self.x_ref <= 9.0:
        count += 1
        # Find all the coins that lie within the circle of radius 1 unit
        coins = self.find_coins(x_list, y_list)
        print("Circle# {num}, center:({x}, {y}), coins: {gold}".format(
            num=count, x=self.x_ref, y=self.y_ref, gold=len(coins)))

        # Update the main list that keeps record of all collected coins.
        total_collected_coins.extend(coins)

        # Move to the next position along positive X axis
        self.x_ref += self.move_distance

    print("Total_collected_coins =", len(total_coll
```

The code depends on the instance variables x__ref and y__ref. These are updated every time we advance to the next search circle. Wouldn't that be a blocker here?

> *You are spot on! The existing* `play` *method serially runs the search operation. It starts with the leftmost circle, finds the coins, and moves on to the next circle by updating* `x_ref`. *Note that we have chosen* `y_ref` *as* `0.0` *in this example.*
>
> *When we run this search operation on parallel processes, each circle will have its unique center coordinates. We need to provide appropriate values of these coordinates to each parallel process. To do this, let's remove the dependence on* `x_ref` *and* `y_ref`. *The center coordinates of all the circles will be determined and stored in a list before parallelizing the search operation.*

The `play` method with the preceding changes is shown below:

```python
def play(self):
    """Top level logic to play the game"""
    x_ref = self.x_ref                          # Optimization pass-6
    x_centers = []
    circle_numbers = []
    x_list, y_list = generate_random_points(self.field_radius,
                                            self.field_coins)
    # Prepare a list to store all the circle centers (x_ref).
    count = 0
    while x_ref <= 9.0:                          # Circle centers and
        count += 1                              # numbers are the two lists
        x_centers.append(x_ref)                 # used in apply_async
        x_ref += self.move_distance
        circle_numbers.append(count)

    # Parallelize the find_coins operation. Choose the
    # number of processes depending on your machine specs!
    pool = multiprocessing.Pool(processes=3)
    results = [pool.apply_async( self.find_coins,
                                args=( x_list, y_list, x_ref, num))
                for x_ref, num in zip(x_centers, circle_numbers)]

    pool.close()
    pool.join()

    # The elements of results list are instances of Pool.ApplyResult.
    # Use the object's get() method to get the final values.
    # Optionally You can also use generator expression here.
    output = [p.get() for p in results]
    # Merge the results
    total_collected_coins = list(itertools.chain(*output))
    print("Total collected coins =", len(total_collected_coins))
```

Let's talk through the important changes in this method:

- In a `while` loop, we will first determine the centers of all the search circles and store the coordinates in a list called `x_centers`. The y coordinate (`y_ref`) is not updated because we have chosen it as constant (`0.0`) for all the circles.

- In the same `while` loop, another `circle_number` list is populated to represent the circle ID. This is just for printing purposes so that we will know which search operation is being performed.

- After preparing the list, a pool of worker threads is created and then `apply_async` is called in a list comprehension.

- Recall that the first argument to the `Pool.apply_async` method is the name of the function (`self.find_coins`), whereas the second argument, `args`, is used to specify all the arguments to this function.

- The rest of the code is similar to what we saw in the introduction of the `multiprocessing` module. The `apply_async` call returns a list containing objects of the `ApplyResult` class. Then, the `get()` method of this class is used to obtain the final values.

> If you are using Python 2.7.9, you may have to create and use a global function as the first argument to `apply_async`. This global function can then return the `GoldHunt.find_coins` method. This is a workaround to avoid a `PicklingError` exception noticed while testing the code. For Python 3.x, there is no problem. This code is provided in the supplementary code bundle. See the Python 2 equivalent of the `goldhunt_pass6_parallel.py` file for details.

Finally, there are some changes to the `GoldHunt.find_coins` method. It now takes the `process_x_ref` and `circle_number` functions as two new arguments. The `process_x_ref` function represents the x coordinate of a given search circle. The `process_` prefix is added just to distinguish it from `self.x_ref`, and indicate that its value will be different for each worker process.

Using `apply_async`, we will run this method on separate parallel processes. Each process gets its own circle center and number to be given as an input for the `find_coins` method. The method is shown in the following code snippet. The highlighted code indicates the changes in comparison with the previous optimization pass.

```
def find_coins(self, x_list, y_list, process_x_ref, circle_num):
    """Return list of coins that lie within a given distance..."""
    collected_coins = []
    # Compute the square of the search radius needed later
    search_radius_square = self.search_radius*self.search_radius
    # Assign collected_coins.append to a local function
    append_coins_function = collected_coins.append

    # Create a single 'points' array from           Optimization pass-6
    # (x_list, y_list) representing x, y coord
    points = np.dstack((x_list, y_list))
    # Array representing the center of search circle
    # process_x_ref is the x-coordinate of the current search circle
    center = np.array([process_x_ref, self.y_ref])
    diff = points - center

    # Use einsum to get array representing distance squares
    distance_squares = np.einsum('...i,...i', diff, diff)
    # Convert it to Python list (list of 'distance squares')
    dist_sq_list = distance_squares[0].tolist()

    for i, d in enumerate(dist_sq_list):
        # i is the index, d is the value of the list item
        if d <= search_radius_square:
            append_coins_function((x_list[i], y_list[i]))

    print("Circle# {num}, center:({x}, {y}), coins: {gold}".format(
            num=circle_num, x=process_x_ref, y=self.y_ref,
            gold=len(collected_coins)))
    return collected_coins
```

The rest of the code remains the same as the previous optimization pass. The source code is provided in the `goldhunt_pass6_parallel.py` file. Let's run this code and see the profiler output:

```
$ python goldhunt_pass6_parallel.py
```

This will print information on the search circles as it did earlier. Here is the profiler output:

```
    6382 function calls (6329 primitive calls) in 13.625 seconds

Ordered by: internal time
List reduced from 251 to 6 due to restriction <'goldhunt'>

ncalls  tottime  percall  cumtime  percall filename:lineno(function)
     1    0.150    0.150    0.207    0.207 goldhunt_pass_parallel.py:41(generate_random_points)
     1    0.001    0.001   13.625   13.625 goldhunt_run_master.py:37(play_game)
     1    0.001    0.001   13.624   13.624 goldhunt_pass_parallel.py:149(play)
     1    0.000    0.000   13.302   13.302 goldhunt_pass_parallel.py:171(<listcomp>)
     1    0.000    0.000    0.004    0.004 goldhunt_pass_parallel.py:169(<listcomp>)
     1    0.000    0.000    0.000    0.000 goldhunt_pass_parallel.py:93(__init__)
```

Note that the `find_coins` call is not shown in the profiler output. It is hidden inside the reported timing of the `play` method. Comparing the cumulative time (`cumtime`) of the `play` method should give a reasonable estimate on the performance gain with parallelization.

In summary, the parallelization has helped improve the total timing from earlier, ~21.5 seconds to ~13.5 seconds.

 Depending on your machine specifications, you can try increasing the number of worker processes by updating the argument to the `Pool` class. For example, instead of three processes you can run the program with four processes. However, this is a simple case and the runtime is so short that you will hardly see any further improvement. In fact, the overhead of the sub-processes may even result in a slightly degraded performance. Also, depending on the problem, beyond a certain number of processes, the performance gain due to parallelization can fade away.

Other methods for parallelization

Is the `apply_async` method the only way to parallelize this problem? Certainly not. There are other methods in the `multiprocessing` module that can do this efficiently. `Pool.starmap_async` is one such method available in Python 3.3 and beyond. We are not going to discuss this here, but the following code shows how to invoke it along with the `itertools.repeat` function:

```
results = pool.starmap_async(self.find_coins,
                             zip(itertools.repeat(x_list),
                                 itertools.repeat(y_list),
                                 x_centers,
                                 circle_numbers))
```

For more information on such methods, refer to the `multiprocessing` module documentation.

Further reading

In the series of the three chapters on performance, we covered several important aspects. The things learned here will help you with the majority of common application performance enhancement tasks. Where do we go from here? There are some other important topics that you can explore, among those are JIT compilers and **Graphics Processing Unit (GPU)** programming. This section aims at providing some basic information on these two topics. You can follow the links provided here for further understanding.

JIT compilers

Python is an interpreted language. In simple terms, it means that the code is parsed and executed directly without involving any code compilation. Although this offers a great deal of flexibility, the program typically runs slower.

In high-level programming languages such as C++, the code is compiled ahead of time or before the execution. Generally speaking, a compiled program (C++) runs faster compared to the equivalent interpreted program (Python).

Thus, we have an interpreted code on one side which offers flexibility and a compiled code on the other that runs faster. The JIT compiler gets the best of both worlds. It compiles the code, but instead of compiling it ahead of execution, it does this just-in-time or during the program execution.

PyPy is one such project that provides an alternative implementation of the Python language that comes with a JIT compiler. Python programs often run faster with PyPy. It is also memory efficient and offers high compatibility with the existing Python code. To learn more about PyPy, check out `http://pypy.org`.

Numba is another project aimed at speeding up the application. It provides a JIT compiler and a very simple syntax to mark a function for optimization using a JIT compiler. You just need to use the `numba.git()` decorator. In other words, add `@jit` above the function name to mark the function for optimization. If you are using the Anaconda Python distribution discussed in *Chapter 1, Developing Simple Applications*, it already provides the `numba` module by default. To learn more, visit the project home page (`http://numba.pydata.org`).

GPU accelerated computing

GPU is traditionally used for applications involving heavy rendering, such as game applications. It is now widely used for applications involving scientific simulations, neural networks, financial modeling, and so on. The massively parallel architecture of a GPU offers tremendous performance improvement (of the order of 100x or more) over the CPU-based parallelization. A typical strategy is to identify the most compute intensive part of your application, and then send it to a GPU. The rest of the code can continue to use CPU. However, it is not as simple as it sounds, especially if you are working on a legacy code. In such cases, the challenge can be to make it compatible to fully utilize the GPU acceleration.

PyCUDA (`https://pypi.python.org/pypi/pycuda`) is a popular Python package that provides a wrapper to access Nvidia's CUDA parallel API. CUDA is a parallel computing platform by NVIDIA. More information can be found at `http://www.nvidia.com/object/cuda_home_new.html`.

PyOpenCL (`https://pypi.python.org/pypi/pyopencl`) is another Python package. It provides an easy access to the **Open Computing Language** (**OpenCL**) API. OpenCL is a framework for parallel computation. Refer to `https://en.wikipedia.org/wiki/OpenCL` for further information.

Summary

With this chapter, we end the series of chapters focused on performance improvements. Let's first summarize what you learned in this chapter. We started with a basic introduction to the NumPy library and saw how to leverage it to further speed up the *Gold Hunt* application. In particular, we used the array (`numpy.ndarray`) data structure and other functionalities, such as `numpy.random.uniform` and `numpy.einsum` to achieve the speedup. The final optimization pass involved parallelizing the code. The chapter briefly introduced you to the basics of parallel processing. We used functionality from Python's `multiprocessing.Pool` class to further trim down the application runtime.

Finally, let's summarize the three performance chapters together. We started by profiling the code to identify the performance bottlenecks and learned about the big O notation. We gradually addressed these bottlenecks to improve the application performance. This was accomplished by several means, ranging from changing the algorithm and implementing efficient data structures to using the functionality from a Python standard library. We further improved the runtime by using NumPy and also by parallelizing the code.

The timings reported by the profiler will vary widely. It depends on your machine specifications, and also on the current running tasks. So, the timings observed in your case will likely be different than the numbers reported in this book.

For the *Gold Hunt* example discussed in these chapters, the total runtime was reduced almost by an order of magnitude, from an initial value of about 106 seconds to a final runtime of nearly 13.5 seconds.

So far, in this book, you learned several key aspects of application development using command-line programs. In the final chapter, we'll see how to develop simple GUI applications in Python.

10
Simple GUI Applications

All the chapters so far were about learning to write better application code in Python. Starting with a simple program, we saw how to develop robust and efficient applications. We touched upon several important areas of software development. More specifically, we covered exception handling, deploying applications, documentation, adopting best practices, unit testing, refactoring, design patterns, and performance improvements. The key concepts were explained using various command-line applications that were progressively improved.

Where do we go from here? Beyond the command line, there are applications that present an interactive user interface. Desktop, mobile GUI applications, or web applications come under this category. Also, there are applications targeted for specific domains such as network and database programming. These are broad topics, and each has its own set of goodies that will help make the application robust. Nonetheless, the techniques we have learned in this book provide a solid foundation for all these domains.

This last chapter is designed to give you just a flavor of one such domain. It will be a superficial introduction to desktop GUI application development using Python.

 GUI programming is too big of a beast to fit into a single chapter. Let's do that anyway, keeping in mind that there is plenty of opportunity to learn beyond what is discussed here. The chapter won't show you how to create full-fledged, complex GUI applications. Rather, we will just dip a toe into GUI application development using Python's Tkinter library.

Here is how the rest of the chapter is organized:

- The chapter will start with an overview of the available GUI frameworks.
- Next, we will see what event-driven programming is, followed by a primer on the Tkinter library.

- What follows next is our first project, a simple GUI application that uses Tkinter. It is essentially the GUI version of the first ever application we developed in *Chapter 1, Developing Simple Applications*.

- The next section will serve as an introduction to the **Model-view-controller (MVC)** architecture. This will be followed by our second project, where the earlier application is rewritten to implement the MVC architecture.

- The chapter will also talk about testing GUI applications. This will be a high-level discussion, and won't involve writing any code.

- This being the last chapter, we will conclude it, and hence the book, with a brief discussion on various application frontiers.

Overview of GUI frameworks

A user interface is typically something that a user can see and use to communicate with the application. So far, we have presented a text-based user interface. For example, in the *Attack of the Orcs* application, the user was prompted to specify a hut number, and based on the number entered, further actions were taken.

A **Graphical User Interface (GUI)**, on the other hand, presents an interface to the user that may have buttons, icons, text fields, graphics, and so on. There are several Python GUI frameworks available. Many of these are based on cross-platform technologies such as Tk, Qt, wxWidgets, and others. Let's briefly discuss some of the most popular frameworks. The purpose is to just make you aware of the GUI technologies available.

Tkinter

Tkinter provides Python bindings or interface to the open source Tk GUI widget toolkit. For more information on Tk, see its official website, `http://www.tcl.tk/`. It is available as a standard module in Python. What this means is that as long as Python is installed, we do not need any additional installations to use it. In this book, we will demonstrate basic GUI concepts using the Tkinter library.

PyQt

PyQt (`https://wiki.python.org/moin/PyQt`) is a widely used Python GUI library. It is one of the most mature frameworks out there. It essentially provides Python bindings for a popular Qt GUI application development framework. In order to use this framework, you need to install Qt first.

It is worth noting here that Qt has different licensing schemes depending on the project. For example, if your project is an open source distribution, licensed under the terms of LGPL or GPL, you can use Qt freely. If you are using it for a commercial purpose, you have to purchase a license. Visit the Qt website, `https://www.qt.io/`, for more details.

PySide

PySide is another Python binding for the Qt GUI framework. It is a free software, released under the LGPL license. PySide supports Windows, Mac, and Linux OS. For more information, see `https://wiki.qt.io/PySide`.

Kivy

This is one of the most promising open source frameworks for creating cross-platform interactive user interfaces. With kivy, you can rapidly develop native multi-touch apps for mobile or desktop. It provides a design language called Kv for GUI design. The kivy website lists many supported operating systems including Windows, Mac OS X , Ubuntu, and Android for which an installer is available.

 If you are using a different OS not listed on the kivy website, the installation could be a challenge. For example, at the time of writing this book, there is no installer available for **Red Hat Enterprise Linux (RHEL)** version 6.x. The other option is to build it from source code. But that could be a challenge if you are not familiar with the code compilation and building process. If you really want to use it, you could also install it in a virtual machine running one of the supported OS.

wxPython

This package provides a wrapper for **wxWidgets**, a cross-platform GUI library. It is an open source toolkit, and according to the project website (`http://www.wxpython.org`), the supported platforms include 32-bit Windows, many Unix-like operating systems, and Mac OS X.

While there are many choices available at our disposal, in this chapter we will use the built-in Tkinter module mentioned earlier. The scope will be limited to developing a simple application that demonstrates some of the major components of GUI-based application development.

GUI programming design considerations

Although the focus of this chapter is on developing simple GUI applications, it is worth taking a moment to briefly discuss some important practical design considerations or guidelines for developing user interfaces. These guidelines will also come in handy for web-based or mobile applications. Some aspects that we are about to discuss should actually be part of your GUI application development life cycle.

Understanding user requirements

The first and foremost task is to put yourself in the shoes of the end user. You are developing the GUI application for consumption by the end users. It is important to take their feedback on the features that they would like to see. This is typically a part of requirements gathering.

Developing a user story

OK, so you know what features are requested, and have prepared a list that would be supported in the upcoming version. It is often useful to prepare a mock user interface that illustrates how various features could be accessed and how they interact. The mock user interface could be in the form of a simple presentation. You can then take feedback from the development team as well as from the key users of the product. This will allow you to immediately identify the problems, if any, or refine your design strategy even before writing a single line of code. Such discussions with the key stakeholders could also unearth future requirements that you have not thought through. This, in turn, will help you refine the software architecture to make provisions for such requirements. Next, let's learn about some of the design principles.

Simplicity and accessibility

The GUI should be simple enough to make the most frequently used tasks easy to access. What the developers think as *simple* may not always go well with the end users. Getting user feedback and going through design iterations play an important role. In general, keep the following things in mind when designing for simplicity:

- It matters how you lay out the various components in the application window. Is it intuitive? Is it easily accessible?

- Place frequently used and important functionality prominently in the UI.

- Try to hide advanced or less frequently used features. If possible, you could create an expert level mode in your GUI where these features appear prominently.

- Have default values wherever applicable.

- Common user actions should be easy to execute. For example, if changing the background color is a common task, allow users to access this option with a click of a button or with a keyboard shortcut.

- Try not to put too many things in the default display. Reduce the clutter.

Of course, this is not a complete list, and things will change depending on the application and the domain.

Consistency

The user interface should be consistent. If you have similar features, they should have a similar look and feel, similar steps to execute, and so on. The placement of standard features or functions should not change. For example, in a text editor, the **Open** button is typically placed near the top-left corner of the application window. This default position should remain constant.

Predictability and familiarity

When a button is clicked, the user should be able to predict the next course of action. A trivial example is the **Save As...** button—when clicked, the user anticipates a dialog with the option to specify a location and file format. Why? Because he or she is familiar with using a similar function in some other application. Further, the user would anticipate some default directory location to save the file. The UI should not surprise the user by changing this behavior.

Similarly, when you design an icon, it should speak for itself. For example, a gear icon typically indicates some sort of configurable settings. The UI design should be such that the user can easily guess the next action to perform in a particular situation, be it exiting the current mode or going back to the previous step, and so on.

Miscellaneous design considerations

We have covered some of the important factors you should know before designing a GUI. There are many other design principles. Some of these principles are tied to the aspects that we've already discussed. A few of these can be listed as follows:

- The GUI should have a visual appeal and clarity.

- It should be comprehensible. In other words, new users should quickly get up to speed.

- It should anticipate common problems, and gracefully handle user errors.

Event-driven programming

In an algorithm-driven program, the flow of the program is dictated by the predefined steps written in that program. The program may prompt the user with these instructions for an input. An example is a command-line application asking for user input in a predefined order.

In contrast, applications with a graphical user interface let the user dictate the program flow. The application waits for the user actions, and then responds to those actions. For example, if you are reading a PDF copy of a book, you can perform actions like jumping to the next page, zooming-in, scrolling down, or closing the window by clicking on the appropriate buttons. Here, you are essentially telling the application what to do next. This is called event-driven programming. Here, the control flow of the program is governed by the triggered events. The application responds to these events as they occur. The response could be changing the state of the graphical element or running some background task, and so on. For example, if the user clicks a button representing the next page, the application will display the next page of the book. Next, let's briefly talk about a few important concepts in event-driven programming.

Event

In simple terms, an event represents an action happening inside the GUI window. An event could be triggered by various sources. For example, when a user clicks a mouse button, it generates a click event; pressing a key on the keyboard is recognized as another event, and so on. An event could also be generated without a direct user input. For example, the application might have completed running some calculations in the background, and now wants to update the contents presented by the GUI. This could automatically trigger some update event that would redraw the view.

Event handling

When an event is triggered, the application responds to that event. For example, when you click on the close button of a browser, you expect the browser window to close. In this example, closing the window is the application's response to the click event generated due to user action. In other words, the application has a *listener* object that *handles* this click event. Every GUI framework provides a way to *bind* (or *connect*) an event to a handling function.

Event loop

The event loop is the main controlling loop of the GUI program. When you start the application, the main loop is started, and it waits for the events to occur. It monitors the event sources, and dispatches the events when they occur.

With this short introduction, let's summarize what we have learned about event-driven programming:

- The overall flow of program execution is governed by events
- The application runs (the main loop starts) and waits for events to occur
- When an event is triggered, the application code, which is listening to the events, responds by running a specific handling function
- Thus, the flow of a program depends on the triggered events

GUI programming with Tkinter

As mentioned earlier, a GUI provides a way to interact with an application. Instead of a text-based input, the user is presented with elements such as text boxes, radio buttons, tool bars, and so on. This section will introduce you to the basics of GUI programming with Tkinter. This library is available as a standard module in Python.

Tkinter documentation links

Let's document some links for a handy reference. The official Tkinter documentation page can be found at `https://docs.python.org/3/library/tkinter.html#module-tkinter`. This page lists several external references. A good introduction is available at `http://effbot.org/tkinterbook`. Of course, you can always perform a web search with search terms like python and Tkinter to find more resources.

Alternatively, you can quickly find the supported functionality and documentation using the Python interpreter!

```
>>> import tkinter
>>> dir(tkinter)
```

The preceding command lists the supported classes, functions, and so on. To pull out a docstring, you can call the __doc__ on a given attribute. The following example shows a docstring for `mainloop()` in Tkinter:

```
>>> tkinter.mainloop.__doc__
'Run the main loop of Tcl.'
```

The mainloop() in Tkinter

In the discussion on event-driven programming, we learned about the main controlling loop. Writing an event loop or the main loop in Tkinter is very simple. The following code fragment shows the main loop in action. This is the simplest possible GUI application that you can write using Tkinter:

```
from tkinter import Tk

if __name__ == '__main__':
    mainwin = Tk()
    mainwin.mainloop()
```

Let's talk through this code:

- The first statement imports the Tk class from the tkinter module.
- Next, we create a main application window by instantiating the Tk class. It is represented by the variable mainwin. In Tkinter terminology, it is often referred to as root or master. In this chapter, we will call it mainwin.
- The main event loop is started by calling the mainloop() method.

The output of this simple program is shown next. You can run it as any other Python program. The code can also be found in the supporting material for this chapter (see the file mainloop_example.py). Depending on your operating system and environment, the look and feel of this window may vary.

```
$ python mainloop_example.py
```

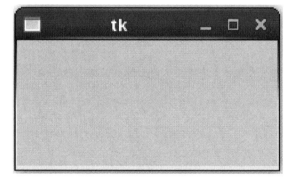

In Python 2.x, there is a minor change in the `import` statement. The module `tkinter` is available as Tkinter (first letter capital) for Python version 2. The supporting code already takes care of this with the following conditional `import`. The rest of the code remains the same.

```
if sys.version_info < (3, 0):
    from Tkinter import Tk
else:
    from tkinter import Tk
```

Simple GUI application – Take 1

We just saw how to start a `mainloop()` method. Let's go one step further, and add some widgets to this application. Observe the following code. You can also see the file `simple_application_1.py` in this chapter's code bundle.

```
from tkinter import Tk, Label, Button, LEFT, RIGHT

if __name__ == "__main__":
    # Create the main window or Tk instance.
    mainwin = Tk()
    mainwin.geometry("140x40")          size specified as 'width x height'
    # Create a label widget and 'pack' it in a row (or column)
    lbl = Label(mainwin, text="Hello World!",  bg='yellow')
    lbl.pack(side=LEFT)
    # 'Exit' button that calls mainwin.destroy when clicked
    exit_button = Button(mainwin, text='Exit', command=mainwin.destroy)
    exit_button.pack(side=RIGHT)          layout option that puts the widget along the right edge

    mainwin.mainloop()
```

The code comments pretty much explain what the code does. It is summarized next:

- We start by importing the necessary classes and options from the `tkinter` module. Note that you could also do the following: `from tkinter import *`. However, the best practices that we saw earlier in the book do not recommend doing that.

- Next, the main window size is specified using the `geometry()` method. This is optional.

- The next few lines of the code create two widgets, a `Label` widget that will show the text `Hello World!`, and a `Button`, which will terminate the application on being clicked.

- We need some way to arrange these widgets inside the application window. This is referred to as geometry or layout management. There are three options to do that. What is illustrated here is the `pack()` method. More on geometry management later.

- When the **Exit** button is clicked, we need some way to process this event. This is accomplished with the command option that is assigned to a callback function. In this example, we simply terminate the application window and also the `mainloop()` by calling `mainwin.destroy()`.

 Recall that Python functions are first-class objects. See *Chapter 6, Design Patterns* where we discussed on this. The callback function, `mainwin.destroy`, is assigned to the command variable.

Running this application from the command line displays a simple GUI window like so:

```
$ python simple_application_1.py
```

If you click on the **Exit** button, it will terminate the main application window.

Looks like Sir Foo is not quite impressed with this simple script...

For bigger and complex applications, it is better to follow the object-oriented programming approach.

Let's rewrite this application, and wrap it in a class. However, keep in mind that it is just a baby step towards creating a better application. Later in the chapter, you will learn about the MVC architecture, and a basic example on implementing it in your GUI application.

Simple GUI application – Take 2

It is time to add some object-oriented flavor to the mix. The application in the previous section can be rewritten as follows:

```
from tkinter import Tk, Label, Button, LEFT, RIGHT

class MyGame:
    def __init__(self, mainwin):
        lbl = Label(mainwin, text="Hello World!",  bg='yellow')
        exit_button = Button(mainwin, text='Exit',
                             command=self.exit_btn_callback)
        # pack the widgets
        lbl.pack(side=LEFT)
        exit_button.pack(side=RIGHT)

    def exit_btn_callback(self):
        """Callback function to handle the button click event."""
        mainwin.destroy()

if __name__ == "__main__":
    # Create the main window or Tk instance.
    mainwin = Tk()
    mainwin.geometry("140x40")
    game_app = MyGame(mainwin)
    mainwin.mainloop()
```

The callback function. We could also directly write: command=mainwin.destroy

New class to hold the main logic and widget creation code.

Let's briefly discuss the preceding code:

- Compare this code against the previous code.

- The `MyGame` class is where we create the widgets and define the main logic.

- Notice that the command callback function for the button is set to `exit_btn_callback`.

- What this means is that when the **Exit** button is pressed, it will invoke `exit_btn_callback()` instead of calling `mainwin.destroy()` directly.

- This is just to show you how to specify a different callback function. You can always set it back to `command=mainwin.destroy()`.

The rest of the code is self-explanatory. You can execute it to get the same `Hello world!` window as in the first program. The command is shown next:

```
$ python simple_application_2.py
```

The `simple_application_2.py` file in the supporting code bundle essentially has the program we just reviewed.

> In all the examples, we will use the `Tk` instance `mainwin` as the master or parent object of the widgets created. In practice, it is often useful to create a container to hold other widgets in the GUI. The container could be an instance of the `Frame` class or any other widget depending on the application. For example, you could write the following:
>
> ```
> mainwin = Tk()
> container = Frame(mainwin)
> some_label = Label(container, text="blah blah")
> ```

Now that we know how to create a simple application with a graphical user interface, let's move ahead and talk about the various widgets available in the Tkinter library.

GUI Widgets in Tkinter

In this section, we will briefly cover some of the frequently used widgets. Note that the widgets we are about to cover are not specific to a GUI library. However, the following discussion is tailored for the Tkinter library. For example, you will find a `Menu` widget in many GUI libraries. Tkinter provides it with the class `Menu`, the PyQt library calls it `QMenu`, and so on.

> What we are about to see is far from being a comprehensive list. You are encouraged to explore the following wiki page that lists several other GUI elements: `https://en.wikipedia.org/wiki/List_of_graphical_user_interface_elements`.

A widget is an element of a graphical user interface that enables user interaction. In other words, the user can do certain actions like pressing a button and interacting with the GUI.

We already saw how to create the `Label` and `Button` widgets. The following table summarizes some important widget classes in Tkinter.

Widget Class	Basic Syntax	Description
Menu	`menubar = Menu(parent)`	This widget represents a menu, such as a menu bar or a pop-up menu. It contains menu items.

Frame	`container =`
	`Frame(parent,`
	`        width=100,`
	`        height=100,`
	`        bg='white')`
		This is typically used as a container to hold other widgets. The frame widget also has its own grid layout, and like many other widgets, you can specify the background color, border, and other properties.

Canvas	`my_canvas =`
	`Canvas(parent,`
	
	`width=100,`
	
	`height=100)`
		This is a graphics widget. This is where you can draw or write stuff. For example, you can render shapes, plots, images, or use this widget to write text.

Label	`lbl = Label(parent,`
	`        text= "some`
	`text",`
	`        bg = 'blue')`
		In a label, you can add a text or an image. When you click on a label, no event is triggered. Instead, you can update a label in response to some other event generated elsewhere.

Button	`ok_button =`
	`    Button(parent,`
	`        text="OK",`
	
	`command=parent.quit)`
	
	The optional `command` argument could also be assigned to any user-defined function.
		A simple button widget. When pressed or released, it triggers an event.

Widget Class	Basic Syntax	Description

Radiobutton	`rbutton_1 =`
	`    Radiobutton(parent,`
	
	`text="Option 1",`
	
	`variable=var,`
	`        value=1)`
	`rbutton_2 =`
	`    Radiobutton(parent,`
	
	`text="Option 2",`
	
	`variable=var,`
	`        value=0)`
	
	A group of radio buttons is tied to a common variable, `var`. When you click on a radio button, the value of that variable is changed to a predefined one given by the value.
		The radio button widget allows a user to choose only a single value from a given set of values. It can contain a text or an image.

Checkbutton	`c_button =`
	
	`Checkbutton(parent,`
	`    text="Enable Audio",`
	`    variable=var)`
	
	The variable `var` has value of 1 when the check button is selected, otherwise the value is set to 0. This is the default behavior.
		This widget allows setting two different values to a variable. Typical usage is to toggle the state (on or off selection) of a variable.

Listbox	`lstbox =`
	`Listbox(parent)`
	
	You can then add elements to this list box using the `insert()` method as follows:
	
	`lstbox.insert(END,`
	`"item1")`
		This widget is used for showing a list of alternatives. The user can select one or many elements from the `Listbox` widget.

Entry	`text_edit=` `Entry(parent)`	This is a text entry widget that allows you to display or input text. In some other GUI frameworks, it is referred to as a line-edit widget.

The basic syntax shown in the previous table is for illustrative purpose only. You can specify many other options. The `parent` argument given to the widget represents the parent or the base widget.

> In this book, we will just use the bare minimum options while creating widgets. You could further configure each of these widgets by specifying the appropriate optional arguments, or by calling the relevant methods. For further learning, follow the various references listed on the official Tkinter documentation page at the following link: `https://docs.python.org/3/library/tkinter.html#module-tkinter`.

Geometry management

Layout or geometry management is about organizing various widgets within the GUI. In Tkinter, this layout management is accomplished with something referred to as geometry managers. There are three different geometry managers to organize the widgets, namely *grid*, *pack*, and *place*. Among these, the grid manager is the recommended choice. Further in this chapter, we will demonstrate the use of a grid manager.

Grid geometry manager

The grid manager offers flexibility in arranging various widgets, and is also very easy to use.

- The parent widget of the grid manager (for example, a frame or a dialog) is treated as a table with rows and columns.

- The smallest element of this table is a cell, which has a height and a width.

- You can place other widgets in such cells. It is also possible to have a widget that spans more than one cells.

- The height of each row in the table is determined by the height of the tallest cell (or a widget) in that cell. Likewise, the width of each column in this table is governed by the widest cell in that column.

- Each row and column in a grid geometry manager can be configured with a weight option. Weight determines how much a specific row or column can expand if the master widget has free space available. The weight can be specified using the methods `grid_rowconfigure` or `grid_columnconfigure` for rows and columns respectively. The default value for weight is 0.

The following screenshot shows a representative grid layout:

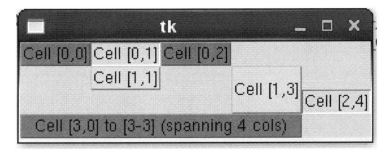

In the preceding image, some `Label` widgets are arranged in a grid layout. The label text **Cell[0,0]** indicates that we have put this label in row 0 and column 0 of the grid. Observe that for **Cell[3,0]**, it shows a label whose width occupies four columns. Similarly, **Cell [1,3]** is a label whose height spans two rows.

Pack geometry manager

In our first Tkinter application, we've already used the pack geometry manager to arrange the widgets. As a refresher, here is the relevant piece of code (the `pack` method):

```
lbl = Label(mainwin, text="Hello World!",  bg='yellow')
lbl.pack(side=LEFT)
```

The pack geometry manager provides options such as expand, fill, and side to control widget placement. It is useful when you want to arrange multiple widgets, either side by side or overlapping each other. The other use case is when you want the widget to occupy the whole container that is holding it.

> Using both grid and pack geometry manager in the same main window could lead to undesirable results. Do not use these layout managers together.

Place geometry manager

The place geometry manager allows you to specify the absolute or relative position of the widget and its size. It finds use in some special scenarios. We will not be discussing this geometry manager further. In most cases, you could, instead, use the grid geometry manager.

Events in Tkinter

Let's briefly talk about the various events supported in Tkinter, and the syntax that describes them.

Event types

The following table shows some of the most frequently used event types. Read the documentation to learn about other event types not listed here. The next section, *Event descriptors*, will elaborate on how to use an event type to describe an event.

Event name	Description
Button (or ButtonPress)	One of the mouse buttons is pressed. Which one? That is determined by the detail field of the event descriptor (see the next section).
ButtonRelease	One of the mouse buttons (that was pressed earlier) is released.
Enter	The mouse pointer entered a widget. This has nothing to do with the *Enter* or *return* key on the keyboard.
Leave	The mouse pointer left a widget.
KeyPress	A keyboard key is pressed. Which one? That is determined in the detail field of the event descriptor.
KeyRelease	A keyboard key is released.
FocusIn	A widget gets an input focus.
FocusOut	A widget no longer has the input focus.

Event descriptors

Tkinter has a special syntax for describing an event. It is a string with the following general form:

```
<[modifier-]type[-detail]>
```

- The event specified is enclosed within the angular brackets <>.
- The type specifies the type of the event, such as a mouse click.
- The modifier and detail specifiers are optional.
- The modifier is the event modifier. Imagine that the Control button is pressed along with a mouse button. Here, the Control button is the event modifier, whereas the mouse button press is the type of the event.
- The detail specifier gives more information about the type of the event. If the type is a mouse click, the details will describe whether it is the left mouse button, the right button, or the middle one.

The following table summarizes some of the common event specifiers.

Event syntax	Description
`<Button-1>`	Mouse button 1 pressed (the left mouse button).
`<Button-2>`	Mouse button 2 pressed (middle button, if available).
`<Button-3>`	Mouse button 3 pressed (the right-most button).
`<KeyPress-B>`	The *B* key is pressed. Likewise, you can write for other keys, such as `<KeyPress-G>`.
`<Return>`	Return key pressed.
`<Configure>`	Size of the widget is changed (for example, window resized). The new size is stored as the width and height attributes of the event object.
`<Shift-Button-1>`	The *Shift* key is pressed along with the left mouse button.

Event object attributes

An instance of the `Event` class holds the information that describes the event. The following table lists some important attributes of the `Event` class.

Event attribute	Description
`widget`	The widget object which triggered this event.
`x, y`	The current mouse position in pixels.
`x_root, y_root`	Mouse position in pixels, relative to the top-left corner.
`width, height`	The changed size (width and height) for the `<Configure>` type of events.

Event handling in Tkinter

Earlier in the chapter, we learned about events and event handling (see the section *Event-driven programming*). In this section, we will see how to bind the various events triggered due to user interactions, with the appropriate handling functions.

Command callback (Button widget)

Recall that when we wrote our first Tkinter application, we tied a callback function to the `command` argument of the `Button` widget. The relevant line of code is reproduced next for easy reference:

```
exit_button = Button(mainwin,text='Exit',command=mainwin.destroy)
```

When you click on the **Exit** button, it calls `mainwin.destroy()`, represented by the `command` argument. It should be noted that while the `Button` widget supports command callback, this feature is not available for all the supported widgets. For that, Tkinter provides the `bind()` method, which is defined on all widgets. The `bind()` method is just one of the levels of event binding in Tkinter. Let's talk about a few event-binding levels next.

The bind() method

This method provides an instance level binding. It binds an event to a specific widget instance. Another way to think of this is as an ability to specify the exact GUI element that is sensitive to a particular event. The basic syntax is as follows:

```
widget.bind(sequence=None, func=None, add=None)
```

It should be noted that you can also use this method for the `toplevel` window.

For ease of understanding, let's represent the optional argument sequence as `even_descriptor` and `func` as `event_handler`. The third optional argument add can be specified as a string +. It allows you to add a new function to an existing binding. We will not discuss the `add` argument here. Refer to the documentation for further details.

```
widget.bind(event_descriptor, event_handler)
```

In the preceding statement, `widget` is any widget that generates one or more events. For example, the widget could be a `Button`, an `Entry` widget, and the like. The `event_descriptor` is the actual event triggered, for instance, a key press, or a click, and so on. `event_handler` is the function that gets called when the event is triggered.

Let's see how to use this method for the `Button` widget, in place of a command callback. Apart from the syntax, we also need to define a callback function that handles the generated event. Let's rewrite the code illustrated in the section, *Simple GUI application*.

```python
from tkinter import Tk, Label, Button, LEFT, RIGHT

def exit_btn_callback(evt):
    """Callback function to handle the button click event."""
    print("Inside exit_btn_callback. Event object is: ", evt)
    mainwin.destroy()

if __name__ == "__main__":
    # Create the main window or Tk instance.
    mainwin = Tk()
    mainwin.geometry("140x40")
    # Create a label widget and 'pack' it in a row (or column)
    lbl = Label(mainwin, text="Hello World!", bg='yellow')
    lbl.pack(side=LEFT)
    exit_button = Button(mainwin, text='Exit')
    # Bind the button click event to function exit_btn_callback
    exit_button.bind("<Button-1>", exit_btn_callback)
    exit_button.pack(side=RIGHT)

    mainwin.mainloop()
```

Observe that we have defined a new event handling function, `exit_btn_clicked()`, that takes the event object (`evt`) as an argument. The first argument to bind represents the type of event or the event format. In this example, `<Button-1>` represents a left mouse button press over the widget. In this chapter, we will only use the `bind()` method. But before we go further, let's briefly talk about the other levels of binding.

The bind_class() method

This method provides a class-level binding. It binds an event to a specific widget class. The basic syntax is shown next:

```python
bind_class(className, event_descriptor, event_handler)
```

In the preceding syntax, `className` is a string representing the name of the widget class. The other arguments are the same as discussed in the previous section.

Imagine that all the `Button` widgets in your application represent some numbers. You can configure all of them to respond to the right mouse click event such that each returns the square of that number. In this example, you can use the `bind_class` method like so:

```
bind_class('Button', '<Button-3>', compute_square)
```

Here, it is assumed that you have defined a function, `compute_square`.

The bind_all() method

This method provides an application-level binding. As the name suggests, this method binds an event to all the widgets at the application level. For example, in some game application, you might want to configure a key to pause the game regardless of the widget under focus. In such situations, you can use this method. The basic syntax is as follows:

```
bind_all(event_descriptor, event_handler)
```

Tkinter supports something referred to as bind tags. Every widget has its own list of bind tags. These determine the order in which the events associated with a widget are processed. The built-in method `bindtags()` can be used to set or get the tags associated with a widget. See the documentation for further details.

Project-1 – Attack of the Orcs V10.0.0

*You have developed a robust and popular command-line application, **Attack of the Orcs**. While the users are happy with the current version, there is a new and growing demand. The users now want a graphical user interface for the application!*

It is time to work on another simple program. Remember the first ever command-line application we wrote in *Chapter 1, Developing Simple Applications*? Let's use the same theme, and develop an equivalent GUI program.

Background scenario

As a refresher, here is the game theme we saw in *Chapter 1, Developing Simple Applications*:

On his way through a dense forest, Sir Foo spotted a small isolated settlement. Tired and hoping to replenish his food stock, he decided to take a detour. As he approached the village, he saw five huts. There was no one to be seen around. Hesitantly, he decided to enter a hut...

Problem statement

The task is to design a simple GUI program. The player selects one of the five huts where Sir Foo can rest. The huts are randomly occupied either by a friend or an enemy. Some huts might also be left unoccupied. The player wins if the selected hut is either unoccupied or has a friendly unit inside.

The following screenshot shows what's coming up. But don't get too excited! It is quite a simple game that will help you learn some important GUI programming aspects.

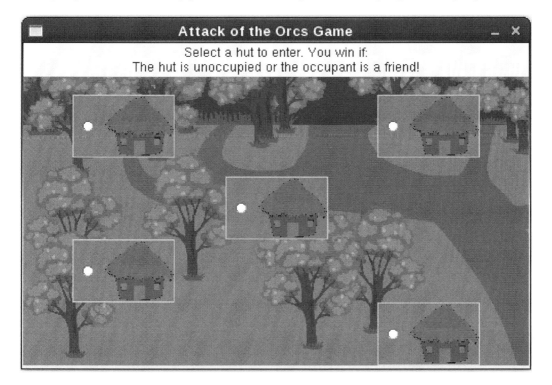

When you click on a hut, it will check who the occupant is, and then pop up a message box declaring the winner. That's pretty much it!

Writing the code

We will use the code provided in the hutgame.py file. Download this file and also the two images, Hut_small.gif and Jungle_small.gif from the code bundle for this chapter.

 It is recommended that you open the file hutgame.py as a handy reference while reading the following discussion. Quite often, it is useful to skim through the full code in a source code editor for better understanding!

We will start with the main execution code:

```python
if __name__ == "__main__":
    # Create Tk instance. This is popularly called 'root' But let's
    # call it mainwin (the 'main window' of the application. )
    mainwin = Tk()
    WIDTH = 494
    HEIGHT = 307
    mainwin.geometry("%sx%s" % (WIDTH, HEIGHT))
    mainwin.resizable(0, 0)
    mainwin.title("Attack of the Orcs Game")
    game_app = HutGame(mainwin)
    mainwin.mainloop()
```

Let's talk through this code:

- Compare this with the main execution block in the section *Simple GUI application – Take 2*. Notice that there isn't much of a difference.

- We set the size and a title for the application window with the geometry and title methods. The mainwin.resizable call freezes the window size. This is optional, but will make sure the background image nicely fits the window.

- The HutGame class is where we create the widgets and define the main logic.

- The main event loop is started by calling mainloop().

Overview of the class HutGame

Before reviewing any code in the class HutGame, let's get the big picture first. The important methods of this class are shown in the following diagram:

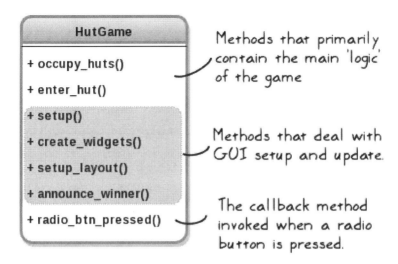

As illustrated, these methods can be broadly divided into three groups based on the functionality. We will talk about this grouping later when we discuss the MVC architecture. Let's review the various methods in this class next.

A note to more experienced readers!

In the following few sections, we will discuss the methods of the class HutGame. You might find this discussion a bit verbose! Optionally, you can just review the code from the file hutgame.py. The code is documented reasonably well. If something is not clear, come back and read the relevant section!

The __init__ method

Take a look at the code that gets called when HutGame is instantiated:

```
class HutGame:
    def __init__(self, parent):
        """A game where the player selects a hut where 'Sir Foo' to rest...
        self.village_image = PhotoImage(file="Jungle_small.gif")
        self.hut_image = PhotoImage(file="Hut_small.gif")
        self.hut_width = 40
        self.hut_height = 56
        self.container = parent

        self.huts = []
        self.result = ""
        # The preparatory work that populates the self.huts list
        # (no UI involved)
        self.occupy_huts()
        # Setup the user interface
        self.setup()
```

The following is a description of the __init__ method:

- The PhotoImage class is used for displaying a background image in widgets such as labels, buttons, and so on. It supports the GIF image format. There is also a way to load an image using **Python Imaging Library** (**PIL**). We won't discuss those details here.

- We will use hut_image on a RadioButton, and village_image will be set as the application background.

- The self.setup() call ensures that widgets are created and appropriately placed in the application window.

The occupy_huts method

The following method is the same as the one illustrated in the first example of *Chapter 1, Developing Simple Applications*:

```
def occupy_huts(self):
    """Randomly occupy the huts: enemy or friend or keep unoccupied."""
    occupants = ['enemy', 'friend', 'unoccupied']
    while len(self.huts) < 5:
        computer_choice = random.choice(occupants)
        self.huts.append(computer_choice)
    # Alternatively you can also use list comprehension like so:
    # self.huts = [random.choice(occupants) for _ in range(5)]
    print("Hut occupants are:", self.huts)
```

There are exactly five huts. This code essentially populates the `self.huts` list with a random choice of occupant from the given `occupants` list.

The create_widgets method

As the name suggests, this method is about creating the widgets for our application. Actually, there aren't many widgets. We just have a label to display some information and a bunch of radio buttons to represent the huts. The method is shown next:

```
def create_widgets(self):
    """Create various widgets in the tkinter main window."""
    self.var = IntVar()
    self.background_label = Label(self.container,
                                  image=self.village_image)
    txt = "Select a hut to enter. You win if:\n"
    txt += "The hut is unoccupied or the occupant is a friend!"
    self.info_label = Label(self.container, text=txt, bg='yellow')
    # Create a dictionary for radio button config options.
    r_btn_config = { 'variable': self.var,
                     'bg': '#A8884C',
                     'activebackground': 'yellow',
                     'image': self.hut_image,
                     'height': self.hut_height,
                     'width': self.hut_width,
                     'command': self.radio_btn_pressed }

    self.r1 = Radiobutton(self.container, r_btn_config, value=1)
    self.r2 = Radiobutton(self.container, r_btn_config, value=2)
    self.r3 = Radiobutton(self.container, r_btn_config, value=3)
    self.r4 = Radiobutton(self.container, r_btn_config, value=4)
    self.r5 = Radiobutton(self.container, r_btn_config, value=5)
```

The preceding method can be explained as follows:

- `self.var` is a Tkinter variable. It is an instance of a variable class supported by Tkinter. Here, it represents an integer variable (`IntVar` class). Likewise. there are other classes such as `StringVar` to deal with string variables, and so on.

- Simply put, the Tkinter variables enable tracking changes. We have five radio buttons that are tied to the single Tkinter variable, `self.var`. A value option can be specified for each radio button. This value gets assigned to `self.var` when the radio button is selected.

- The dictionary `r_btn_config` is used to set configuration options common to all the radio buttons. It is passed as an argument to `Radiobutton`.

- An example would help in understanding how a radio button works. The button `self.r4` has an associated value of `4`, which represents the hut number. When you select the button, this value gets assigned to `self.var`. This invokes `self.radio_btn_pressed()`, the command callback for the button.

- `self.background_label` is used to set a village background for our application window. There are other ways to accomplish this. We won't be discussing such customization details in this book.

Certainly! Have a look at the following application window where some of these widgets or configuration options are annotated.

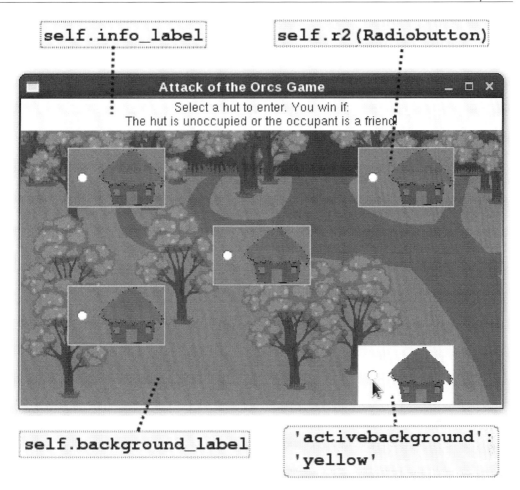

The setup_layout method

The following code fragment shows the setup_layout() method. and how it is invoked in the top-level setup() method:

```python
def setup(self):
    """Calls methods to setuo the user interface."""
    self.create_widgets()
    self.setup_layout()

def setup_layout(self):
    """Use the grid geometry manager to place widgets."""
    self.container.grid_rowconfigure(1, weight=1)
    self.container.grid_columnconfigure(0, weight=1)
    self.container.grid_columnconfigure(4, weight=1)
    self.background_label.place(x=0, y=0, relwidth=1, relheight=1)
    self.info_label.grid(row=0, column=0, columnspan=5, sticky='nsew')
    self.r1.grid(row=1, column=0)
    self.r2.grid(row=1, column=4)
    self.r3.grid(row=2, column=3)
    self.r4.grid(row=3, column=0)
    self.r5.grid(row=4, column=4)
```

 The grid layout offers a lot of flexibility in arranging widgets. In this illustration, we are just scratching the surface of Tkinter! To gain expertise, you should create your own GUI widgets, and experiment with different layout configuration options. Refer to the documentation for other available options.

Now let's talk through this code snippet:

- Recall that we can assign a relative weight to a specific row or a column in a grid layout. This is accomplished using the grid_rowconfigure and grid_columnconfigure methods. weight determines how much free space the row or column will occupy relative to the others. A default value of 0 means it won't grow even if there is free space available.

- In this example, row 1 of the container is given a relative weight or 1, allowing it to expand and occupy more free space. Likewise, the column 0 and column 4 are assigned with a relative weight of 1. Experiment with this option, and see how it influences the layout. The other option to try out is pad, which adds padding to the widget.

- For background_label, we use the place() geometry manager. The label is anchored at (0, 0). The arguments relwidth and relheight indicate the fraction of the height and width of the parent. The value of 1.0 means the label size will be the same as its parent (the main application window).

- The `sticky` option for `info_label` ensures the widget is aligned along the four edges of the cell. The value `nsew` aligns the widgets along the north, south, east, and west cell edges respectively. You can also specify a few values, for example, `sticky='ew'` will align the widget along the left and right edges.

The radio_btn_pressed and enter_hut methods

Let's review these methods together. In the `create_widgets()` method, we specified the command option as indicated in the following code fragment:

```
# Create a dictionary for radio button config options.
r_btn_config = { 'variable': self.var,
                 'bg': '#A8884C',
                 'activebackground': 'yellow',
                 'image': self.hut_image,
                 'height': self.hut_height,
                 'width': self.hut_width,
                 'command': self.radio_btn_pressed }

self.r1 = Radiobutton(self.container, r_btn_config, value=1)
```

`radio_btn_pressed` is a command callback for all the radio buttons. It is shown next:

```
# Handle Events
def radio_btn_pressed(self):
    """Command callback when radio button is pressed..."""
    self.enter_hut(self.var.get())
```

The method just calls `self.enter_hut`. When the radio button is selected, it updates the value stored in the Tkinter variable, `self.var`. This value is nothing but the hut number assigned to the selected hut, and can be obtained by calling the `get()` method of Tkinter's `IntVar` class.

Let's take a look at the `enter_hut` method:

```python
def enter_hut(self, hut_number):
    """Enter the selected hut and determine the winner...."""
    print("Entering hut #:", hut_number)
    hut_occupant = self.huts[hut_number-1]
    print("Hut occupant is: ", hut_occupant)

    if hut_occupant == 'enemy':
        self.result = "Enemy sighted in Hut # %d \n\n" % hut_number
        self.result += "YOU LOSE :( Better luck next time!"
    elif hut_occupant == 'unoccupied':
        self.result = "Hut # %d is unoccupied\n\n" % hut_number
        self.result += "Congratulations! YOU WIN!!!"
    else:
        self.result = "Friend sighted in Hut # %d \n\n" % hut_number
        self.result += "Congratulations! YOU WIN!!!"

    # Announce the winner!
    self.announce_winner(self.result)
```

The preceding code is self-explanatory. It checks the occupant, and announces the result. The winner announcement is done with a `messagebox` widget.

The announce_winner method

This is the last method we will review:

```python
def announce_winner(self, data):
    """Declare the winner by displaying a tkinter messagebox...."""
    messagebox.showinfo("Winner Announcement", message=data)
```

In the preceding method, we use the `messagebox` module in Tkinter to show an information box. This module provides several other types of dialog boxes. Refer to the documentation for more details.

Running the application

It is time for some action! Run this application as follows:

```
$ python hutgame.py
```

This last command should display the GUI window shown earlier. The following screenshot shows the game in action. First you select one of the huts:

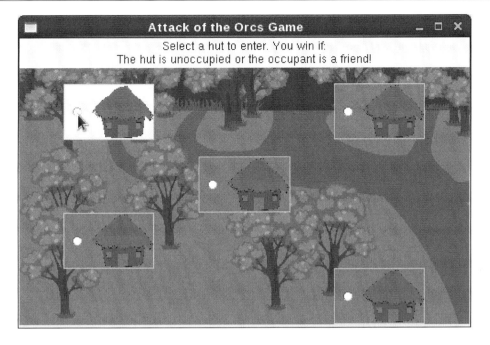

When you click on the radio button, it displays the information box notifying the winner.

MVC architecture

MVC is a widely used software architectural pattern in GUI-based applications. It has three components, namely a *model* that deals with the business logic, a *view* for the user interface, and a *controller* to handle the user input, manipulate data, and update the view. The following is a simplified schematic that shows the basic interactions between the various components:

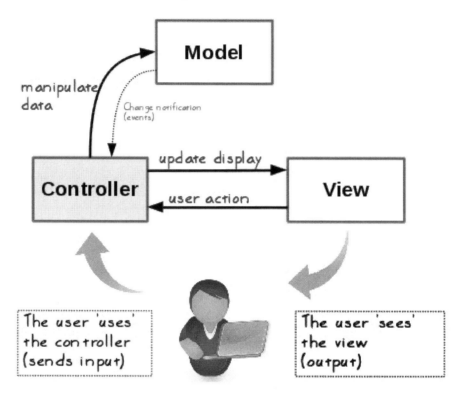

Let's further discuss each of these components.

Model

The model component of the MVC architecture represents the data of the application. It also represents the core business logic that acts on such data. The model has no knowledge of the view or the controller. When the data in the model changes, it just notifies its listeners about this change. In this context, the controller object is its listener.

View

The view component is the user interface. It is responsible for displaying the current state of the model to the user, and also provides a means for the user to interact with the application. If a user action (like the click of a button) changes this state, the view is refreshed to display that change.

Controller

In some sense, the controller enables a handshake between the model and the view. It monitors the changes to the model. When the user interacts with something in the view, the controller works in the background and handles the events triggered by the user actions, such as a mouse click. The handling function can further update the model. When the model's state changes, the controller updates the view to reflect those changes.

It's confusing. Perhaps an example of 'MVC' would help better understand these components!

You are right. The individual MVC components and their working would be better understood with an illustration. Let's use a trivial example given earlier in the section **Event-driven programming**.

Imagine you have opened a PDF file for reading. In this context, MVC and its components could be explained as follows:

- The PDF reader is the running application.

- It will show the contents of the file you have opened, and will also have buttons to navigate through the file. This is the view component that deals with the user interface.

- To jump to the next page, you interact with the view and click on the next page button. This is a user input that generates an event.

- Such an event is internally handled by the controller, which then updates the model, or, in this context, retrieves the relevant data on the requested page.

- The model 's state has changed. The controller further communicates with the view for updating it with the new contents.

- The view is refreshed, and finally, you see the desired page.

Advantages of MVC

The MVC architecture has been traditionally used in desktop GUI applications, and is also widely used in web application development. As this is a three-component architecture, one major advantage it offers is code reuse across several applications. For example, imagine you have multiple applications with different user interfaces, all needing the same business logic. With MVC architecture, you could just reuse the business logic represented by the model object across these applications.

Moreover, the MVC enables user interface developers to focus on the UI code without worrying much about the code that handles the business logic. Likewise, the developers working on the business logic can concentrate on that piece of code alone without losing sleep over the choice of UI widgets and the related code. This is referred to as *separation of concerns*. The model is concerned about the business logic or data, the view worries about the user interface, and the controller code is concerned about things such as enabling view manipulation and handling the input.

Project 2 – Attack of the Orcs v10.1.0

Let's work on another small project. In fact, this is exactly the same hut game we developed in *Project-1 – Attack of the Orcs V10.0.0* earlier. The difference is the underlying architecture. We will rewrite the program to implement the MVC architecture.

Revisiting the HutGame class

In the first project, we wrote the HutGame class. Let's pull up the diagram representing the high-level structure of this class:

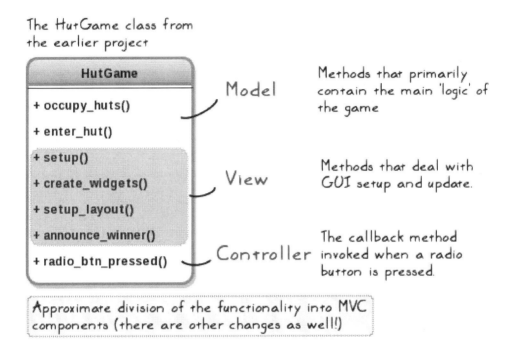

Based on the functionality, the methods of this class can be roughly placed into three categories, namely model, view, and the controller. The preceding diagram shows this division. We also need to further update a few of these methods.

Creating MVC classes

In the previous section, we earmarked the methods of the old class HutGame into three broad categories. It is now time to say goodbye to this class. We will break it down and split its methods among the three new classes, Model, View, and Controller. Of course, you can give more descriptive names to the classes, but let's continue to call them by the aforementioned names.

Observe the following UML-like representation that shows the classes in which these methods are parked. Only the important attributes are listed here.

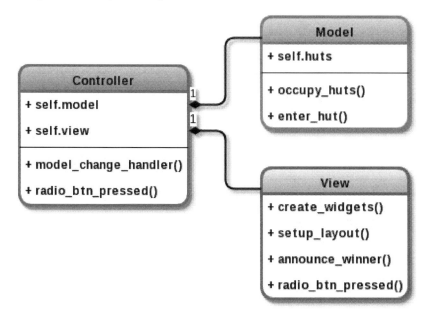

In *Chapter 1, Developing Simple Applications*, we briefly talked about UML-like representation. One way to create such diagrams is to use `https://www.draw.io`. It is a free, online diagram software for making flowcharts, UML diagrams, and so on.

Now that we know how the classes are laid out, let's understand how these classes exchange information.

Communication between MVC objects

Before diving into the details on how MVC objects communicate, let's first list down a few important points about the MVC architecture:

- The controller knows about the model as well as the view
- The model is unaware of the other two, namely the controller and the view
- The view (just like the model) knows nothing about the controller and the model

There could be some other variants of the MVC architecture. In this book, we will stick to the aforementioned points, and design a solution.

Controller to Model or View communication

Let's begin the discussion by learning how a controller sends the information to either the model or the view.

The `Controller` object can directly talk to the `Model` and `View` instances using `self.model` and `self.view` respectively. For example, it can just call a `View` method like so:

```
self.view.announce_winner(data)
```

This is pretty straightforward. Now let's see how it receives the data from either the model or the view.

Model to Controller communication

How does the controller receive information from the model? For example, in the hut game scenario, a winner is determined depending on who is inside the selected hut. Once the winner is determined, the `Model` class needs to communicate it to the `Controller` class. This is accomplished with the `model_change_handler()` method of the `Controller` class. It is invoked whenever the state of the `Model` class changes.

Good question! The Model *class knows nothing about* Controller *and* View. *Then how does* Controller *know that* Model *has changed? Let's see that next.*

The `Controller` class can receive information from the `Model` class in various ways. Let's briefly talk about two such approaches.

Using method assignment

Recall that in Python, you can assign a method to a variable. The chapter on design patterns talked about the first-class objects in greater detail. The following line of code can be added to `Controller.__init__`.

```
self.model.changed = self.model_change_handler
```

Then, in the `Model` class, you could call `self.changed()`, like so:

```
def enter_hut(self, hut_number):
    # Some code goes here (not shown)
    self.changed()
```

This automatically notifies `Controller` that the model has changed. While this is very convenient, we will instead use a publish-subscribe API which makes things even simpler.

Using a publish-subscribe pattern

Publish-subscribe is a messaging pattern. The publisher can be any program that broadcasts some data to a topic. There could be one or more applications that are listening to this topic. These are called the subscribers, who receive the published data. The publisher does not know (or does not need to know) anything about the subscribers. Similarly, a subscriber has no knowledge of the publisher. The following schematic gives a high-level overview of a publish-subscribe system:

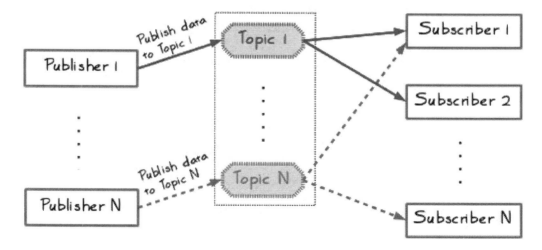

The publish-subscribe concept can be better understood with a real-world analogy. Imagine an online retailer running a weekly flash sale. You have opted in to receive notifications in the form of SMS or e-mail alerts. There are several other customers who would also like to get notified about the sale.

In a publish-subscribe world, the online retailer is a publisher who broadcasts the sale information (the data) to a topic, say *flash sale*. You and several other customers are the subscribers to this topic. Likewise, the online retailer can publish some other information as different topics, for instance, *Friday sale*, *Half price sale*, and so on. Each topic could have several subscribers. If you are not subscribed to *Friday sale* , you won't get any notifications sent to that topic.

PyPubSub package

How do we implement a publish-subscribe framework in Python? One option is to write the code from scratch. Instead, we will just use a Python package called pypubsub. It provides a publish-subscribe API that simplifies the design and improves code readability and testability. The package can be installed as follows:

```
$ pip install pypubsub
```

Here is a simple example that shows a typical usage. In fact, this syntax is all we need in this chapter.

```python
from pubsub import pub

# A Subscriber function
def model_change_handler(data):
    print("In model_change handler function, data=", data)

# Register the subscriber
pub.subscribe(model_change_handler, "WINNER ANNOUNCEMENT")

# 'Publish' a message. the data is any optional argument
pub.sendMessage("WINNER ANNOUNCEMENT", data="Player Won!")
```

When you run this script, it produces the following output:

```
$ "In model_change handler function, data= Player Won"
```

The first argument to pub.subscribe() is the function you want to subscribe to a given topic. The topic name here is WINNER ANNOUNCMENT. The last line of the code shows how to broadcast a message to a specific topic using pub.sendMessage(). The first argument to pub.sendMessage() is the topic name. You can specify any number of optional arguments, just make sure that the subscriber function accepts all those arguments! In this example, it sends data as the only optional argument.

For more information on the PyPubSub package, see the project home page: http://pubsub.sourceforge.net/

PyDispatcher is an alternative to the PyPubSub package. While we won't be using it, here is a link to the project: https://pypi.python.org/pypi/PyDispatcher

View to Controller communication

Just like Model, there is no direct communication link from the View object to the Controller object. When the user presses a radio button, the controller needs to be notified. We can employ similar approaches, as discussed in the previous section. For example, you can assign a method of Controller to a View method. Alternatively, you can use the publish-subscribe API to talk to the Controller object.

Communication between View and Model

Let's discuss how View and Model talk to each other:

- When the user presses a radio button, View communicates with Controller using one of the approaches discussed earlier

- The Controller object then talks to Model instructing it to update

- The state of Model is updated, and the results are communicated back to Controller

- Controller asks View to update the display

View and Model communication using a publish-subscribe API:

You could potentially use the publish-subscribe framework to establish a communication channel between the Model and the View object. Note that this still keeps the basic rules intact. Model does not know anything about the View object. It just publishes the data to a given topic. View doesn't have any knowledge of the Model object. It is just registered as a subscriber to the same topic where Model is broadcasting the data. Thus, whenever there is a change of state in Model, View could get a notification through the publish-subscribe API. Likewise for the communication from View to Model. The potential flip-side is that these publish-subscribe signals are essentially global variables, and could bring in the painful issues associated with them. So use it with caution!

For this project however, we will stick to the classical approach, where the communication happens through Controller.

Reviewing the code

So far, you have got a high-level overview of the new classes and how they communicate with each other. In the first project, we already reviewed most of the methods listed under each new class. That said, to implement the MVC architecture we need to make a few changes. Let's review only a few important methods from the file `hutgame_mvc.py`. Note that all the classes have been put in the same file. As an exercise, split the individual classes in their own module!

As we won't be reviewing each and every line of the code, you should download the file `hutgame_mvc.py` and also the two images, `Hut_small.gif` and `Jungle_small.gif` from the code bundle for this chapter. Keep the source file handy while reading the upcoming discussion. Quite often, it is useful to skim through the full code for better understanding!

The main execution code is shown next. It is almost identical to the one we saw in the first project. The only difference is `game_app` (shown highlighted). It is now an instance of the `Controller` class instead of `HutGame`. In fact, there is no `HutGame` class for this project! Recall that we broke it down, creating three new classes.

```
if __name__ == "__main__":
    # Create an instance of Tk. This is popularly called 'root' But let's
    # call it mainwin (the 'main window' of the application. )
    mainwin = Tk()
    WIDTH = 494
    HEIGHT = 307
    mainwin.geometry("%sx%s" % (WIDTH, HEIGHT))
    mainwin.resizable(0, 0)
    mainwin.title("Attack of the Orcs Game")
    game_app = Controller(mainwin)
    mainwin.mainloop()
```

The Controller class

The Controller class is quite small, as shown next:

```
class Controller:
    def __init__(self, parent):
        """The Controller class of the Hut game (MVC architecture)...."""
        self.parent = parent
        self.model = Model()
        self.view = View(parent)
        self.view.set_callbacks(self.radio_btn_pressed)
        self.view.setup()
        # 'Subscribe' to the topic 'WINNER ANNOUNCEMENT'
        pub.subscribe(self.model_change_handler, "WINNER ANNOUNCEMENT")

    def radio_btn_pressed(self):
        """Command callback when radio button is in the view pressed...."""
        self.model.enter_hut(self.view.var.get())

    def model_change_handler(self, data):
        self.view.announce_winner(data)
```

Let's talk through the code. You can skip reading these bullets if you have already understood it!

- The Controller class is composed of Model and View instances. This allows it to directly call the functionality from these classes.

- The self.view.set_callbacks() function essentially assigns the radio_btn_pressed method to an appropriate attribute of View. What this simply means is that whenever the user presses a radio button, this method is invoked. See the section *View to Controller communication* for more details.

- The Controller class receives data from the Model instance by subscribing to the topic, "WINNER ANNOUNCEMENT". We have already seen an example of the pub.subscribe() function. Simply put, the method model_change_handler is called whenever the winner is announced.

- The method model_change_handler calls the appropriate View method to display a message that announces the winner.

The Model class

There aren't many changes in the `Model` class. The only significant change is the highlighted line of the given code (the call to `pub.sendMessage`) in the `enter_hut` method. The details of the other methods are not shown. These methods are shown with their code collapsed in the editor.

```python
class Model:
    def __init__(self):...

    def occupy_huts(self):...

    def enter_hut(self, hut_number):
        """Enter the hut, determine the winner and 'publish' the result....
        print("Entering hut #:", hut_number)
        hut_occupant = self.huts[hut_number-1]
        print("Hut occupant is: ", hut_occupant)

        if hut_occupant == 'enemy':
            self.result = "Enemy sighted in Hut # %d \n\n" % hut_number
            self.result += "YOU LOSE :( Better luck next time!"
        elif hut_occupant == 'unoccupied':
            self.result = "Hut # %d is unoccupied\n\n" % hut_number
            self.result += "Congratulations! YOU WIN!!!"
        else:
            self.result = "Friend sighted in Hut # %d \n\n" % hut_number
            self.result += "Congratulations! YOU WIN!!!"

        # 'Publish' a message to notify the 'subscribers' (Controller).
        pub.sendMessage("WINNER ANNOUNCEMENT", data=self.result)
```

Compare this method against the one we wrote in the first project. Notice that it does not call `View.announce_winner` directly. Instead, it notifies the `Controller` instance using the `pub.sendMessage()`. The rest of the code remains unchanged, and you can have a look at the `hutgame_mvc.py` file for further details.

As noted in the section *Communication between View and Model*, you could potentially use the same publish-subscribe framework to notify the `Model` state changes to the `View` and vice versa.

> **Object-relational mapper (ORM):**
>
> Simply put, it is a library that enables you to use an object-oriented language like Python to access and update the data sitting in a database. In Python, DJango ORM and SQLAlchemy are among the popular ORM libraries. You can do a web search on these libraries to find useful resources.
>
> Model classes and ORMs: This book does not cover anything related to web or database application programming, but it is worth mentioning the following. It is quite common for the Model classes to inherit from the ORMs, and represent database tables where each object is a row in the table. Writing unit tests for such systems could be a challenge, as you typically don't want to actually hit the database every time these tests run. In *Chapter 5, Unit Testing and Refactoring* we saw how to use Python's mock library. Quite often, mock is useful for unit testing such systems (it is not covered in this book).

The View class

The View class is illustrated next. The only significant change is the method by the name set_callbacks. The other methods are shown with their code collapsed.

```python
class View:
    def __init__(self, parent):...

    def setup(self):...

    def set_callbacks(self, callback_function):
        """Assign the given function (argument) to a method in this class.
        self.radio_btn_pressed = callback_function

    def create_widgets(self):...

    def setup_layout(self):...

    def announce_winner(self, data):...
```

Recall that in the Controller.__init__ method, we have the following code:

```python
self.view.set_callbacks(self.radio_btn_pressed)
```

The preceding code states that the radio_btn_pressed attribute of the View class represents the method radio_btn_pressed() of the Controller class. The rest of the code is identical to the one seen in the first project.

Running the application

In this project, we did not add any new features to the GUI. The idea was to just show a rudimentary example on implementing the MVC architecture. You can run this application as follows:

```
$ python hutgame_mvc.py
```

This should show the same GUI window and features as in the first project.

Testing GUI applications

In a complex and feature-rich GUI application, the user is presented with many choices of widgets, menus, keyboard shortcuts, and so on. As seen earlier in the chapter, the event-driven nature of GUI programs lets the user dictate the program flow. This often presents many possible ways for the user to perform certain operations to arrive at the desired output.

> It should be noted that we are not going to write any code here. This is just a high-level discussion that touches upon a few important testing considerations. For further learning on this topic, start with the following wiki page: https://en.wikipedia.org/wiki/Graphical_user_interface_testing.

Imagine a GUI application that allows selecting some object in the application window, for example, a folder icon on the desktop. The user can hover the mouse over the icon to highlight that object, and then click on it to select it. Alternatively, he can do a window selection, where a selection window is drawn around the object to select it. Yet another alternative could be using a combination of keys on the keyboard. While the user is happy that he can accomplish the task in different ways, it becomes a challenge for the developer to write a bug-free code.

The nature of event-driven programming makes it difficult to write a robust code and comprehensive tests to account for the majority of the user input scenarios. The bugs would creep in one way or the other. Of course, this varies depending on the application and testing strategy, but it is typically a problem for large and complex GUI applications.

Testing considerations

There are various testing strategies to make the GUI application code more robust. Let's touch upon a few important testing considerations.

Unit testing and MVC

A unit test helps you test an individual chunk of the code. An integration test is where you have many unit tests grouped together to test a larger functionality. In a regression test, you typically have a combination of unit and integration tests. Here, the tests are rerun to ensure that nothing is broken. A good regression test framework is crucial as the first line of defense against the bugs. Unit testing generally helps in addressing some common problems. In an earlier chapter, we already covered this topic with examples from a command-line application.

The MVC architecture of the GUI program further helps in making the code robust. The separation of concerns or breaking down of the code into the model, view, and controller components allows us to write unit tests for particular types of error. For example, in some applications, you may anticipate `ZeroDivisionError` in the `Model` class instead of the `View` class. So you could write focused unit tests for the `Model` class to gracefully handle such situations.

Manual testing

While having a good regression test suite helps with the common issues, the event-driven nature of the program often presents scenarios that are not accounted for. In manual testing, the software tester manually checks the working of the application by playing with different features provided in the GUI. If something is not working as expected, the tester creates a bug report to document the instructions to reproduce the problem. Many hidden bugs surface in the manual testing phase.

With the growing complexity of the program, the repetitive manual testing job becomes overwhelming for the testers. This is where automated GUI testing comes to the rescue.

Automated GUI testing

Here, the testing tool records the user actions to create tests. If you run such a test, the user actions are repeated automatically in the same sequence. This allows quick identification of the broken functionality.

Automated testing should not replace manual testing. Unless the tool has artificial intelligence built into it, you still need someone to test the new features, and use the existing ones in ways not tried before. In general, automated testing should complement the manual GUI testing activity.

There are several open source and commercial tools available for automated GUI testing in Python. The following table summarizes a few prominent, freely available tools for GUI test automation. For a comprehensive list, see the Python wiki page at `https://wiki.python.org/moin/PythonTestingToolsTaxonomy`.

Tool name and link	Notes
Sikuli (SikuliX) `http://www.sikuli.org/`	Supported on Windows, Mac, and some Linux OS. Visit the website to check if your OS is supported.
StoryText `https://pypi.python.org/pypi/StoryText`	Supported GUI frameworks include Tkinter, PyGTK, wxPython, and others. See the website for the complete list.
Dogtail `https://fedorahosted.org/dogtail/`	Intended for Linux OS like Fedora. Check if it is compatible with your OS.

One of the frailties of such automated testing systems is that the innocent-looking GUI changes may require you to change a lot of tests, and depending on the complexity of your GUI application, this could be a hassle.

Exercises

Here is a list of a few things you could do to further improve the GUI application. With one exception, the solutions are not provided for these exercises.

1. Put the `Model`, `View` and, `Controller` classes in their own modules!
2. Use the publish-subscribe API for communication from `View` to `Controller`. You can refer to the file `hutgame_mvc_pubsub.py` for a solution.
3. Add more widgets such as a menu bar and buttons. Implement the **Restart Game** button. When clicked, the game should restart. Do the following when this button is clicked:
   ° Randomly distribute the occupants again by calling `occupy_huts()`.
   ° Clear the state of the radio buttons. All the buttons should be deselected.
4. Add exception handling to the application.
5. Try to generalize the `View.add_callbacks` method so that it can be used to set more callback functions.

Further reading

This book has touched upon several important aspects of application development. The key concepts were taught primarily by developing command-line applications. As noted earlier in the chapter, there are many applications that require you to learn domain-specific techniques. For example, in this chapter, we learned about the MVC architecture commonly implemented in GUI applications. Let's conclude this chapter, and hence the book, with a brief discussion on some of the important application domains. This will just give you some useful pointers (with lots of links!) to the relevant libraries or application frameworks. To avoid clutter, the URLs with further information are provided separately at the end of this section. The following is a list of other important application domains; however, this is far from being an exhaustive list:

1. Web and mobile application development:

   These are important application development domains. To learn Python Web application development, you can start exploring the Flask or DJango frameworks in Python. Knowledge of MVC will also help you here. For mobile application development, the kivy library is probably a good start.

2. Applications involving databases:

   A **database management system (DBMS)** is another important application domain. In a nutshell, DBMS provides you a way to create, access, and manage your data. Python has several libraries that enable talking to a database.

   SQLite3 is a simple, light-weight relational database system. The module sqlite3 is a built-in Python module that provides a DB-API 2.0 compliant SQL interface. There are several client libraries written in Python that provide a way to talk to a database. For example, the PyMongo module provides tools to work with MongoDB, and so on.

3. Machine and deep learning:

   In the data science domain, the use of machine learning and deep learning libraries is growing rapidly. The knowledge of GPU programming would help here.

 Data science applications almost always involve visualizing some data. It is very convenient to use IPython or Jupyter notebooks to write and share interactive data science applications. See `http://jupyter.org/` for more details.

For machine learning, you can explore Apache Spark. This is a general-purpose cluster computing system that provides high-level APIs in Python and other languages. MLlib is Apache Spark's scalable machine learning library. For deep-learning applications, Caffe and Tensorflow are among the popular deep-learning frameworks.

4. Internet of Things:

   This is is yet another rapidly emerging field where Python is one of the favored languages for developing applications. Here you could use Python to not only process data (Analytics applications) on the server side but also have a Python client running on the end device. You can find use of the publish-subscribe messaging pattern in such applications, where the device publishes data to a topic, and the server side application is a subscriber that receives this data.

5. Multimedia and game applications:

   This is broad topic, and there are several frameworks and libraries available for developing multimedia applications:

   ° Python wiki documents many tools that deal with audio and video processing. **GStreamer**, **MoviePy**, and **MLT** are among the popular frameworks. See also the PyMedia module.

   ° There are quite a few options for image processing. Check out scikit-image, Opencv, and pillow (a fork of Python Imaging Library or PIL).

   ° There are many libraries useful for developing game- and animation-related applications. Check out PyGame and Pyglet. Again, you can find a comprehensive list on the Python wiki page.

The following table lists a few useful web links that provide more information on various tools or domains discussed earlier.

At the time of writing this book, all the web links (URLs) presented throughout the book are accessible. As noted in *Chapter 1, Developing Simple Applications*, these links might end up being broken over time. If that ever happens, do a web search with the appropriate search terms. For example, if you find the link to the PyMongo module broken, you can Google search PyMongo Python MongoDB to find some useful resources!

Tool or application domain	Web link for further information
Flask	`http://flask.pocoo.org`
Django	`https://www.djangoproject.com`
Kivy	`https://kivy.org`
sqlite3	`https://docs.python.org/3/library/sqlite3.html`
PyMongo	`https://api.mongodb.com/python/current/`
Jupyter notebook	`http://jupyter.org/`
Apache Spark	`https://spark.apache.org`
Caffe framework	`http://caffe.berkeleyvision.org`
Tensorflow	`https://www.tensorflow.org/`
Internet of Things (IoT)	`https://en.wikipedia.org/wiki/Internet_of_things`
Audio, video processing	`https://wiki.python.org/moin/AudioVideo`
Game and animations	`https://wiki.python.org/moin/PythonGameLibraries`

Summary

This chapter served as an introduction to the Python GUI programming. Starting with an overview of the different GUI frameworks, it touched upon some important practical design considerations for developing user interfaces. You saw what event-driven programming is, and learned about events and event handling. With a quick introduction to Tkinter library, we developed a simple Hut Game, an equivalent GUI version of the first ever application developed in *Chapter 1, Developing Simple Applications*.

The second half of the chapter introduced you to the MVC architecture, and we transformed the Hut Game to implement this architecture. The chapter concluded with a high-level discussion on testing GUI applications.

Index

A

S

SciPy
  about 333
  reference 333

Scrum methodology
  reference 183

shared memory parallelization
  about 341
  reference 341

Sikuli (SikuliX)
  reference 407

simple factory
  about 220
  design, rethinking 222, 223
  problem 221, 222
  Pythonic approach 225-227
  recruit feature 220, 221
  traditional approach 224, 225

Sir Foo 10

slicing 312, 322-324

sorted array 275

sorting algorithm
  reference 280

sorting options
  reference 265

Sphinx
  about 109
  reference 116

sphinx-build tool
  using 125

StoryText
  reference 407

strategy pattern
  about 205
  attempted solution 209-211
  design, rethinking 211
  jump feature 205, 206
  problem 207, 208
  Pythonic approach 218, 219
  traditional approach 212-217

structural patterns 195

T

test case 145

test execution
  controlling 148-150

test fixtures 145

testing considerations, GUI applications
  automated GUI testing 406
  manual testing 406
  unit testing, and MVC 406

test modules
  creating 160, 161

test runner 145

tests
  creating, with unittest.TestCase 146-148

test server, PyPI
  reference 82

test suite 145

timeit
  reference 263

timeit documentation
  reference 297

Tkinter
  about 360
  documentation links 365, 374
  reference 360
  widget classes 372, 373

tools, for GUI test automation
  Dogtail 407
  reference 407
  Sikuli (SikuliX) 407
  StoryText 407

TortoiseMerge
  reference 120

U

unhandled exceptions 49

Unified Modeling Language (UML) 33
  reference 184

unit testing
  about 144, 145, 189
  new class, creating for 154, 155

11361122R00243

Printed in Great Britain
by Amazon